TWELVE YEARS
AMONG THE
WILD INDIANS

CHIEFLY FROM

THE DIARIES AND MANUSCRIPTS

OF

GEORGE P. BELDEN

BY GEN. JAMES S. BRISBIN, U.S.A.

1881

Contents

PUBLISHER'S NOTES

James Brisbin notes towards the end of this updated version of his book on Belden that he had written the first edition twelve years previous to this one; that would be 1869. In the September 30, 1869 edition of the War Department's register of civil, military, and naval service, Brisbin and Belden appear on the same page. Brisbin was then a major and Belden a first lieutenant.

James Sanks Brisbin lived an active and remarkable life. He was a lawyer, publisher, author, Civil War general commanding the 5th United States Colored Troops, and a cavalry officer in the frontier army after the war. He is best known to Custer scholars today as a member of Colonel John Gibbon's Montana Column during the Yellowstone Expedition that resulted in the death of Custer and over two hundred of his 7th cavalry troopers. Brisbin was a major under Gibbon and at the mouth of Rosebud Creek had offered his cavalry troop to Custer the day before the latter marched off to his destiny at the Little Bighorn. Custer refused the additional troops. Brisbin was later critical of Custer, blaming him for the Little Bighorn disaster. You can read a letter written by Brisbin to Edward Settle Godfrey (the lieutenant commanding K Company of the 7th Cavalry at the Little Bighorn) in Brininstool's excellent *Troopers with Custer*. Brisbin was a prolific writer, contributing to many magazines and books. He died in 1892 and is buried in Minnesota.

George P. Belden was born in Ohio in 1842, served in the Civil War, and was also a writer of some merit, mostly about Native American life. As the title suggests, Belden lived among the tribes for twelve years. Only 29 at the time of his death, he had already lived an adventurous life and published what was described as a rather "imaginative" biography. Running away from home at thirteen, his parents followed him and for a time, he and his father ran a newspaper in Nebraska. Soon bored with this life, he again left and began his wanderings among the western tribes, closely studying their languages, dialects, and customs. When the Civil War erupted, he obtained a commission as a cavalry lieutenant but found military discipline unendurable. He resigned his commission and returned to the plains. He was shot after leaving the Grand River

Agency in Dakota Territory on September 1, 1871. A contemporary article in the *Boston Daily Advertiser* stated that he was unarmed when killed, which seems unlikely, and that his assailant was thought to have been an Uncpapa Sioux.

Brisbin took on the task of arranging the Belden papers into a coherent manuscript that the public could consume. This book is the result.

BIG BYTE BOOKS

ORIGINAL PUBLISHERS' PREFACE

THE attention of the Publishers was called to the Belden papers something over a year ago, since which time a few of them have been published in the New York *Tribune* and the Chicago *Tribune*, and in the Cincinnati *Gazette*. The papers thus published, although the less important and interesting of the collection, excited a great deal of interest, and were read with a great deal of satisfaction by thousands. In fact, so great was the satisfaction that the whole series was eagerly sought for publication in serial form before its issuance in book form; but we are happy to state that we secured the entire series, and herein present it to the public, fresh and unhackneyed.

It will be observed that nearly every chapter is complete in itself, each presenting a different phase of Indian or frontier life and character, but all so systematized and arranged as to form a connected and *complete* whole.

THE PUBLISHERS.

St. Louis, 1881.

OUT IN THE OPEN AIR—OFF FOR THE PLAINS

IT is no very difficult task for me, at one hundred yards, to send a rifle-ball against the head of a brass nail, or to cut with an arrow, at half the distance, the string that suspends a squirrel by the tail; but the pen is a weapon with which my hand has long been unfamiliar. It matters little where a man may have been born in this country, or what his earlier life may have been; for Americans consider more what men are than what they have been. To those who read these pages, and who may be curious to know, I will, however, say I was born in the good State of Ohio, and, at the age of thirteen ran away from my parents to seek my fortune in the then almost unknown West.

The wild life I have led, and the many adventures I have passed through, may seem almost incredible to those accustomed to living in civilized communities; yet I can assure the reader that, although there is a great deal of romance, there is no fiction in these chapters, and that what I am about to re late is as much everyday life among the wild Indians of the plains as is the business of the merchant or banker, who goes regularly to his counter and desk in the great city.

How I got from Ohio to Nebraska is my own affair. Suffice it to say, that I was not yet fourteen years of age when I arrived at Brownsville, then a small hamlet of log houses. Here, on the banks of the murky Missouri, I first saw the "Great West." Emigrants were pouring in from the States; and, filled with the idea of the future wealth and importance of this broad land, I made haste to write to my father, describing the valley, and urging him to move out. That he thought well of what I said, and relied somewhat on my judgment, is evinced by the fact that he came with his family and settled in Nebraska, where now stands the city of Brownsville.

My father had once learned the printing trade, and our first enterprise was to establish a weekly newspaper, called the *Nemaha Valley Journal*. It was a sickly affair, but through its influence many a well-to-do farmer was induced to leave his home in the States to try his fortune in the Far West; and of all who came, not one, I believe, regrets the day he left the East. Many of them now count their herds by thousands and number their acres by miles of land, while all who have labored and practiced economy own beautiful homes, and have abundant wealth.

In two short years brick houses began to appear; the buffalo, game, and Indians were gone, and I felt Brownsville was no longer my home. I burned for adventure, and when our little weekly paper was announced as a "daily," I knew it was time for me to be off. I wished to see the mountains covered with perpetual snow; I longed to chase the buffalo and wild deer over boundless plains. I wanted to dress as a trapper, and live in the open air far away from the habitations of men. The case and the setting of type being no longer tolerable, I flung down my stick, and, seeking my father, told him of my craving for wild life and adventure. I was a sickly boy, and, naturally, he endeavored to dissuade me from my purpose to cast myself loose on the prairies. Finding I could not gain his consent, I determined to run away once more and, consulting with a friend, I begged him to buy me a horse. In two days I had a stout pony, saddle, and bridle concealed in the stable of a Mr. Hill, and awaiting my order. My rifle and revolvers, which had already become my familiar companions and most trusted friends, were carefully cleaned, oiled, and laid away. I overhauled my shot-pouch, and purchased a good supply of powder, ball, and caps. All these warlike preparations did not escape the attention of my good mother and sisters, who anxiously inquired what I meant to do. God forgive me for the story I told them, but I desired only to avoid giving them pain, and said I intended taking a short hunt someday .on the prairies. It is now many years ago, but that short hunt is not yet ended, and, probably, never will be until death ends the hunter.

It was a beautiful starlight night when I stole down the stairs, and, quietly opening the street door, stepped into the open air. For a moment I paused on the threshold, and an intense desire to go back seized me. I wished to look once more on the faces of my dear mother and sisters. Should I ever see them again? All, who could tell? I stood irresolute, but the sound of approaching footsteps on the street aroused me, and, crushing down the great lump in my throat, I brushed aside the gathering tears I could not suppress, and hastened to the stable where my horse was concealed.

To saddle and bridle him, mount and gallop out of the town, was the work of but a few minutes on the rising ground overlooking the city I paused for one last look of home. How quietly the houses lay in the moonlight! how peacefully the hundreds slept! And is it not strange that I, a mere boy, was possessed of a restless spirit that would not let me sleep, that was driving me from home, plenty, and friends to the wilderness, to take upon myself hardships, privations, and dangers that, if foreseen, were well calculated to appall the stoutest hearts? I said, "O, fool, how long?" and turning my horse's head to the northward, plunged my spurs into his sides, causing him to rear wildly, and then bound furiously over the broad prairie.

The die was cast; a life of adventure decided upon, and I was off for the boundless plains, where the buffalo roamed at will; where I could hunt the elk, a rub trap the beaver; dwell in a wigwam, and make my home with the children of the "Great American Desert."

JOINING THE INDIANS

FAST and furious I rode forward, never pulling rein until I arrived at Nebraska City, then a small village, though now a considerable place. Halting to rest for an hour or two, I suddenly remembered that my parents had friends in the town, and' that a telegraph ran from there to Brownsville, and, fearing lest I should be telegraphed or taken charge of by relatives, I mounted my pony, and, striking boldly out on the prairie, kept in what I supposed the direction to Omaha, and just as the sun was going down I saw the city, and by dark was in it, having ridden eighty-five miles in less than twenty-four hours. The heat had visibly affected me, and I felt fatigued, though my tough little pony seemed fresh almost as when starting. Opposite Omaha is Council Bluffs, so named from a famous Sioux Indian council once held in the hills above the city; and feeling I should be more secure there than in Omaha, I crossed the Missouri and put up at a small and obscure hotel.

It was now late at night, and I was completely exhausted. Putting the pony in the stable, and seeing him well supplied with hay, I went to bed and slept for many hours, until the sun shining through the window awoke me, and, hastily dressing myself, I breakfasted and sallied out to see the town and buy some more ammunition. I had determined to stay several days at the Bluffs, but, while standing in a store, I saw a neighbor from Brownsville pass, and, imagining he was looking for me, I slipped out, and, going to the hotel, saddled my pony and departed in haste.

I had purchased many shells, beads, ribbons, and pieces of colored cloths, to trade with the Indians, and with great difficulty managed to carry them along.

Following up the eastern bank of the Missouri, I passed over high hills, through deep cations, across wide meadows and prairies, and climbed precipitous bluffs. It was in August, that season of the year when the prairie strawberry is ripe. The ground, at times, for miles was covered with this delicious fruit, arid many were the halts I made to rest my pony and gather the luscious berries.

7

I was riding to reach a hunter's cabin, forty miles up the Missouri, but the day was hot, and I made slow progress. Night came down upon the prairies, and still no cabin was in sight. It soon became so dark I could with difficulty follow the trail, and was about to give up all effort to go further and camp on the prairies, when my pony pricked up his ears and set off at a gallop.

I gave him rein, and he traveled rapidly on what seemed to be a well-beaten wagon road. Suddenly halting, so as nearly to pitch me over his head, the little fellow began snorting and exhibiting unusual signs of terror. I held him firmly, and, although I strained my eyes, it was so dark that I could see nothing. While I was endeavoring to force the beast forward, a rough voice close by my stirrup inquired:

"Who are you, and where are you going?"

"A man going to Sioux City, and looking for a cabin here abouts," I answered.

"All right," replied the voice; "follow me."

"Do you live nearby?" I inquired.

"Yes; come along."

Thus urged, I rode on in silence, and presently entered a patch of timber, where I saw a light shining among the trees. In a few minutes we were before the door of a hut, and my companion, with a bluff "Get down, stranger," entered the house.

I did not like the movements of my host; but, dismounting, followed him into a snug room, the walls and floor of which were completely covered with the furs of wild animals. Softer than any carpet were the white wolf skins beneath our feet, and the walls were rich with the beautiful coverings of antelope and red deer, while in the corners were antlers of elk, on which hung clothing, shot-pouches, and Indian bead-work.

By the light of a rag burning in a saucer of grease, I saw my host was a large, powerfully-built man, with bushy black beard, and a big, honest face. In a moment I felt perfectly at ease, for I knew I was in the home of a hardy frontiersman, than whom no honester [*sic*] or braver men ever lived.

"Darned if I didn't take you for a half-breed at first," he said, laughing heartily; and then added, "Where on earth are you going to, youngster?"

"To Sioux City," I replied

"Got friends there?"

"No, only on a pleasure trip."

"Well, you're after fun, sure, and if you don't look out you'll get it," said my host, breaking out into an immoderate fit of laughter.

"What news have you?" I inquired.

"News enough," said my host, growing serious. "Haven't you heard that the red devils have broke loose again, and are just murderin' everybody above here? But hold on till I put your pony up, and get you a bite to eat, and then, while we smoke, I'll tell you all about it."

Here he rose to his feet, and, uttering a loud shrill whistle, an Indian squaw came in at the door, and my host, saying something to her in the Indian tongue, went out.

The squaw, with noiseless tread, moved about the room, making a fire, cutting meat, and putting the coffee on to boil, never once seeming to notice my presence. In a few minutes the host returned, and, seating himself, began: "You see, them Sioux of the upper country had a big pow-wow with the Minneconja Sioux, and they all have agreed to go to war. A party of the dirty, stealin' cusses were down at Randall the other day, and drew all their annuities .and ammunition, and then went over to see the Yanktons, and get them to join in the war. I tell you, they are bound to give us thunder this fall, and swear they will clear every white off the Missouri before spring. They say we must leave; but I reckon I'm too old a duck to get skeered at a darned Sioux."

So he talked on until the squaw had cooked the supper and set it out on the floor, using a white blanket for a table-cloth. The repast was a hearty one of boiled corn, fried elk, 'coon meat, and corn bread. The coffee was poured into tin-cups, and the host, rising, said: "Come and eat." Seating himself opposite to me, on' a corner of the blanket, he drew his knife from a sheath by his side, and, looking at me, inquired if I had any eating tools. I told him I had a knife and fork in my saddlebags, and, with the remark, "Better get'em," he cut off a large slice of the elk and commenced eating. Having secured my knife and fork, I ate heartily, for I was very hungry. Picking up the tin cup, I took a sup of coffee, and was obliged to spit it out to keep from scalding my mouth.

"Darned hot, ain't it?" said my host, bursting into a loud laugh.

Instinctively I looked at the squaw, but not a smile, not even a muscle moved in her stolid face. An Indian, unless addressed, never laughs or notices what happens to others.

When supper was over, my host filled a long-stemmed pipe, and pointing with the stem toward the sky, turned it to the earth, and ejaculating "How! Wa-con Tan Ka!" (Good, Oh God!) handed it to me. Supposing the pipe was for me to smoke, I thanked him, and began pulling away at the fragrant tobacco. Looking at him, I saw an angry scowl on his face, and he said, roughly, "Guess you've smoked enough." I handed the pipe back quickly, asking, "Did you not fill it for me?" "Yes," he replied, "but it is a peace pipe, and not for much smoke." I now saw that this white man was Indiana, when assembled together in council of friendship, use the peace pipe. They never use but one pipe, all sitting in a circle, and the man on the right smoking first. Each Indian takes three or four puffs and then passes the pipe to the Indian on his left. When it reaches the last Indian on the left, it is passed across to the Indian on the right, and commences its journey again. No Indian will smoke a pipe coming from the left, unless it is the Indian from whom the pipe started, who receives it from the man on the extreme left of the circle imbued with some of the strange customs of his savage neighbors, and, fearing to offend him, said nothing.

The squaw moved about so noiselessly that I did not hear her remove the dishes, but, on looking around, they were all gone, and the blanket taken up. How she had cleared away the things, without so much as jostling a dish, I could not conjecture, and-I feared to give offense by making inquiries, though I was burning with curiosity to learn more of this strange family.

"So you are going to Sioux City?" abruptly inquired the host, after having remained quiet for half an hour.

"Yes," I replied; and guessing he wished to know the object of my visit, added: "I'm going on up to the Yanktons, and, perhaps, as far as the Santee village."

"What," he inquired, rising to his feet, and eyeing me suspiciously.

"I'm going to the Yanktons to live and trade," I answered.

"You'll be scalped, as sure as thunder."

"Tell me all about the Indians' action's."

"Their what?"

"What they have been doing of late."

"Well," he replied, filling up and handing me a pipe, "that's what I was going to do. You see, the brutes came down to the settlement across the river, and after getting something to eat, killed all they could. They said they were hungry, and-while one old man was giving an Indian some bread another one shot him. They went into one man's house, and after eating at his table, shot him dead and carried off his wife. The fact is, they stole all they could, killed all they could, and then went up to the fort and traded off their

"What did they do with the woman?" I inquired, all my sympathies aroused.

"Do with her!" he exclaimed. "Why, kept her to gamble with, of course."

"How's that?" I pursued.

"I guess you ain't been much on the frontier," he replied, laughing.

I admitted that such was the case, and he said:

"You see, when they take a white woman they gamble her off every day until she gets pretty much passed round the tribe, and then she

11

is turned over to the squaws, who kill her, because they're always jealous of white women."

I could not help shuddering at the thought of a fate so terrible, and paid little more attention to what he said.

Feeling tired, I asked where I would sleep, and, my host pointing to a corner of the room, I spread down my blankets and soon fell asleep.

At dawn of day I was awakened by a loud pounding at the door, and my host, springing from a pile of buffalo robes in the opposite corner of the room, went to see what was the matter.

He soon learned that a party of miners had come down the Missouri from the Yellowstone, in Mackinaw boats, and seeing his hut from the river, had tied up and came over to find out who lived there, and how far they were from Omaha.

My host promptly opened the door and cordially welcomed the strangers. After a hearty breakfast, we went to the river and saw the boatmen off. As they shoved out from shore my host looked wistfully after the boat, and said: "How I do wish I had all the robes and beaver skins them fellows have; I'd leave this tarnal country if I had."

"Did you hear anything more of the Indians?" I inquired.

"No, they didn't see any," he answered; "but, depend upon it, they're not far off."

"Will your pony eat corn?" he inquired.

"I don't know," I replied.

"Well, we'll try him." And ordering the squaw to bring him the corn bag, he took from the limited household store about two quarts, and carried it to the stable, where I saw a superb hunting horse and two splendid hounds, who leaped upon their master and licked his hands and face.

"Do you not feed your own horse with corn?" I inquired.

"No, we can't afford it," he replied; "but if you are goin' to Sioux City, your nag will need something stronger than grass."

Returning to the cabin, we found the breakfast cleared away and the squaw chopping wood.

I talked an hour with my new-found friend, and then, saddling my pony, proposed to be off. I wanted to pay my host for what I had received from him, but the kind-hearted man refused, saying to me: "Keep your money, young man, for you will need it. We never charge here for what little we have to give travelers."

Cordially thanking him for his hospitality, I spurred up my pony, who sprang down the little knoll on which the cabin was built, and galloped over the prairie. It was a bright morning, and the air was fresh and bracing. Millions of beautiful flowers covered the ground for miles, and their perfume filled the air. It was a glorious sight, and my pony, seeming to partake of my spirits, went forward at a rapid pace.

It was high noon when I halted for an hour to graze the pony and eat a few slices of dried beef—the only lunch I had.

At sundown I reached Sioux City, sixty-five miles distant from where I had started in the morning.

I remained at Sioux City a day, and learned during that time that the Sioux had been again to see the Yanktons, and it was believed the Yanktons were going to war against the whites. Not a little dismayed at this intelligence, I set forward, and after two days' hard riding arrived at Fort Randall. I had seen some Indian squaws on the road, going to Yankton, on the Missouri, to trade, but being ignorant of the Indian tongue could not converse with them.

At Randall I found a Frenchman, named La Frombe, who lived with the Indians, and, joining him, we set out for the Yankton tribe.

In one month after turning Indian, with the aid of my friend La Frombe, I had mastered the language so I could speak Sioux quite fluently. I liked the wild life of the Indians, and built me a house in the village, composed of nine poles and ten robes.

I had now been in the village nearly two months, and, as it was drawing near to the time when the Indians would go on their fall hunt for winter provisions, I expressed to La Frombe my determination to join the hunt and remain through the winter. He said it would be best for me to regularly join the tribe, and offered to see the chief about the matter. I agreed to leave all to my friend, and do as he advised. Two days later Frombe came to me and said it was all arranged. I was to be received into the tribe at the next full moon, and was to have the squaw, Washtella, for a wife. This-was more than I had bargained for, and I told La Frombe that I did not want a squaw; but he said it was best to do as the chief wished, if I remained in the tribe. It was two weeks yet until the moon was full, so I promised La Frombe I would think over the matter.

One evening soon afterward Frombe came to my lodge, and said he would take me to see my sweetheart. I followed him, and we went out of the village to where some girls were watching the Indian boys play at ball. Pointing to a good-looking Indian girl, Frombe said: "That is Washtella."

"Is she a good squaw?" I inquired.

"Very," he replied.

"But perhaps she will not want to marry me," I said.

"She has no choice," he answered, laughing.

"But her parents," I interposed; "will they like this kind of proceeding?"

"The presents you are expected to make them will be more acceptable than the girl," he answered.

I did not feel at ease, but determined to follow my friend's advice, and obey the chiefs wishes in all things. The day of the full moon came, and with it my nuptials and adoption. I made the usual presents, and received a wife in return.

La Frombe gave me a nice new lodge-cover of tanned elk and buffalo hides; and, pitching my house in the midst of the village, I settled down to the business of a warrior of the first class.

The marriage, funeral, baptism, christening, and ether ceremonies of the Indians, will be described in a chapter devoted to that purpose.

A FAMILY MAN

I HAD not lived long with the Indians before I perceived a jealousy growing up in the tribe against me. Many of the old men were my friends, but the young warriors hated and despised me. There were many reasons for their dislike, for, not only was my squaw the handsomest woman in the nation, but I could run, ride, or shoot with the best young Indian, and I did much of my own work, and carried wood and water for little Washtella, which the young warriors thought was a degrading thing for a man to do. But Washtella was one of the kindest and best of women, and I really liked this wild maid of the forest, and, as is common among white men, I was willing to work for my wife. So I pretended not to see the sneers of the young Indians, and kept close to my lodge, for Washtella was teaching me her language.

One evening, while lying on the bed in my teepee, I heard a great beating of drums and rattling of gourds in the lower end of the camp, and asked Washtella what it all meant. She replied:

"The big medicine man calls the warriors to the medicine teepee."

"What for, Washtella?"

"To make arrows; then go on a big hunt; kill heap buffalo," she replied.

Gathering, my blanket about my shoulders (for I had now ceased to wear a coat or vest), I strode out of my lodge and made my way to the medicine lodge. Arrived there, I saw a number of old men seated around the walls of the lodge, and looking very solemn. One old Indian made room for me by his side, and I sat down on the ground, crossing my leg, and saying not a word. No women or children are allowed to enter the medicine lodge, and so none were present. We sat as silent as Quakers for half an hour, the drums and gourds meanwhile rattling vigorously without. The lodge now was full, and a great crowd of Indians, who could not get in, wert assembled about the door.

Presently, all the chiefs having come, the drums ceased to beat, and the medicine man (there is but one to each tribe) arose and built

16

a small fire in the center of the lodge. Casting on some brambles and a few light branches of wood as soon as it began to blaze, he harangued the crowd, telling them it was good time to go on a hunt, and that every sign in the sky and on the earth was favorable to their success. His speech was pretty 'long, and outlasted the fire, which burned down so now he had to rekindle it at the close of his oration.

When it burned bright again he began to chant an invocation to the Great Spirit, in which he asked blessings from We-ton-ka (God) on the hunters, the game, they killed, and on the guns, bows, arrows, knives, and ponies. He begged most earnestly that the hunters might be permitted to find plenty of buffalo, and that they might be successful in killing them, so that all the. Indians would be fat and comfortable during the coming winter.' The deep solemnity and reverence manifested by the Indians while this prayer was being offered up exceeded anything of the kind I had ever witnessed among white men. Not a sound was heard within, and the crowd without stood with bowed heads and outstretched necks anxious to catch every word of the great medicine man.

Taking a bunch of scented grass, he strewed it over the coals, when it emitted a sweet perfume, which completely filled the lodge and almost intoxicated the senses. While burning the grass, he chanted a wild song, keeping time with his foot. At length, sitting down, he tossed blades of grass on the fire, and the chiefs and warriors arose, and, moving to the left around the fire, kept slow time and step to the monotonous beating of the drum, which had struck up again.

When this had continued for some time, the leading chief laid on the fire a new arrow, which was gaudy with feathers and paint, and had a bright steel point. Then, the next chief in rank selected a fine arrow and threw it in the flames; so every chief and warrior did, when, seeing La Frombe cast in his arrow, I felt badly, for I had none, having come to see arrows made instead of destroyed.

I noticed that I was observed by the Indians, who kept going around the circle, although everyone but myself had cast in his arrow, and I began not only to wish myself safe out of the lodge, but to wonder how I would get out, when, chancing to look around, I saw the next Indian in the circle behind me was the old man who had given me a seat when entering the lodge. I passed my hand back to him, when, seeming to understand what I wanted, he slipped, unobserved, a new arrow into my fingers, and, drawing it through as if from under my arm, I advanced and threw it into the flames. The pile of arrows was quite high, and a bright red flame leaped up nearly to the roof of the lodge, the dry shafts making a crackling noise as they burned.

All the time the ceremony Aras going on, the medicine man sat by the fire, muttering to himself, and easting on scented grass. When each man had burned his arrow he left the lodge, and another warrior entered to replace him in the circle. Seeing my arrow consumed, I stepped out of the lodge, and went to my teepee, as did the other warriors to theirs.

It was now quite dark, and I found Washtella waiting supper for me. You may be curious to know how we lived in a wigwam, and I will tell you. We had no chairs, but sat on skins of wild animals laid on the ground. We had gourds for cups, and platters of both wood and tin. For food we had corn, prepared almost as hominy is in the States; then roast elk, boned buffalo, roast artichokes, flour, biscuit, buffalo tallow and water, and fried brains. We never used salt, as the Indians abominate it. At first I could hardly live without it, but soon became accustomed to fresh victuals, and even now I do not use a pound of salt in a year. Few Americans appreciate how much salt they eat—salt in everything of food kind, and pounds of it.

Coffee and tea, Washtella and I had none; but we had plenty of pure cold water, and I can assure you it is no bad substitute for the stronger beverage they were not unpleasant. While I shaved an arrow-shaft, Washtella made Some pretty head-work, or braided a buffalo hide with porcupine quills. Then we talked; and Washtella told me the curious tales of her people; how they had once lived far to the east, and had a great war with a fierce tribe, who drove the Yanktons from their hunting grounds and forced them far up the Missouri. Then she told me how the tribe wasted away from many thousands to a few hundreds, and how their towns had once been seven in number, built of wood and clay, and the buffalo, deer, elk, and antelope came and grazed within sight of the villages. Once, too, there had been a great chief in their tribe, who was famous in war, and so skillful he slew or defeated all their enemies; and his name was so terrible, that he was feared "every-where, and his people grew rich, and had many horses and much corn, and gave laws to all the other nations, who made presents and sent horses and corn, so they would not make war upon them. But the chief died, and then the fame of the nation decayed, and nobody feared them any longer or brought them corn or horses, but made war upon them and took away their horses and corn. So my dark-eyed companion, woman-like, rattled on with her tongue, now telling quaint stores of old times or curious legends of the lands where they had dwelt. The little maid was always cheerful, and made me tell of the great towns in which the pale faces live, and their tall houses where people slept far above the ground, all of which was very wonderful news to her.

In the mellow fall days we walked in the wood, or I joined the young men and played at ball. I must tell you how this game is played among the Indians, for it is curious.

A great noise of shouting is heard in the camp, and the young men, with bat or club three feet long and crooked at the end, go out on the prairie near the camp. Having found a smooth spot they halt, and two of the youths, by common consent, take opposite sides and pick out' the players, first one and then the other, until enough are had.

One morning I heard the young' men shouting for ball, and I went out with them to the play-ground. The two chiefs, A-ke-che-ta (Little Dog Soldier), and Ma-to-sac (White Bear), were picking sides, and a number of Indians were already seated facing each other, and bantering on the game. As each man was selected he spread down his buffalo robe and sat upon it, facing his opponent. I was selected by A-ke-che-ta, and silently took my place in the line. Presently all the young men who were to play were selected, and then several old men were appointed to act as umpires of the game. These advanced and seated themselves between the contestants, and then the warriors rose and commenced betting on the game. First one warrior advanced and threw down a robe before the old men; then a warrior from the other side came forward and laid a robe upon it; and so all bet, one against the other. Presently there was a great number of piles of stakes, some having bet moccasins, head-dresses, bead-work, ear-rings, necklaces, bows and arrows, and even ponies. All these were carefully watched over by the old men, who noted each stake and the deposition on a stick. If you did not wish to bet with any particular warrior you laid your wager on the big pile, and instantly it was matched by the judges against some article of corresponding value from the pile of the other side. Thus I bet a hunting-knife, half a pound of powder, a pair of moccasins, and a small hand-mirror, which articles were appropriately matched with others by the judges. All was now in readiness for the game to begin, and the parties separated. The two lines were formed about one hundred yards apart. In front of each side, twenty feet from each other, two stakes, smeared with paint, are driven firmly into the ground, and the object of the game is to drive the ball between the stakes. Whichever side shall first force the ball through the opposite, stakes wins the game. The ball, made of rags and covered with buckskin, is carried to the center of the ground between the combatants, and there deposited, by one of the old men, who then returns to his post. The judges then give the signal, and with loud shouts the players run to the ball, and commence knocking it to and fro with their crooked sticks. The ball is about the size of a large orange, and each party tries to prevent its coming toward their stakes. No warrior must touch the ball with his hands; but if it lies in a hole, he may push it out with his foot, and then hit it with his stick.

In the game which I am telling you about, Ma-to-sae's party reached and struck the ball first, lifting it clear over our heads, and sending it far to our rear and close to our stakes. Then we all ran, and Ma-to-sac's and A-ke-che-ta's warriors fell over me another, and rapped each other on the shins with their clubs, and there was great confusion and excitement, but at length one of the party succeeded in hitting the ball, and sent it to Ma-to-sac's stakes. Thither we ran, but no one could find the ball. After much search, I discovered it m a tuft of grass, and, bidding one of our men run quickly to the stakes, I hit it and drove the ball to him. Unfortunately, it fell in a hole, and before our warrior could get it out and hit it, a dense crowd of Ma-to-sac's men were around the spot and in front of the stakes. The contest was violent, so much so, indeed, that no one could hit the ball, though it was continually tramped over. At length someone called out,

"There it goes," and the warriors scattered in all directions looking to see where it was; but one of Ma-to-sae's men, win had called out, stood fast, and when the crowd had scattered L saw him attempting to conceal the ball beneath his foot. Running against him from behind with such force as to throw him on his face, before he could recover his feet, I hit the ball and, seeing all Ma-to-sac's men off their guard, with the aid of a young man, easily drove it between their stakes, only a few yards distant.

The judges at once declared the game was ours, and many and loud were the cheers sent up by our party, in token of the victory, while Ma-to-sae's men retired sullen and disappointed. I was declared the winner, and A-ke-che-ta thanked me for my services, while the young warriors gathered around and congratulated me on my success. Then we all smoked, and went over to the stakes to receive our shares. As winner, I was entitled to a general share of the spoils; but I declined in favor of the young Indian who had helped me drive the ball, saying that, as he had last hit it, and actually forced it between the stakes, he was, in reality, the most deserving. This argument was loudly applauded by the old men, and the young warrior, who had not been friendly for some time with me, was so touched by my generosity that he came and thanked me, saying frankly, "You, and not I, won the game."

However, I forced the general stake upon him, at which he was much pleased. I found that the stakes had won a saddle, half a pound of powder, six yards of wampum beads, and a handsomely braided knife-scabbard. When the judges had awarded all the winnings, among which were fourteen ponies, each took up his trophies and returned to the village, where, for the remainder of the day, the game was fought over again and again in the teepees.

It was now four days since we had made buffalo medicine (burned the arrows), and the time to go upon the hunt had come. The chief, on the fourth evening, sent a crier through the village to notify all to be in readiness, and we at once began packing up our lodges, mending bows, and grinding knives, etc. Poles, like shafts, were made for the ponies, and fastened across their backs by broad wampum belts at the small ends, while the large ends dragged on the ground. On these, behind the pony, were lashed robes and bedding, and cooking utensils; and on them sat the children. Even the dogs had packs to carry, which were tied on their backs with thongs of buffalo skin. The squaws walked and led the ponies, having charge of all the property and children, while the warriors, mounted on the best animals, rode ahead, behind, and on the flanks of the column, which, when drawn out, was several miles long—each pony following the one in front of him. So, we went on the great annual buffalo hunt.

The knives of Indians are generally ground on one side, like a carpenter's chisel; and this is always done when going on buffalo hunts, as they less liable to cut the skin when sharpened in that way.

AT THE HUNTING GROUNDS

IT was a bright, clear morning when the whole village was aroused by beating of drums, blowing of horns, and the barking of dogs. While the squaws cooked the breakfast, the warriors set about pulling down the lodges, and soon almost the whole village had disappeared. The few wigwams left standing were for the sick, the aged, and those who were too infirm to go on the hunt. Bidding good-bye to the Indians who were to remain, we set out, as gay a party as ever was seen seeking pleasure.

Those first packed were first off, and, as I was one of the laggards, when I pulled out, the column was streaming over the hills for miles ahead.

I had two ponies, one for myself and the other for Washtella and our household goods. The cha-a-koo, or saddle, had been fastened to the little pony's back, and to this were tied our teepee, or lodge poles, three on each side. They we-fastened by the small ends, and the large ends dragged on ground. To prevent the poles from spreading apart, a crosspiece of dry wood was lashed with rawhide just behind the pony's hams. On the poles were piled our bedding, lodge covers, and cooking utensils, while the provisions in flesh-bags were slung across the pony's back. Some of the families who had children, slung wicker-baskets between the poles, and in these were put the papooses. The squaws walked and led the ponies, and the dogs and larger children trotted alongside. When tired, the squaws or children rode on the pony by turns, and one was on his back all the time. It is astonishing what burdens these little beasts can carry, and still keep fat and lively. I have frequently seen them travel hundreds of miles, loaded down almost out of sight, and thrive every day. They have greater powers of endurance than the mule.

My spare pony was led by Washtella, who tripped joyfully along singing her Indian songs. One of these ran as follows: "Tish-ah, be moak sa-ura Ma-mo, za na geezing Ma-ino zali na ahkee Ma-mo yah na. "Bai me sa yah na geezhigeny Bai me sa yah na Wa bun ong tuz-ze Iwai Ise wah ween ne go ha za."

Which might be rendered thus:

> "We are riding to seek the war path;
> The earth and the sky are before us.
> We walk by day and by night,
> And the evening star is our guide."

Another was:

> "We devote our bodies to the fight,
> And charge with the speed of eagles;
> We are willing to lie with the slain,
> For then our name will be praised."

Still another:

> "Look how beautiful is my face and form,
> And hear the sweet song of my voice;
> All my thoughts are of you, darling,
> And I speak to you with my naked heart."

It was in vain I urged the little maid to ride; to all my appeals she replied, "Never mind, pony will be tired enough, and I will ride him plenty when we find the buffalo."

Our first day's journey was only fifteen miles, and early in the afternoon we came to a limpid stream where the chief ordered ns to halt and camp. While the warriors pitched the teepees the squaws brought wood and water, and soon the fires were blazing and the kettles boiling for supper. Leaving the preparation of the meal to the women, we hoppled our ponies and picketed them out on the green grass near the camp. Several warriors remained to guard them, and the rest returned to the village. The Indians never leave their horses or camp without a guard, and, no matter how secure the country may be, they steadily keep out their pickets or runners.

After supper, the warriors played at ball, made arrows, repaired their horse equipments, wrapped the loose sinews on their bows, or gathered in groups and smoked. The women cleaved away the supper, made up the beds in the lodges, and carried wood and water for the morning.

In the evening I strolled out with Washtella, and, going to the edge of the woods, saw one of those glorious sights only to be witnessed in perfection at sea or on the prairie, a glorious sunset.

A great red globe of fire hung in the west, sinking slowly and grandly behind the hills, lighting up the horizon and clouds with molten gold. I gazed long and earnestly at the beautiful scene, and stood lost in thought until aroused by my companion, who said, "Let us return to the lodge; it grows late." Through the gloaming we walked back to the village, and, entering my teepee, I bade Washtella bring me my pipe, and, while I smoked, tell me a story. She brought the pipe, and, seating herself by my side, related the following extraordinary tale:

Once there were giants on the earth, and they devoured little children. The great medicine man of our nation told the chief he should bet all the little children of his nation on a race he would run with the giants, and, if he beat them, no more children would ever be eaten by the big men. The chief was very anxious to rid himself of the giants, besides it was evident they would eat up all the children at any rate, so they might as well be bet as not. A great council was called, and' after three days' debate, it was agreed the children should be put up and the race run with the giants by the medicine man. All the nation was present to witness the contest, but the giants easily won the race; so they demanded the children should be given up that they might devour them. Now, there was one old man who had a grandchild that he loved dearly, and when the race was lost, he took the child on his back, and traveled for many days to the west, until he came to a great wood, and in the depth of the forest he built a hut, and hid away the child, hoping the giants would not find him.

The prophets had foretold that a child would be born in the tribe, who would wear a white feather, become a mighty man, a great warrior, and slay all the giants the old man kept his grandson in great ignorance, telling him they were the only people in the world besides the giants, and that if the giants found them out they would kill and eat them. The boy was very much afraid, and hid away at every noise he heard.

One day, while out hunting, he shot a bird, and, as it had pretty white feathers in its tail, he pulled them out and put them in his hair. When he returned home in the evening, his grandfather saw the white feathers, and, remembering what the prophets had said, he knew at once that his grandson would be a great man and destroy the giants. But the old man was still afraid the giants might kill and eat the boy, for he was yet a small lad; so he did not tell him of what great honors were in store for him.

Not many days after he had shot the bird, the boy was out hunting in the woods, and, as was his wont when tired, he laid down in the shade of a great tree to sleep; and as he slept, he heard a voice, saying, "Go home, you wearer of the white feather, and when you sleep, you will dream of a pipe and sack with a great white feather, and when you wake up you will find them, and see that you keep them." When the boy heard these words he jumped up and looked whence the voice proceeded and saw a wooden man fixed firmly in the earth. He was greatly astonished, for he did not know there were any men in the world beside his grandfather. So he ran home and slept and sure enough he dreamed he saw a pipe and sack, and a great white feather in it; and when he waked up the articles were there. He had told his grandfather all about his dream in the wood, and at once accused him of putting the sack and pipe with the feather by his bed while he slept. But the old man would only answer, "Put the feather in your hair, and you will one day become a great man and destroy all your enemies." So the boy braided the feather in his hair, and immediately he felt very strong, and, to see if his strength was real, he went out and easily overthrew a great tree, and he became very proud of his strength. Next day he said to himself, Now that I am so strong I will go out and pull up the wooden man and bring him home, so that I can talk with him. And he went to the wooden man in the forest, and tried to pull him up; but, although he could uproot great trees, he could not get the wooden man out of the ground; whereat he got very angry, and struck the man in the face, but only hurt himself, for the man had an iron head. The wooden man laughed heartily at his rage, and said to the boy, "See, my son, strength is not the only thing we must have in the world, and, in a man or a nation, it is of little use without

26

wisdom; now, if you will dig about me, you can easily lift me." Then he dug about the man and lifted him out, and carried him home on his back. When the old man saw the wooden man he fell to the earth on his face, and was mightily afraid, for he knew it was the god the giants had stolen when they overcome his nation, since which time no luck had come to his people. The boy bade his grandfather get up and tell why he was afraid. Then the old man said, "My son, whatever you wish will be so, for this is the all-powerful god the giants stole and hid away." The young man at once lighted his pipe, and wished for some pigeons for his dinner, and immediately great flocks issued from the smoke of his pipe; then he wished for some rabbits, and hundreds of them came jumping out of the woods. He took good care of his pipe and the wooden man, and wore his white feather, and lived in the wood with his grandfather until he grew to be g tall man.

One day the wooden man said to the boy, who was now called Chacopee, "You are big and strong; go, slay the giants, but be not foolish, for wisdom, and not strength, must win the victory. If you think of nothing else until it is done, you will kill all the giants. Go and be wise."

Early the next morning the young man set off alone, and after traveling a hundred sleeps he came to the land of the giants. When they saw him and observed that he wore a white leather in his hair, they laughed, and scoffingly said, "So this is the little man who has come to kill us all! Let the cooks put on some water to boil him in, and we will soon make an end of him by eating him." "Come, short legs," cried one of the giants, "dance us a jig while the water is heating." But Chacopee only said, "If my legs are short, they are long enough to beat yours, if you will give me a start." "Agreed," cried the giant; "go out to yonder tree, and I will catch you before you have run half a mile." Then Chacopee walked out to the tree, and all the way along he thought how he should out-wit the giant. Unperceived he tied the grass across the path, and cried to the giant to come on. So the giant ran, and tripped his foot in the grass, and fell to the ground with great force, which so stunned him, that before he could rise Chacopee hit him on the head with a war-club and beat his

27

brains out. Another giant came running to help his brother; but Chacopee fell flat on the earth, and the giant stumbled over him p so he beat out his brains.' Now, there was still another giant, who was a very wise man, who had the power to take whatever shape he wished, and, seeing the fate of his brothers, he immediately changed himself into a beautiful woman, and came to Chacopee and said,

"Come and be my husband, for I love you, and have traveled a long way to marry you." But Chacopee remembered what the wooden man had told him, and at once lighting his pipe he wished himself an elk, and immediately he was an elk. The woman upbraided him, and cried so bitterly that he repented, for she was very beautiful, and he wished himself a man again.

He became a man at once, and kissed the woman's lips and cheeks, and laid his head-on her lap and fell asleep. While he slept, she took the feather out of his hair, and, taking his pipe, the giant at once became himself, when he called in a loud voice to Chacopee to wake up; and, on waking up, poor Chacopee found the woman gone and himself as weak as any other man. So the giant broke his back with his great club, and then, changing Chacopee into a dog, bade him follow him. Putting the feather into his own hair, the giant and his dog set out for the north, where two famously pretty women lived whom the giant wished to marry! These girls were the daughters of a great chief, who had sworn they never should marry anyone but a great chief who, the prophets foretold, would come from the south and wear a white feather in his hair. When the giant and his dog came to the village the giant went in to stay with the eldest sister, while the dog stole off to the other sister's lodge and slept beside her. In the night the younger sister dreamed if she took good care of the dog she would become a great chief's wife, far greater than he of the white feather. Next morning she would not look at the giant, but walked out of the village followed by the dog, and when they were alone the dog ran to the brook and took up a stone in his mouth, which immediately became a beaver, and the chief's daughter took it home for their dinner. The giant hunted every day, but he could kill nothing, so he and his squaw were nearly starved, and the chief was very angry because the giant Kept his

28

daughter so poorly. The giant, seeing how well the younger sister and her dog lived, watched the dog, and when he had taken a stone from the brook and saw it turn to a beaver, the giant drew out a stone from the water and it also became a beaver. Greatly rejoiced, he tied the beaver to his belt and carried it home, where he skinned it, and his wife put it in the pot to boil. But when she took off the lid to see if it was done, only the stone was there which her husband had taken from the brook.

The dog, finding his secret was discovered, went out into the woods and broke a dry twig from a bush that had been burned by the fire, and the black twig at once became a black bear. The giant watched again, and seeing how the dog got his game, he broke a twig off, and immediately it was a black bear. So he tied it to his belt and brought it home. But when his squaw went to get some of the bear, she saw only a charred stick tied to the belt. Then the giant went to the chief and told him of the disgraceful manner iii which his daughter was living with a dog; but the chief said it was impossible for a dog to take game as the giant related. However, the chief, to satisfy himself about the matter, appointed several young men to go and see about it. When the dog heard this he told his mistress by bow-wows to sweat him as the Indians do sick people. Then she built a pit and left it open at the top, and in the pit she' put the dog, and put several heated stones in with him, and closed the opening. So he sweat prodigiously, and when the young men came and opened the pit, the dog was no longer there, but a nice young man in his stead.

Then they took him out of the pit and brought him to the chief, but he had no speech, and could tell them nothing The chief called all the wise men together, and they took council. All of them smoked, and the giant smoked, but when the young man smoked, behold great flocks of pigeons flew out of the smoke. The wise men knew by this token that the young man was the real Chief of the White Feather, and the giant an impostor. So the wise men smoked again, and then took the white feather from the giant's head and put it in Chacopee's hair, for it was he, and immediately Chacopee's speech returned, and he related to the wise men all that had happened to him; how he had been raised in the wood; how he had got the white feather; how he carried home the wooden man and conversed with him; how he had slain the giant's brothers; how he had been beguiled by the beautiful woman, .transformed into a dog by the giant, and brought hither. When he had made an end of speaking, the wise men rose up and told the chief all they knew, and the chief ordered the giant to be beaten to death with clubs. But when the warriors came near him, he changed himself into a wolf, and ran away so fast that neither the warriors nor the dogs could catch him. Until that day no wolf had ever been seen, and all the wolves now living are the giant's children, and that is why they eat little boys and girls.

After the giant had run away the chief made a great feast, and married both his daughters to Chacopee, who took his wives to his people, where he brought also the wooden man and his old grandfather, who was still living. And Chacopee became a great chief, and had many brave ones and beautiful daughters. And his sons still rule all that country, which is toward the setting sun and along the sea.

Thus ended Washtella's story of Chacopee, and, when she had done, I asked if she really believed there ever were giants on the earth.

"Yes," she replied, "hundreds of lives ago the men and women were all as tall as trees; but they have grown smaller and smaller, until now they are no higher than bushes, and a hundred lives hence they will be no taller than the buffalo grass. Then they will go into the ground and live like rabbits."

"Washtella, tell me where your people first came from."

"Long, long ago," she said, "they lived in the earth, which is hollow; but one day they came to an opening and came out, when, liking the outside best, they staid and would not return. My own father once saw the hole they came out of, but I never saw it, as it is far down the Missouri, where the white man lives."

It was now late, and, wrapping ourselves in our blankets, we lay down and soon fell asleep.

30

Early the next morning we resumed our journey, and on the fifth day began to see buffalo warders. On the sixth day we came upon the herds, and pitched our camp on the banks of a pleasant lake. The whole evening was consumed in putting up the lodges, for the winds often blow terrifically on these lakes, and it is necessary to make the teepees very strong. Hundreds of buffalo were grazing within a few miles of us, and everyone busied himself in making final preparations for the great hunt which was to begin on the morrow.

The old bulls that are feeble, and whose horns are dull, are driven away from the herd by the young bulls. They stay near the herd, but not with it. In approaching buffalo these stragglers or warders, as they are called by the Indians, are always met long before you come on the main body. When they see the hunters they run to the herd, and give notice of approaching danger.

AT PEACE WITH ALL THE WORLD

WHEN our camp was pitched, I walked out along the banks of the beautiful lake, to see what I could discover. Its waters were clear as crystal and full of fish. Not a boat, and perhaps not even a canoe, had ever rippled its bosom, and I could not but imagine, as I gazed across the blue expanse, that one day commerce would spring up, and towns and cities be built upon its green shores.

Looking to the north, I was startled from my reflections by seeing a large buffalo cow coming down to the water to drink, Hastening back to the village, I quickly procured my Hawkins' rifle and ran over the little eminence that hid the lodges from the animal. She had approached quite near the water, and was not more than one hundred and fifty yards distant from me, when, hearing a noise in my rear, I looked back and saw several Indians running toward me with their guns. The row at the same moment saw them, and turned to make off, but too late, for I had drawn a bead on her heart, and at one shot dropped her dead. All the village came running and shouting, and the squaws gathered around the dead buffalo, jostling and elbowing each other as they tore off the meat. Tt is the Indian rule that game is common property, and my buffalo was soon reduced to a pile of bones by the knives of the busy squaws. I could not help laughing as I watched them struggling for the choice morsels. First, the skin was carefully removed, and then the muscles and gristle cut away, when, just as a squaw was about to take the coveted part, she would be rudely thrust aside, and some other .squaw would take it. These exploits were received with loud shouts of laughter, and no ill-temper or quarreling was observed among the excited crowd of women who surrounded the carcass.

On returning to my lodge, I found Washtella in great glee over my good luck, and she explained that it was no small matter to have killed the first buffalo slain in the hunt. Presently I received a message from the chief, and was informed by an old Indian that, having killed the first buffalo, I would be entitled to lead the hunt on the first day. Meat was brought me, and the skin or robe, which,- according to the Indian custom, is always given to the one who kills

32

the animal. So proud was Washtella, she did nothing all the evening but talk of my good fortune and I could not help being amused at the boasts of the little maid. Nothing could possibly have happened that would have given her more pleasure.

The next morning, as soon as it was daylight, I was aroused, and told that the warriors were waiting for me, to lead them in the chase. Assembling all of them before my lodge, I addressed them, saying I was a young man, and lacked experience, but if they would allow me, I would name one worthy to lead them in my place. This was received with loud shouts of approval, and as soon as quiet was restored, I pointed to a young warrior, and said: "He is a good man go and follow him." The warrior I had selected was my bitter enemy, and had formerly been a lover of Washtella. Ever since my marriage he had abhorred me, and omitted no opportunity to show his dislike. As his animosity was well-known in the tribe, the honors thus thrust upon him, by one from whom he had expected no favors, surprised and pleased, them. For a moment the brave hung his head, and then came forward, and, amid the shouts of the warriors, gave me his hand. Feeling unwell, I did not go upon the hunt that day, but in the evening, when the party returned, my old enemy came to my lodge, and as a token of his friendship, presented me with two fine robes he had taken during the day.

On the second day I went out with the hunters, and joined in a most exciting chase. Under the directions of a chief, we deployed at wide distances, and then, closing in, surrounded a herd of buffalo on three sides; and as soon as the herd began to move, the chase began. Our tough little ponies bore us swiftly along, and soon the herd was hard pressed. Presently it began to scatter, and then each Indian, selecting a buffalo, followed the beast up until he had killed it. It is astonishing how fast the great lumbering animals can run, and although they do not seem to go-over the ground very rapidly, it takes a good horse to come up with them. Their shambling "lope" is equal in speed to an American horse's gallop, and they can climb steep hills and get over rough ground faster than a horse. They run with their heads near the earth, and a hundred of them will make a mighty noise, resembling the rumbling of distant thunder. The hunter approaches from behind, and, when opposite the beast, fires, aiming at the spine or side, immediately behind the fore-shoulder. One shot in the spine or heart will bring a buffalo down, but it generally takes from three to ten balls in the vitals to kill one.

In the second day's hunt I killed seven buffalo, which was considered a good day's work, only one other warrior killing as many. The warriors do not stop to touch the game after it is dead, the skinning and packing of the meat being the work of the squaws, who follow in the wake of the hunters. For this purpose they have pack-ponies, and two women will skin and pack three or four buffalo in a day. The meat is brought to the villages, where it is cut in narrow slices, about an inch thick, and three or four inches long. These slices are then hung on poles, or stretched on small willows laid across a frame-work of poles. The meat is frequently turned, and allowed to remain in the sun and air for three days. It should be covered, or brought in at night, and must not be allowed to get wet by rain while it is curing. This is called jerking buffalo, and is a simple and easy process of curing meat. The pure crisp air of the plains soon dries it, and then it has a sweet, pleasant taste. I have known climates on the plains where nearly all the year carcasses could be hung up and left without spoiling until used. Meat, when jerked, is only about half the weight and size it is when in a raw state. If soaked in water it will swell greatly, and then, unless used immediately will spoil. "When the buffalo flesh is dried sufficiently, it is put into parfleches, or wrappers, made of raw-hide, cut square, and which will hold about half a bushel. They are sewed up at the bottom and sides, the laps at the top being left open until they are filled. The meat is then laid flat, and packed tightly, like plugs of tobacco. When two or three layers of meat have been put in, hot buffalo fat is brought and poured over it until all the interstices are filled up. Then more layers of meat are put in, and more fat poured on, until the parfleche is full, when the laps are folded over each other and tightly sewed up with sinews. The meat is now ready for winter use, and two parfleches are fastened together like a pair of saddle-bags, and slung across the back of a pony when the Indians travel. To prevent these bags or wrappers from hurting the ponies' backs, the under ide is lined with fur or bear skin.

We had hunted four days from our camp on the lake, and although we had taken the utmost precaution not unnecessarily to alarm the buffalo, most of them had gone a long distance from the village. A council was called, and it was determined we should go over to the lakes that lay on the Jim River, sixty miles distant. We immediately set out, moving around the lake to the right of the buffalo, so as not to disturb them. Our route lay across a beautiful level country, through which meandered little streams eight or ten miles apart. These streams are unwooded, and we were compelled to use buffalo chips for cooking. We traveled leisurely along, however, halting on the creeks, and making about sixteen miles per day, for many of our pomes were already heavily laden with meat.

On the fourth day we reached the lakes, and again pitched our village. .Here we found plenty of buffalo and a great many calves, which were very acceptable to us, as we wanted some parfleches of veal.

We hunted four days, and took a great deal of meat. Each family had from three to six parfleches, according to its size which was as much as it could use during the winter, and enough for the infirm besides. So the hunt was announced at an end, and we began to prepare for our return. I had been exceedingly fortunate, and had taken no less than nine parfleches of meat and had twelve robes.

There are several methods of killing buffalo beside the regular chase. One of these, as practiced by the Indians, is as follows:

The buffalo are watched until they graze near a precipice, when two or three Indians put a buffalo skin on sticks, and concealing themselves under it, approach near the herd slowly, as if grazing. This must be done when the wind is favorable, and blowing from the buffalo. If the decoy is successful, other Indians make a wide circuit, surrounding the herd on all sides, except that toward the bluff. Then they steal up as close as possible, anti when the buffalo discover them they shout, shake their blankets and poles, and close in upon the herd. The animals are greatly alarmed, but seeing the mock buffalo (which has managed to attract attention) set off for the bluffs, they rush madly after it. When the baiters reach the bluff, they fling the mock buffalo over the precipice, and betake

35

themselves to holes in the bank or crevices among the rocks. It is in vain the leaders of the herd halt when they see the chasm; the mass from behind, crazed by the poles and blankets of the Indians, who are now close upon them, rush madly on, and press those in front over the cliff.

It is exceedingly dangerous to bait buffalo, as the herd frequently overtake the false buffalo and trample it beneath their feet, or the great beasts, falling among the rock, crush the Indian baiters to death. Many reckless young Indians, who as baiters have gone too far inland, have, after the chase, been found dead on the plain, or their mangled bodies lay at the foot of the precipice with the carcasses of the animals they had so cruelly deceived. It takes a brave Indian to be a baiter, but there are always plenty of young and foolish boys who are anxious to engage in the dangerous sport.

After the buffalo have fallen and killed or maimed themselves, a party of Indians who have been concealed near the foot of the precipice suddenly advance and finish them with axes or rifles. As many as a hundred animals are frequently taken in a single day in the way I have related.

Another method of capturing buffalo is in this wise: When the Indians have been engaged at war, or, for any reason, have not been fortunate in securing, during the fall, a supply of meat for winter, they go to a lake or river where there is game, and crossing the country in a wide circuit, fire the prairie. The buffalo, alarmed by the fire, and finding themselves surrounded by flames, plunge into the water, when the Indians easily kill them. Another way is to drive them on the ice, where they slip and fall, while the Indians can run rapidly in their moccasins on the ice.

When the Indians get out of provisions in the winter, early in the spring they will fire the grass on the opposite side of a river from where the buffalo are grazing, and the buffalo are tempted to cross the ice in search of the green grass which springs up immediately after the fire. The ice, being already soft, breaks beneath their great weight, and the animals are drowned or killed. Sometimes a large buffalo will get on a great cake of ice and float down the river, when the Indians will kill him and tow him ashore. It is wonderful how the

Indians can run on the floating ice. They will frequently press a piece no more than a foot square, and yet cross in safety. Their moccasins render their footing sure, and they spring lightly from one cake to another, never halting for a moment, for to halt is to go down.

Our hunt having ended, the chief ordered that the usual feast and rejoicing should take place. A long pole was provided, a buffalo head put on the top of it, and a number of tails nailed, at right angles, to the sides. The pole was then set firmly in the ground, in the center of an open space before the village, and buffalo heads were piled up around it. The heads are set in a circle, and arranged to look as hideously as possible. Immense quantities of buffalo meat were now brought, and the feast made ready. Nothing but buffalo meat is eaten, and everyone makes it a point to gorge himself to the fullest extent. Even the dogs are stuffed, and the women and children persuaded to eat while they can force down a bite. The greater the quantity of meat eaten, the greater the honor; and some starve themselves for two or three days in advance, in order to do justice to the occasion; The meat is prepared in every form—boiled, fried, broiled, roasted, and raw. When one is full, he goes to the pole, and as soon as a sufficient number have collected, the dance begins. The warriors sit in a circle around the pole, and the squaws, gaudily dressed and painted, form a circle around the warriors. At a signal the drums beat, and all rise and stand. Then the squaws sing, and the warriors move around to the right and the squaws to the left, each keeping time to the drums with their feet. The dance is a slow, shuffling motion, but soon makes one very tired. When a warrior or squaw gets tired, they step out of the circle and others take their places. As soon as it is dark wood is brought, fires made around the pole, and the dancing is kept up all night. The feasting frequently continues for three days, and at no time is the pole without its set of dancers. The amount of buffalo consumed is prodigious, when we consider that, besides the vast quantities eaten by the Indians, each family has from six to ten dogs.

Not to dance on such an occasion would seem to be ungrateful for the good luck I had had in taking meat, so I joined-in heartily, but by midnight, was completely worn out. Calling to Wash tell a, I told her I was so tired I must go to my lodge, and she readily acceded, and went with me. Laying down, I immediately fell asleep, but, on waking at daylight, I was surprised to find Washtella already up and going about her work. I inquired what made her rise so early, and she then confessed that as soon as I was asleep she had stolen out and gone back to the dance, from which she had but just returned. Poor child! she had done no more than her white sisters often do— that is, had a night of it—so I readily forgave her.

The feast over, we began to prepare in earnest for our return. The meat was carefully distributed, so that no pony would be overloaded, and everything was neatly packed. It took both my ponies and all my dogs to carry my meat and lodge, so Washtella and I had to walk. We considered this no great hardship, however, as nearly the whole village was on foot. We made only eight or ten miles a day; but at last, after a most fatiguing march, reached the Missouri, and entered our old camp near Fort Randall.

I was glad to be at home once more, and I felt very comfortable, for I had made a good reputation as a hunter, formed new friendships, and won over some of my old enemies. Indeed, why should I not be comfortable? My domestic relations were most happy. I had an abundance of winter's fowl, twelve robes, and Washtella had provided me with a good supply of tobacco. So I sat down with my favorite pipe and was at peace with all the world.

The eha-sha-sha, or Indian tobacco, is made of red-willow bark. The squaws gather great quantities of the sprouts or small limbs, and reel off the bark, which, when dried, is broken into pieces of about the consistency of Kinnikinick. When properly preserved, red willow is equal to the best Kinnikinick; and when smoked has a sweet, pleasant taste, and emits a delicious perfume.

INDIAN DOCTORS

INDIANS have the reputation among white people of being great natural physicians, and although it cannot be denied that they have some knowledge of herbs and simple remedies, yet their claim to extensive medical learning is wholly fictitious. Among my earliest recollections are pictures on bottles of well-proportioned female Indians receiving "from angels" herbs which were to cure all the ills of the flesh, and the knowledge of which some venerable chief, while on his deathbed, kindly communicated to a missionary. Hence we have Red Jacket's Bitters, when Red Jacket, in fact, never drank any bitters. It would somewhat destroy the efficacy of these nostrums to inquire to what church the missionary belonged who received the information of the medical properties of the herbs, and also of what tribe the famous Chief Whangdoodleds was the head. We shall recur to this subject again, but now give place to the following incident, as illustrative of the character of the Indian doctor.

There were several young girls who came nearly every day to my lodge to talk with my squaws, and one day one of these, while out gathering brushwood for the fire, was bitten in the arm by a rattlesnake. This I was told by a girl who came running to ray lodge crying bitterly, and saying her sister was going to die. I asked Washtella what the medicine man did in such cases, and she said nothing at all but pray for the spirit of the unfortunate. I told her to run over to the medicine-lodge quickly, where the girl had been taken, and tell the "Great Medicine Man" I could cure her. Washtella laughed in my face, and said she would not dare do such a thing, as no women but the immediate relatives of the afflicted were allowed to approach the lodge on such occasions. I threatened to punish her if she did not go instantly, and no doubt thinking my anger was more to be dreaded than that of the medicine man, she ran off, but soon returned to say she could not gain admittance. I hastened to the lodge, and on approaching saw several poles stuck up over the door with charms and feathers tied to them. I heard a great beating of drums and wailing within, and while others stood at a respectful distance I walked boldly up to the door and entered. Within I saw the old doctor crouched at the head of the girl, who lay extended on

39

a buffalo-robe, her arm bare to the shoulder. Her mother was seated at her feet, moaning bitterly, and rocking herself to and fro. The doctor was singing vigorously and rattling a gourd over the girl's head; then he would take up a drum made of raw hide and beat it industriously,-raising his humdrum tone to a shrill key, when he would resume his gourd and guttural song. So intently was this learned doctor engaged in making medicine that he did not notice my intrusion, but kept on with his chant. Feeling that I was standing on forbidden ground, and making myself liable to a severe punishment, if not death, I determined to act quickly, not only for my own sake but the girl's. Stepping up to the gray-headed and shriveled doctor, I cried in a loud voice:

"Let the father be silent and hear."

For a moment or two the sharp rattling of the gourd continued, and the song rose higher and higher, then suddenly it ceased, and the old doctor, rising to his feet and drawing up his shrunken frame to its full height, demanded:

"Why come you here?"

"In His name I come," I answered, pointing to the sky.

In a moment the old man was bowed on his knees, and muttered, "How is this, O God!"

"Behold," I continued, "the Great Spirit has sent me to eat the poison and cure the girl;" and so saying I knell down by the side of the poor sufferer. She had now been bitten some fifteen or twenty minutes, and already the swelling had commenced, and two small purple-looking circles were formed around the wound. There were two small red spots where the fangs of the reptile had entered the arm, and I feared it was too late to save the poor creature's life, but determined to try. I applied my lips to the wound and sucked it vigorously, but nothing came from it; then I bit it gently and a few drops of black looking blood came out. Presently it bled freely, and I sucked it as long as the blood seemed impure. I next ran over to my lodge and sweetened nearly a pint of whisky, which I fortunately had, and gave it to the girl to drink. Then I heated a wire, and, thrusting it into the wound, cauterized it to the depth the snake's teeth had penetrated. The girl held very still, and never once moved or complained. Very soon the whisky caused her to fall into a deep sleep, and I left the lodge motioning the mother and doctor to follow. They had looked on with feelings of wonder and awe, and when we were outside I said, "Let the maiden sleep as long as she will, and when she awakes she will be well."

I started toward my lodge, when the medicine man followed me a few steps, and, seizing my hand, said, with deep feeling, "Farewell, my son; I am sorry for you."

I asked him what he meant, and the venerable ass then explained that, having eaten the poison from the girl's arm, of course I would die. I said I hoped not, for I intended to spew it up, and I believed the Great Spirit would not let me die for doing as he had commanded me. He replied, "O God, I guess this is good!"

"You bet it is, old donkey," I replied in English, knowing he did not understand a word of that language. He bowed deeply, no doubt thinking I had paid him a great compliment, and departed to his lodge.

I hastened home, and found my poor Washtella in great distress, for she had heard already that I had eaten the poison, and of course would die. I bade her be of good cheer, and, drinking nearly a quart of rum, lay down to sleep. In truth, I was a little uneasy lest some of the poison had got into my system, but hoped to neutralize it with the effects of the rum.

When I awoke, the morning sun was shining, and a great crowd of men and women had collected around my lodge, curious to know if I were dead or alive. My first care was to inquire after my patient, and to my inexpressible delight found she was not only living but well.

I had slept many hours, but the effects of the liquor were still upon me; and, after smoking the great medicine pipe, and giving thanks to the Great Spirit for my own as well as the girl's safety, I lay down again to rest.

In the evening I went out, and, knowing the great desire in the village to have the particulars of the cure I had performed made known, I desired all the chief men to assemble, and, when all were present, gave them the following truthful version of the affair:

"As I lay in my lodge, the Great Spirit came to me and said, 'A young girl of thy tribe, while gathering brush, has been bitten by a rattlesnake, and I desire her to live. Arise, and go to the medicine lodge, and eat the poison, and you shall not die. Tell the Great Medicine Man, my servant, that I sent you, and he will know I did; for he is very great and very wise.' (Here the venerable ass nodded complacently and smiled benignantly on us all.) So I went to the lodge, and eat the poison, and the Great Spirit did not let the girl die, nor am I dead, my fathers."

When I closed, the mighty man of medicine arose and modestly said:

"All the brother says is true. When he came, I knew at once the Great Spirit had sent him, and that he would eat the poison and not die, but save the girl's life. Had he not done so, I would have eaten the poison myself; and when any of you are bitten by a rattlesnake, come to me and I will cure you."

I felt very much like kicking the miserable old liar, but dissembled, and then we all smoked, gave thanks for an occurrence so wonderful, and adjourned.

After this I was considered a great medicine man in the tribe, and all the halt, the lame, and the blind in the village came to me. I managed to get rid of most of my patients by sending them to the medicine man, who had become a firm, fast friend of mine.

The girl I had cured wished to marry me, but I declined, and so remained a great lion among the young ladies of the village.

At Forsyth's battle on the Republican,* in 1868, the medicine man of the Cheyennes harangued the young men, and told them to charge the fort, for the medicine was all right, and the Great Spirit had told him the bullets would not hit them. He also said he could catch a bullet in his teeth, and to show them, he rode down toward the fort, when one of Forsyth's men shot him through the bowels and he died. It is said that these men, by long continued imposition on others, come to believe their own lies.—Ed.

The Battle of Beecher Island in September, 1868, was between U.S. Army forces led by Major George Alexander Forsyth, a Civil War Veteran and Cheyenne forces led by Roman Nose. After the Sand Creek Massacre in 1864, Roman Nose had become a prominent warrior leader among the Cheyenne. It was believed he could not be killed. The fight was ferocious and spread out over days. Many were killed and wounded on both sides, including Roman Nose.—Ed. 2015

THE MARCH—THE ATTACK

SOON after the incident related in the last chapter the fall races began, and we had a lively and exciting time. The Yanktons had pitted a number of fine horses against the Santees stock, and the whole village turned out to see the contest. The Indian races present a gay scene, everybody being in their best dress and feathers, and the horses gay with plumage. The running was very fine, and the Yanktons were unusually successful, winning nearly every race over the Santees. I had a horse to enter, but the Santees objected to my running him, so I was not a little gratified to see them so badly beaten.

Two weeks after the races were over, time hanging heavily on our hands, another expedition against the Pawnees was proposed. A large number of Santees were to go with us, and the party was to be larger, better mounted and equipped, than the preceding expedition. All being in readiness, we marched down the Missouri, and crossed over where the river was very wide and shallow. The crossing, however, was difficult, and it was with much labor we effected it. Each Indian tied his ammunition on top of his head, and strapped his gun to the side of his pony's head, with the lock uppermost. Then they drove the ponies into the water, and taking hold of their tails near the root, with the right hand, paddled with the other one, guiding the pony toward the opposite shore. We were carried by the current some distance down the stream, but landed safely among some willows. We marched inland about ten miles to a small stream and encamped, building fires to dry ourselves. Here we remained all the next day, waiting for the Santees, who had not come up yet. Toward night we saw a cloud of dust in the west, and soon the Santee warriors came in sight. Another day was consumed in dividing up the command, and assigning to each warrior his duty. We set out at daylight, and on the following day, at one o'clock, found ourselves within two miles of the Pawnee village. We went into a ravine, and immediately began preparations for the attack. The guns were loaded, forces again divided, and all prepared, when a dispute arose as to whether we should attack them at once, or wait for the cover of night. The Santee chief, who was the senior in

44

command, was in favor of an immediate attack, urging that they would be likely to discover us to the Pawnees and defeat our designs. I did not wish the attacks made until night, for fear some of the white men, who I knew to be with the Pawnees, would recognize me, and afterward give me trouble. My little party of fourteen warriors was, however, easily voted down, and the old chief ordered the assault to begin. Eight Indians were detailed to stampede and drive off the herd while we held the Pawnees in check. We had no idea of capturing the village, but hoped to steal the herd, which was the object of the expedition.

The Santees attacked the village on the west side, and the Yanktons on the north, so as to cover the herd,-which was grazing on that side of the town. The surprise was complete, the ravine sheltering our movements until within a few hundred yards of the teepees; then we dashed up and commenced firing our pistols and guns.

Indians do not fight in line like white men, but 'scatter out, riding furiously about, and firing as often as possible. The Pawnees, although surprised, were not dismayed, and soon the fire from their lodges was very hot. I saw men and women running from shelter to shelter with guns, and was beginning to think about falling back, when I heard the long "Hoo! Hoo! I-Yah-hoo!" of the stampeders, and saw the herd going pell mell over the hill, closely followed by our men. I immediately withdrew, so as to cover the herd, and was soon joined by the Yanktons, who were on my right. We commenced our retreat, and all seemed to be going well, when suddenly, we saw a great commotion in the herd, and our stampeders came riding down the hill, closely followed by a large body of mounted Pawnees. In an instant, the Santee chief called out to us to charge them, and we did so, turning their right and cutting off about one-half of the herd, which we drove rapidly about five miles, whet we saw a cloud of dust rising in our rear, and the Pawnees were upon us again. The chief ordered the captured stock to be driven on as fast as possible to the hills, and halted to give the Pawnees battle.

We had just crossed a little stream, and took up our position among the brush on its furthest bank from the enemy. We saw that

45

all the ponies they had recaptured from us were mounted by warriors, and, thus re-enforced, the original party of Pawnees greatly outnumbered our own. They deployed in a long line, and advancing, began the battle by hurling clouds of arrows against us. Our war-chief was struck in the shoulder and disabled early in the fight. He pulled out the arrow without even a grimace, and, riding up to me, turned over the command, desiring me to hold on as long as I could, and then fall back into the hills nearby, where I would find him. The fighting had lasted half an hour, and the firing becoming slack in front, I was about to withdraw, when I perceived a large body of Pawnees on my left and rear, and almost between me and the herd. While one party had been holding us in front, another body had moved down the stream, under cover, and crossed over, completely outflanking my warriors. I saw the Pawnees making for the herd, and mounting my men, we ran for it, but the Pawnees having the shortest distance beat us, and cut off, not only the herd, but our stampeders and war-chief. The Santees were much concerned about their chief, and cut their way to him. The old man was completely surrounded by Pawnees, and fighting desperately. It was with great difficulty we extricated him, and, although hardly able to sit on his horse, from wounds and loss of blood, he immediately resumed command, and with great skill withdrew us from the fight. The Pawnees fought desperately, being determined to take the old chief's scalp, but we carried him off, and the enemy, having now recovered all their stock, did not follow us far.

Sadly we pursued our march homeward, and on the second day reached the Missouri. The expedition had proved a total failure, and we had lost heavily. Bidding our allies—the Santees—good-bye (they wishing to keep up the other bank of the river to their tribe), we crossed the Missouri, and' soon entered our village, where we were received by the howling of dogs, beating of drums, and wailing of children and women for their dead fathers, brothers, and husbands.

SUPERSTITIONS

I HAD been in the village but a day or two after my return from the disastrous expedition against the Pawnees, when I was made aware, in more ways than one, of a growing dislike to me among the Yanktons. First, Shan-ka Galles-sca—the Spotted Dog—who had his lodge close beside mine, pulled it down and moved away. He it was who had told me to take the Santee robes into the council chamber just before the raid. When my friend Galles-sca abandoned me, I expected to see all the rest of my band follow his example; but, with the exception of one other old Indian, all remained steadfast. I called my warriors together, and explained to them how it was the fault of the Santees, and no fault of mine, or those under my leadership, that we had been defeated. They seemed satisfied, and advised me to lay the matter before the general council. I attended the council at its next session, but as it had been called for the transaction of special business, I could not be heard, and I never attended again.

One day, some weeks later, I was told a party of young men were going out to visit the Poncas, who live on a reservation near the mouth of the Niobanah River. From the secrecy used in their preparations, I suspected something more than .a friendly visit was meant, and sent my brother-in-law, a young warrior of some note, to find out what was going on. He soon returned, and informal me that the party was going ostensibly to visit the Poncas, but in reality to attack the Pawnees. I was cautioned, however, to say nothing, as some Santees were then in the village on a visit, and the Yanktons did not wish them to know of the expedition. That day, much to the gratification of our warriors, the Santees took their departure, .and the necessity of secrecy being removed, the expedition was then publicly talked of.

In the evening, as I was returning home, I met a warrior who was going on the raid, and who I knew did not like me. He came up and asked me if I was going upon the new expedition, and I said, No, I would not go; when he fell to bragging about what they would do, and told me I should go and try to redeem myself in the eyes of the tribe. I became angry at this unjust taunt of the braggart, and made haste to reply.

"I fought the Pawnees as well as any Yankton, and better than you ever will."

He laughed, and asked:

"How many Pawnee ponies have you to trade?"

"More than you will ever capture," I said.

"Come, now," he replied, "you can go with men this time not squaws."

"I had rather have Yankton squaws than you," I retorted at which he became pale with rage, for it is a most deadly insult to call an Indian a squaw.

Stepping up to me, he struck me with the back of his hand on the breast, saying, "Go away, boy! Go away, boy!"

"Stand back!" I cried, "or I will strike you to the earth."

"Does the pale face think because the Yanktons have been kind to him, he is their equal?" inquired the warrior, with a contemptuous curl of his lip.

"Yes, and the superior of a squaw's man, and a warrior whose mother never allows him to use pointed arrows, lest he hurt himself," I answered, hotly.

With a bound, the Indian sprang upon me, but I leaped aside, and gave him a blow on the nose, which made the blood spurt out. Blind with rage, he sought to grapple with me, but knowing he was much the stronger of the two, I kept out of his clutches, and punished him terribly with my fists. In a short time his face was beaten like a prize-fighter's, and, making a furious bound, I struck him in the stomach, and laid him flat on his back.

The fight had been witnessed by many of the warriors, who sympathized with me; and when I had knocked my antagonist down, they set up a great shouting, and my friends took me in triumph to my lodge. Next morning I sent for some whisky, killed a dog, and made a great feast in token of my victory.

The warriors who went on this third expedition against the Pawnees, returned in a few days completely broken down and disheartened. They reported that the Pawnees, under the leadership of a white chief, named Frank North, had surprised them, captured some ponies, and killed one Ponca warrior, and captured another. They had had a hard run to save their lives, and all the ponies were exhausted, and some had died of fatigue before they reached the village.

I was glad I had not gone on the expedition, and wished to go and taunt the Indian I had thrashed with his misfortunes, but my friends persuaded me not to do so.

The summer had now come with its sunshine and flowers; the grass was up several inches high, and the birds caroling in the trees overhead. As the tribe had determined to remain in camp all summer and eat up their buffalo meat, I concluded to go on a journey up the Missouri. I had so far overcome my first antipathies to Indian wives as to take a second one. Polygamy is not only one of the recognized, but one of the most honored, practices of the Yanktons. A man may have all the wives he can keep, after the fashion of Brigham Young and his latter-day saints. As I was a skillful hunter, and might have had half a dozen, whereas I only took two, I claim some virtue and credit on that account.

My second rib was a pale-faced, slender beauty—indeed, a mere child, with a gentle and submissive disposition. Washtella evidently did not like this new-corner to the lodge; but she said nothing, and treated the young squaw with respect and kindness. Often I saw the pain and grief even her Indian stoicism could not conceal, and from the bottom of my heart I pitied her, and regretted having brought another to my lodge to vex my patient and faithful Washtella.

When I had fully determined to leave the camp, I called my wives together, and informed them of the fact. They uttered no words of comment, for what has an Indian wife to do out obey her master? My warriors were next notified of my intended departure, and they

49

said not a word. The old chief spoke kindly to me, and asked wither I was going, but I only pointed to the northward, and said nothing.

It was a beautiful morning in the month of June, when my wives pulled down my lodge, and we began our journey. The lodge cover, and all my effects were packed on two ponies, one of which was led by Washtella, and the of her by Wacheata, my second wife, followed soon afterward, mounted on my horse.

I could not help pitying the "ladies" as they trudged along on foot through the sand, for the day was quite hot, and their skirts narrow and heavy. Tilters would have been of great comfort and benefit to them just then.

At noon we halted in a grove on the river bank, and while the ponies grazed, Washtella set out on the grass a repast of buffalo meat and ash-cake.

I asked the women where the trail we were then traveling led to. I cared not, so it went northward, and away from the hostile Pawnees.

Washtella told me that not far to the north were the lands of the Santees, and that where we were then resting once stood the village of the Yanktons. Not a vestige of it was left, but on the hill beyond the wood I could see the burying-ground.

I directed Washtella and Wacheata to pack our kitchen furniture on the poles behind the pony, and we would go up to the grave-yard, for I wished to have a look at it. At this their great eyes opened wide with horror, and the held up their hands to signify that they did not dare commit such a sacrilege, and so I bade them stay where they were. Not having the fear of Indian gods before me,

I rode boldly up to the hill, and there saw hundreds of bodies wrapped in blankets, buffalo robes, and bark, and laid out to dry on scaffolds made of poles and forked sticks. These scaffolds are seven to eight feet high, ten feet long, and four or five wide. Four stout posts with forked ends are first set firmly in the ground, and then in the forks are laid cross and side poles, on which is made a flooring of small poles. The body is then carefully wrapped, so as to make it water-tight, and laid to rest on the poles. The reason why Indians bury in the open air, instead of under the ground, is for the purpose of protecting their dead from wild animals. In new countries, where wolves and bears are numerous, a dead body will be dug up and devoured, though it be-put many feet under the ground.

An Indian grave-yard is a curious sight, with its silent sleepers. Here was an old fellow, whose scaffold had fallen down at one end, and his skeleton rested with its head on the ground, and its bony feet in the air. There the long black hair of a woman, falling through the decaying poles, streamed in the wind. There were skulls and bones all around, and flocks of ravens screamed and wheeled in the air. I saw stout warriors, old men and old women, resting as peacefully as if they slept in the beautiful cemeteries of the East. Maidens' lay there, too, all unconscious of the flowers that were springing up on the prairies around them, girls who had died long before my two young wives (who were then praying in the grove for my safety) had opened their seductive orbs on this world of glass beads and buffalo intestines.

I noticed many little buckets and baskets hanging on the scaffolds, and when I returned to the grove I asked Washtella what they were for. She said that when an Indian dies the body is carried to the grave-yard, where, amid much smoking and speech-making, it is hoisted upon the scaffold and left to rest. All then return to the village except the immediate friends and relatives of the dead, who remain to howl around the grave.

After death the soul goes on a journey to the happy hunting-grounds, where there is plenty of game, clear streams, beautiful groves, pleasant wild fruits, and no wars. While the soul is performing this journey it must be fed and have drink, the same as though it had remained in the body. The buckets and baskets I had seen had contained food and water for the dead.

I asked Washtella if she was sure the soul ate and drank on its journey, and if the food did not remain untouched in the basket?

She replied, "Oh, no; the water and food is always gone, for the dead are very hungry." I looked at the hundreds of ravens perched on the scaffolds, and could, account for what became of most of the

51

food and water, still I could not help thinking there were lazy Indians in every village who got the most of their living out of the grave-yards.

I asked Washtella how long it took a soul to reach the happy hunting-grounds, and she replied: "About one month; and during all that time the wife or nearest relation must go every day with a fresh supply of bread and water for the journeying spirit. When the dead person is rich, a couple of ponies are killed and buried under the scaffold, so the spirit can ride to the happy home."

I asked Washtella what the Indians did when there was no timber to build scaffolds, and she replied that they never camped far from timber; and if anyone in the village died while on the march, the body was packed on the teepee poles, and carried along until they reached a grave-yard, where it was buried.

Having finished my pipe, and satisfied my curiosity in regard to the mode of burying dead savages, I ordered the women to repack the ponies, and we resumed our journey.

In the evening, just as the sun was setting, we spied a beautiful willow grove, and turned off the trail some distance to camp in it. A stream of pure cold water meandered through the trees, and we pitched our lodge on the green grass by its banks.

I had shot an antelope, and while Washtella dressed it and prepared the evening meal, Wacheata put the ponies out to graze and erected the lodge. I sat cross-legged on a buffalo robe, and smoked my pipe, having nothing else to do, according to Indian custom, where the women do all the work.

A more beautiful spot than our camp could not be imagined. The tall, graceful willows, with their yellow arms, shaded the greensward from the sun in summer and broke the wind? in winter.

After supper I caught some fine fish out of the stream, and when the full round moon came up, I watched its bright rays flit and dance among the trees, making a thousand grotesque pictures on the ground.

Next day's journey brought us near Fort Benton. All afternoon we had been marching for many hours along the Missouri. The valley was wide, covered with luxuriant grass, and dotted with many-colored flowers. These flowers, though beautiful to the eye, had no fragrance. The river banks were fringed with a heavy growth of cottonwood, willow, and dogwood trees.

At one time this valley was the resort of vast herds of buffalo, elk, deer, and antelope, and their skulls and bones still lie scattered thick on the ground between the bluffs and the river.

All the game is now gone except a few antelope and deer.

We halted in some cottonwoods by the river, and the squaws, gathering a supply of wood, soon had a supper prepared of dried buffalo meat, corn, 'coon fat, and ash-cakes. We all ate out of the same kettle, so the dishes were easily washed. To eat, smoke, sleep, and march was the same to-day as yesterday, and so the journey wore on for nine long, weary suns, when we came in sight of the Santee village, and here our travels ended for the present.

Ash-cake is the Indian's bread. It is made of flour mixed with water And kneaded into a tough dough. It is then made into little cakes and baked in the ashes. The Indians use no salt in their bread or any of their victuals.— Footnote in original

A STRANGE AND BEAUTIFUL PICTURE

ONE can have no appreciative idea of an Indian village, unless he has been permitted to come across the prairie through a hot summer's sun, and suddenly discovers one nestled under the broad shade trees, beside a clear running stream, in a green valley. How pleasant the grass then looks; how refreshing the bright waters, and how cozy the tall lodges, with their shaded verandahs of thickly interwoven boughs.

All day long we had toiled over the scorching plain, through clouds of grasshoppers that often struck us in the face with sufficient force to make the skin smart for several minutes. Once we had seen a mirage of a beautiful lake, fringed with trees and surrounded by green pastures, which invited us to pursue its fleeting shadows, but we knew all about these deceptions by sad experience, and pushed steadily on over the burning sands.

These mirages often deceive the weary traveler of the desert. Suddenly the horseman sees a river or lake, apparently, just ahead of him, and he rides on and on, hoping to come up to it. For hours it lies before his eyes, and then in a moment disappears, leaving him miles and miles out of his way, and in the midst of desert sands.

Men have ridden all day striving to reach the beautiful river just before them, and then at night turned back to plod their weary way to v here they had started from in the morning. These mirages often lead to death both man and horse.

The mirage we had seen was most delightful, representing a clear lake, with trees, meadows, and villages nestling on its shores, but it scarcely equaled the reality of the scene when, late in the afternoon we ascended a rise in the prairie, and saw below us a wide stream lined with green trees, and on its banks a large Indian encampment.

The ponies pricked up their ears and neighed with pleasure as they smelt the water, and our own delight was unbounded. We halted for a moment to admire the beautiful prospect Through the majestic trees, slanting rays of the sun shivered on the grass! Far away, winding like a huge silver-serpent, ran the river, while nearby, in a

54

shady grove, stood the village—the children at play on the green lawns not made by hands. The white sides of the teepees shone in the setting sunlight, and the smoke curled lazily upward from their dingy tops. Bright ribbons and red grass, looking like streamers on a ship, fluttered from the lodge-poles, and gaudily dressed squaws and warriors walked about, or sat on the green sod under the trees. There were maidens, as beautiful as Hiawatha, or as graceful as Minnehaha, wandering, hand in hand, along the stream, or listening under the shade of some wide spreading tree to words of love, as soft and tender as ever were poured into woman's ear.

The warriors have a war-paint which they put on when they go to battle, and they have also paint which they wear when in love; it is called "love paint," and means that the warrior is "on the path of love, and not the -war-path." Nothing is more common than to see an Indian maiden seated on a buffalo robe, under a shade tree, beading moccasins for her dusky lover.—Note in original.

Near the village were hundreds of horses and ponies, with bright feathers flaunting m their manes and tails as they cropped the rich grass of the valley.

The buffalo-grass is dry and hard, and seems to have little nutriment in it, but its stem and roots are filled with a rich sweet, juice. The cattle and horses get very fat on it, notwithstanding its brown and parched appearance.—Note in original.

A group of noisy children were playing at a game much resembling ten-pins; some boys were shooting at a mark with arrows, and up the stream several youths were returning home with rod and line, and fine strings of speckled trout.

Scores of men and women were swimming about in the river, now diving, and then dousing each other amid screams of laughter from the bystanders on the shore. Here and there a young girl darted about like a fish, her black hair streaming behind her in the water.

While we looked, the little children suddenly ceased from play and ran into the lodges; mounted men surrounded the herd, and the swimmers and promenaders hastened toward the village. We had been perceived by the villagers, and the unexpected arrival of strange horsemen at an Indian encampment always creates great excitement. They may be friends, but they are more often enemies, so the villagers are always prepared for a surprise.

Soon men were seen running to and fro with guns and bows, and in a few minutes, some mounted warriors left the encampment and rode toward us, going first to the top of the highest the mounds to see if they could discover other horsemen in the rear; or to the right or left of us.

No sooner did they ascertain there were but three in the party, than they rode boldly up and asked us our business.

I told them who we were, and where we were from, upon which they cordially invited u$ to the village.

As we approached, men, women and children poured out of the encampment to look at the strangers, and having satisfied their curiosity, the sports and amusements of the evening were renewed.

I asked permission to camp of no one, for I needed none, as this was God's land, and not owned by ravenous and dishonest speculators. So I marched right down to the center of the village, and finding a vacant space, pitched my lodge. Tt was not necessary to purchase a town-lot here, for no one, save Him who owns all, held real estate.

A few Santee women gathered about my squaws and chatted with them, anxious to learn the news from down the river. Seeing they were interfering with the unpacking of the ponies and the erecting of the lodge, I unceremoniously ordered them to be gone, and they went quietly away. The lodge was soon up; the ponies unpacked and put out to graze. Having seen things put in order for the night, I sauntered out through the village to learn the news.

I was agreeably surprised, when I learned there was a white man in the village, who had been sent out to the Indians as a missionary. All the savages spoke of him as a kind-hearted, good .man, who was a great friend of the Great Spirit, and the .Big Father at Washington.

I made haste to pay my respects to my white brother, and found him indeed a good Christian gentleman. He had a white wife and child, and he and they were living comfortably and pleasantly with these wild children of the desert. I talked more than an hour with the good man; it was so delightful to see and speak with one of my own blood and color. When I left him, I promised I would return the next day and dine with him, which I did. It may sound strange to hear one talk of "dining out" in an Indian camp, but I can assure my civilized readers the meal was none the less wholesome or abundant on account of the place in which it was served.

When I returned to my lodge, I found it surrounded by a crowd of dirty squaws and children, who were intent upon examining everything we had. I ordered them off, and could not help laughing when I compared the curiosity of these rude Indian women with that I had seen exhibited at church in the States by white women. They there go to church, not to hear the Gospel, but to see what their neighbors have to wear, and these Indian women had come to my lodge with the same laudable object. I am not certain that human nature is the same every-where, but I am quite certain woman nature is the same all the world over.

I found the Santees a most excellent people. I had heard bad stories about them, but was agreeably surprised to learn that all that had been told to their disadvantage was false. The Omahas, Winnebagoes, Pawnees; Otoes, Sacs, Foxes, Crows, Snakes, Arrapahoes, Cheyennes, Blackfeet, Ogallalahs, and Yanktons are all either thieves or beggars, but here was a tribe of Indians who neither begged nor stole. The women were generally neat in their dress, virtuous, and cleanly in their persons. The warriors were men of great pride and bravery. The chiefs of the Santees were men of few words, but they were dignified, courteous, and truthful in all they said and did. After all my experiences and disappointments among the Indians of the plains, I could not help admiring and respecting these people, for here at last I had found a tribe such as Cooper had represented, and Longfellow characterized in Hiawatha. The longer I lived among the Santees the more cause I found to praise them.

I had built a willow awning over the door of my teepee, and shaded it with brush, so it was quite cool and pleasant.

Every tribe of Indians builds their lodges differently. Thus, the Winnebagoes live in huts made of the bark of trees, closely resembling an inverted teacup on the outside. The Pawnee houses are built in the same shape, but are made of mud, sod, or adobes.

The Santee lodges were tall conical-shaped tents, made of buffalo hide tanned with the hair off, and stretched around twelve poles. These poles are tied together at the top, and set about three feet apart at the bottom, around a circle of one hundred and eight feet. The lodge, when finished, is thirty-six feet in diameter at the ground. The skin or covering is cut bias, the small end being fastened to the top of the poles and the long end wrapped round and round the poles, and finally fastened to the ground with a wooden pin or stone. The poles are not set in the ground, but the edge of the lodge cover is pinned down with short pegs made of hard wood. Au aperture is left at the top of the lodge for the smoke to escape, and the fire is built in the center. When the door is open it draws well, and all the smoke goes up and out at the aperture.

These lodges, although standing on the surface of the ground and apparently very fragile, will withstand the most violent wind and rain storms. I have seen them outlive the strongest modern tents, and stand up when even great trees were blown down.

Many of the teepees were painted, having grotesque representations of men, horses, birds, turtles, deer, elk, and other animals in red, blue, and black colors on their sides. The village contained about two hundred lodges, and represented a prairie-dog town, being laid out with little regularity or order as to the streets.

The village covered a great space, the tents being often one and two hundred yards apart. Having improved and beautified my own lodge to my satisfaction, I sat down to enjoy myself and smoke my pipe in peace among these delightful people, little caring if I never saw the Yankton village again.

WAR ARROWS

IT was during my residence in the Santee village that I saw many curious things, and learned much of the mode of life and ceremonies of the Indians. Some of these are well worth, not only reading but remembering, by persons who peruse this volume.

Most people have seen the bows and arrows used by boys in the eastern States, and those who have observed them know how feeble they are, not even being capable of killing the smallest animal. Do not be surprised, then, when I tell you that an Indian, with his bow, will send an arrow entirely through a horse, man, or buffalo. The shaggy-coated bear or Rocky Mountain lion will fall beneath a few shots from the savage's strong bow, while the fleet, wild deer is not swift enough to escape the flight of his arrow. With unerring aim the hunter sends his deadly shaft, at eighty yards, into the heart or eye of his game, and with ease tips birds from the tops of the highest trees. Of 'course, it requires long practice to acquire such skill in the use of the bow, but the Indian will tell you that more depends upon the manufacture of the weapon than the skill of the marksman. With a good Indian bow and arrow a white man can, in a few hours, learn to shoot very well, while with a bow and arrow of his own manufacture he can hardly hit a tree, the size of a man's body, a rod off.

Let me teach you how to make a good bow and arrow. And first, we will begin with the arrow: The shoots, or rods, must be cut in the arrow season, that is, when the summer's growth is ended. They must not have any branches or limbs on them, but be straight and smooth. The Indians cut their arrows late in the fall, when the timber is hardening, to withstand the blasts of winter. The sticks are not quite so thick as one's little finger, and they are sorted and tied in bundles of twenty and twenty-five. These bundles are two or two and one-half feet in length, and wrapped tightly from end to end with strips of rawhide, or elk skin. The sticks are then hung up over fire in the teepee to be smoked and dried, and the wrapping keeps them from warping or bending. When they are seasoned, which takes several weeks, the bundles are taken down, the covering removed, and the bark scraped off. The wood is very tough, then, and of a yellowish color. The next process is to cut the arrow shafts exactly one length, and in this great care must be used, for arrow s of different lengths fly differently, and, unless they are alike, the hunter's aim is destroyed. Another reason for measuring the length of arrows is to identify them for no two warriors shoot arrows of precisely the same length.

Each warrior carries a measuring or pattern stick, and it is only necessary to compare an arrow with the stick to find out to whom it belongs. But should the arrows, by chance, be of one length, then there are other means of identifying them, for every hunter has his own private mark in the shaft, the head, or the feather. Of many thousands I have examined, I never found two arrows exactly alike when they were made by different warriors.

The shafts being made even, the next work is to form the notch for the bow-string. This is done with a sharp knife, and, when made properly, the bottom of the notch will be precisely in the center of the shaft. The arrow is then scraped and tapered toward the notch, leaving a round head an inch long near the notch, to prevent the string from splitting the shaft, and to make a firm hold for the thumb and forefinger in drawing the bow.

All the arrows are pealed, scraped, and notched, and then the warrior creases them. To do this, he takes an arrow-head and scores the shaft in zigzag lines from end to end. These creases, or fluted gutters, in the shaft are to let the blood run out when an animal is struck. The blood flows along the little gutters in the wood and runs off the end of the arrow. The arrow-head is made of steel or stone. It is shaped like a heart or dart, and has a stem about an inch long. The sides of the stem are nicked or filed out like saw-teeth. Nearly all the wild Indians now use steel arrow-heads, they being a great article of trade among the savages. There are firms in the East, who manufacture many hundreds of thousands every year and send them out to the traders, who sell them to the Indians for furs.

When the shaft is ready for the head, the warrior saws a slit, with a nicked knife, in the end opposite the notch, and inserts the stem of the arrow-head. The slit must be exactly in the center of the shaft, and as deep as the stem is long. When properly adjusted, the teeth of the stem show themselves or each side of the slit. Buffalo, deer, or elk sinew is then softened in water, and the wood is wrapped firmly to the arrowhead, taking care to fit the sinew in the teeth of the stem, which will prevent the head from pulling out.

The next process is to put on the feathers. To do this properly great care must be taken. Turkey or eagle quills are soaked in warm water, to make them split easily and uniformly. The feather is then stripped from the quill and put on the shaft of the arrow. Three feathers are placed on each shaft, and they are laid equidistant along the stem. The big end of the feather is fastened near the notch of the shaft and laid six or eight inches straight along the wood. The feathers are glued to the shaft, and wrapped at each end with fine sinew. The arrow is next painted, marked, dried, and is ready for use It takes a warrior a whole day to make an arrow, for which the trader allows him ten cents.

Arrow-heads are put up in packages of a dozen each. They cost the trader half a cent, or six cents per package, and are sold to the Indians at enormous profits. Thus, twelve arrow-heads will be exchanged for a buffalo robe, worth $8 or $9, and three, for a beaver skin, worth $4. Indians often buy arrow-heads at these enormous prices, and then sell the arrow back to the trader at ten cents, in exchange for goods, beads, or knives. The paints used by Indians in ornamenting arrows are purchased from traders. It is put up in small packages, and sold at 500 per cent, above cost. Of late years there has been a house in St. Louis that has made a speciality of Indian paints, and every Indian tribe on the plains knows their brand. These paints are indelible and excellent, the Indians being willing to pay any price for them. Generally, imitation of Chinese vermillion, yellow and green cromes, indigo, lamp-black, and ink are sold to the savages for paints.

To make war arrows, the Indians manufacture the shafts the same as for game arrows. The head is then fastened loosely in the wood, and when it is fired into the body it cannot be got out. If you pull at the shaft the barbs catch and the shaft pulls off, leaving the arrow-head in the wound. Some war arrows have but one barb, and when this arrow is fired into the body, if the shaft be pulled, the barb catches in the flesh and the steel turns cross-wise in the wound, rendering it impossible to extract it.

Fortunately but few Indian tribes now use the poisoned arrow. This deadly weapon is made like other arrows, except that it has a poisoned point. For years past, in the wars along the Platte, on the upper Missouri, and in all our contests with the Indians, not a single soldier or citizen has been shot with a poisoned arrow. Civilization can never be sufficiently grateful, to even savages, for having discarded a practice so barbarous.

A Santee warrior once showed me the method used by Indians in poisoning arrows, which I will here describe:

A large, bloated, yellow rattlesnake, the most deadly reptile in the world, was caught, and his head held fast by a forked stick. An Indian then tickled him with a small switch, by passing it along his body from head to tail. The rage of the snake was unbounded; he threshed the ground with his body, hissed, rattled his tail, and his eyes grew bright as diamonds. I could not imagine why so simple a thing should make him so angry, but his rage was as great as it was amusing. A small deer had been brought out alive, and when the snake was most furious, the animal was killed, the smoking liver torn out, and, hot and bloody, laid before the reptile. The stick was then removed from his neck, and in an instant he struck it, his teeth sinking deep into the soft flesh. His rage seemed to increase each moment, and he hit it again and again. When he tired, and would have gone away, the forked stick was brought, his neck pinned to the earth, and the tickle used until he became enraged. This was kept up as long as the hideous creature could be induced to strike the liver. He was then killed, a sharpened pole stuck into the liver, and it was carried to the village. It soon became very black, and emitted a sour smell. Arrows were brought, the heads thrust into the liver, and left there for half an hour, when they were withdrawn, and laid in the sun to dry. A thin, glistening yellow scum adhered to the arrow, and if it but so much as touched the raw flesh, it was certain to poison to the death.

Formerly the Indians always carried their poisoned arrows in the skins of rattlesnakes, and they were very careful of them, selecting and poisoning only such as had long shafts, peculiar points, or different marks. Still, mistakes would occur, warrior's horses, dogs, and children, got accidentally poisoned and died and at last the Indians quit using them, more on account of their own safety than for any humanitarian reasons.

A liver prepared in the way I have described, would contain virus enough to poison a thousand arrows. Years ago, each war party carried a poisoned liver, wrapped in a piece of buckskin, and it, with many arrows, was packed on a pony, balled the "dead horse." "When they found arrows of the enemy, they would poison and throw them on the trails, where they would be picked up and used by the foe to shoot game.

Travelers on the prairie have often seen the Indians throwing up signal lights at night, and have wondered how it was done. I will tell you all about it: They take off the head of the arrow and dip the shaft in gunpowder, mixed with glue. This they call making fire arrows! The gunpowder adheres to the wood, and coats it three or four inches from its end, to the depth of one-fourth of an inch. Chewed bark mixed with dry gunpowder is then fastened to the stick, and the arrow is ready for use. When it is to be fired, a warrior places it on his bow-string arid draws his bow ready to let it fly; the point of the arrow is then lowered, another warrior lights the dry bark, and it is shot high in the air. When it has gone up a little distance, it bursts out into a flame, and burns brightly until it falls to the ground. Various meanings are attached to these fire-arrow signals. Thus, one arrow meant, among the Santees, "The enemy are about;" two arrows from the same point, "Danger;" Three, "Great danger;" many, "They are too strong, or we are falling back;" two arrows sent tip at the same moment, "We will attack;" three, "Soon;" four, "Now;" if shot diagonally, "In that direction." These signals are constantly changed, and are always agreed upon when the party goes out, or before it separates. The Indians send their signals very intelligently, and seldom make .mistakes in telegraphing each other by these silent monitors. The amount of information they can communicate, by fires and burning arrows, is perfectly wonderful. Every war party carries with it bundles of signal arrows.

Every tribe of Indians make their arrows differently. The Snakes put but two feathers on their shafts; the Sioux, when they make their own arrow-points, or buy them, always prefer long, slim points; the Cheyennes, blunt points, sharp on the edges; the Pawnees, medium points; and the Crows, Blackfeet, Utes, Omahas, Ottoes, and Winnebagoes, long points. The Pawnees wrap their arrow-heads with elk sinew, the Crows with deer, and the Santees, with sinew taken from the inside of the shoulder-blade of a buffalo bull. Not many years ago, the hunters and frontiersmen could tell to what tribe the Indians who attacked them belonged by their arrows, but now that is impossible. Many tribes trade and exchange arrows, while others pick up and keep all the arrows they find. It is a practice among the Pawnees, to carefully collect all the arrows of their enemies and keep them to shoot again, or trade, while many wily Indians, when they wish to attack the whites, or commit an outrage, purposely use arrows belonging to other tribes. To find a white man dead, with a Pawnee arrow sticking in him, is no longer, as in former days, evidence that a Pawnee killed him, for, most likely, the deed was done by a Cheyenne or Sioux, and the blame thus sought to be thrown on the poor Pawnees.

THE BOW—HOW THEY ARE MADE AND CARRIED

THE bow—the weapon so long in use among the different Indian tribes of this continent, so typical of Indian life, and the mere mention of which always associates our ideas with the-red men—is made of various kinds of wood, and its manufacture is a work of no little labor. Even at this day the bow is much used, and although an Indian may have a gun, he is seldom seen without his long bow, and quiver well filled with arrows. The gun may get out of order, and he cannot mend it; the ammunition may become wet, and there is an end of hunting; but the faithful bow is always in order, and its swift arrows ready to fly in wet as well as dry weather. Thus reasons the savage, and so keeps his bow to fall back upon in case of accident.

Until the invention of breech-loaders, it is a fact well-known to frontiersmen that the bow was a far more deadly weapon at close range than the best rifle. A warrior could discharge his arrows with much greater rapidity and precision than the most expert woodsman could charge and fire a muzzle-loading rifle.

The antiquity of the bow is so great that its origin is, perhaps coincident with war and the necessities of mankind. It is painted on the ruins of Nineveh; it is mentioned in the first book of the Bible, and it is known to have been used on the eastern shore of the Mediterranean Sea, where the human race probably first had its origin.

The Indian boy's first lesson in life is to shoot with a bow. He is furnished with a small bow and "beewaks," or blunt arrows, so he will hurt nobody, and with these he shoots at marks. By and by, when he has acquired some skill in handling his .weapon, he is given small arrow-points, and with these he shoots birds, squirrels, and small beasts. As he grows older he receives the long-bow, and at last the strong-bow.

These strong-bows are powerful weapons, and I have seen them so stiff that a white man could not bend them scarce four inches, while an Indian would, with apparent ease, draw them to the arrows head. A shaft fired from one of these bows will go through the body of a buffalo, and arrow-heads have been found so firmly imbedded in the thigh bones of a man that no force could extract them.

The parents take great pride in teaching young Indians to shoot, and the development of the muscles and strength of v their arms is watched with much interest. A stout arm, ornamented with knots of muscles, is a great honor to an Indian, and no one but those who can handle the strong-bow are deemed fit for war.

Of all the Indians of the West, the Sioux and Crows make the best bows. The Sioux bow is generally four feet long, one and a half inches wide, and an inch thick at the middle. It tapers from the center, or "grasp," toward the ends, and is but half an inch wide and half an inch thick at the extremities. At one end the bow-string is notched into the wood and made permanently fast, while at the other end two notches are cut in the wood, and the string at that end of the bow is made like a slip-knot or loop. When the bow is to be used, the warrior sets the end to which the string is made fast firmly on the ground, and then bends down the other end until the loop slips into the notch. This is called "stringing" the bow. The bow is never kept strung except when in actual use, as it would lose its strength and elasticity by being constantly bent. When unstrung, a good bow is perfectly straight, and, if properly made and seasoned, will always retain its elasticity.

The wood generally used in manufacturing bows is ash, hickory, iron-wood, elm, and cedar.. No hickory grows west of the Missouri, and it is very difficult to get; and an Indian will always pay a high price for a piece of this wood.

When the bow is made of cedar, it need not be seasoned; but all other woods require seasoning, and are not worked until perfectly dry. Every teepee has its bow-wood hung up with the arrows in the smoke of the fire, but well out of reach of the flames. A warrior with a sharp knife and a sandstone, or file, can make a bow in three days if he works hard, but it most generally takes a week, and sometimes a month, to finish a fancy bow. When done, it is worth three dollars in trade.

All the bows differ in length and strength, being gauged for the arms of those who are to use them; but a white man would, until he learned the slight of it, find himself unable to bend even the weakest war-bow. This has given rise 10 the impression that the Indians are stronger than white men, which is an error; for, although only a slight man myself, I learned, after some practice, to bend the strongest bow, and could send shaft as far or as deep as any savage. On one occasion I shot an arrow, while running, into a buffalo so that the point came out on the opposite side; another arrow disappeared in the buffalo, not even the notch being visible. The power of the bow may be better understood when I tell you that the most powerful Colt's revolver will not send-a ball through a buffalo. I have seen a bow throw an arrow five hundred yards, .and have myself often discharged one entirely through a board one inch thick. Once I found a man's skull transfixed to a tree by an arrow which had gone completely through the bones, and imbedded itself so deep in the wood as to sustain the weight of the head. He had probably been tied up to the tree and shot.

The Sioux and Cheyenne bows are generally strengthened on the back by a layer of sinew glued to the wood. This sinew, as well as the bow-string is taken from the back of the buffalo. It starts at the hump and runs along the spinal column to the tail, and is about six feet in length.

The surface of the bow is made perfectly flat, then roughened with a file or stone, the sinew being dipped in hot glue and laid on the wood. The sinew is then lapped at the ends and on the middle, or grasp of the bow. The string is attached while green, twisted, and left to dry on the bow. The whole outside of the wood and sinew is now covered with a thick solution of glue, and the bow is done. Rough bows look like hickory limbs with the bark on, but some of them are beautifully painted and ornamented. I once knew a trader glue some red velvet on a bow, and the Indians paid him an immense price for it, thinking it very wonderful.

The Crows make bows out of Elk horn. To do this they take a large horn or prong, and saw a slice off each side of it, these slices, are then filed or rubbed down until the flat sides fit nicely together,

67

when they are glued and wrapped at the ends. Four slices make a bow, it being jointed. Another piece of horn is laid on the center of the bow at the grasp, where it is glued fast. The whole is then filed down until it is perfectly proportioned, when the white bone is ornamented, carved, and painted. Nothing can exceed the beauty of these bows, and it takes an Indian about three months to make one. They are very expensive, and Indians do not sell them; but I once managed to get one from a friend for thirty-two dollars in gold.

In traveling, the bow is carried in a sheath attached to the arrow quiver, and the whole is slung to the back by a belt of elk or buckskin, which passes diagonally across the breast, and is fastened to the ends of the quiver. The quiver and bow-sheath is generally made of the skin of an ox or some wild animal, and is tanned with the hair on. The quiver is ornamented with tassals, fringe of buckskin, and the belt across the breast is painted or worked with beads. Each Indian has his sign or name on his belt, bow, sheath, or arrow quiver. The celebrated Sioux chief, Spotted Tail, or "Sin-ta Galles-sea," had his-bow-sheath made from the-skin of a spotted ox he had killed in a train his warriors captured, and as the tail was left dangling at the end of the sheath, the Indiana ever afterward called him Spotted Tail, or "The man with the Spotted Tail." You may be curious to know what this Indian's name was before he was called Spotted Tail, and I must tell you many Indians never have a name, while others have half a dozen. Some act of bravery, or an article of clothing, generally fixes an Indian's name, but a new deed, or a new head-dress, may change it.

Mr. Belden is likely mistaken as to the origin of Spotted Tail's name. I have often been told by soldiers and old frontiersmen that when Spotted Tail was a young man he wore a coon's tail in his hair, and from this took his name Spotted Tail, or "The man with the spotted tail." Our soldiers have often seen him wearing this coon tail in battle, and I think it was from it he derived his name.—Note in original.

To shoot with the bow properly, it must be held firmly in three fingers of the right hand; the arrow is fixed on the bowstring with the thumb and forefinger of the left hand, and the other three fingers are used to pull the string. The shaft of the arrow lays between the thumb and forefinger of the right hand, which rest over the grasp of the bow. To shoot, the bow is turned slightly, so, one end is higher than the other, and the arrow is then launched.

Not only is the bow used as a weapon, but it serves as an implement with which to disgrace a man. Thus, an Indian who is struck with a bow is as much disgraced and insulted as a white man who has been cowhided. To strike one with a bow means in the Indian language, "Go, coward; or, "You are not worthy of being killed by arrows;" or, "I do not consider you a brave or honorable man," which is the worst of all insults to a savage.

A REMARKABLE TRADE ENTERPRISE

MOST the Indian tribes of the west have obtained from traders, many articles of civilization, but among the Santees, I found they relied almost wholly upon their own skill to produce tools and household utensils. These were generally manufactured by old men and squaws, except axes, hammers, mallets, files, rasps, and hoes, which were made by the warriors.

The axes were of three different kinds—stone, bone, and flint. The stone ax is made from a large pebble, or river stone. It is first split in two parts, which gives each section a sharp edge and a flat side. The stone is then enveloped in rawhide, except the edge. The bine is put on when green, and strongly sewed with sinew, and when dry, it is almost as hard and tight as the stone. While the hide is still soft, a handle covered with rawhide, and having a long slip projecting, is laid on the fiat side of the stone, and strongly sewed to the skin covering the ax. The slip is then wrapped around the ax-head and handle, and sewed fast, after which the whole is lapped with sinew, and set away to dry. As soon as it is thoroughly dried, the ax is brought out, the edge filed up, or sharpened by rubbing it against a sandstone, and it is ready for use. It is astonishing how firmly the contracted rawhide and sinews hold this rude ax on its handle; the stone often breaks, however, and the ax can only be used for cutting soft wood and brush.. Three or four of these axes can be made by an Indian in a day, so they are of no great value, and are thrown away as soon as they break.

The flint axes are more difficult to make, but are manufactured in the same manner, except that a notch is sawed in the handle, and the ax set in the notch to give it greater firmness.

The bone ax is the best as well as the hardest to make. Buffalo bones (generally the leg or shoulder-blade) are taken, split in two, and trimmed down to the right thickness. A sapling, young tree, or limb, is then split near a knot, and the bone shaved through, where it is left to grow fast. This is done in the spring, and by fall the sap will have filled up the interstices, and the wood become firm around the bone .The wood is then cut at the right length, and the handle

70

shaved out. The whole is next covered with rawhide sewed and lapped with sinew, the bone ground up, and the implement is ready for service. One of these axes will last a year and carry a fair edge, but the great objection to them is, that they are too light for effective chopping. Elk ham-bone makes a very good ax head.

Mallets, hammers, and hatchets, are made in the same manner as described for axes, except that the big mallet, used for driving stakes and tent-pins, is made of a round stone, in the side of which a trench has been pecked, into which the handle is laid. The whole is then covered with, rawhide, and when dry, the hide is pared off one end of the stone, and it is flattened by rubbing it against a rock, or dressing it as a miller does his millstone.

Hoes are made of flat stones and bones, covered with raw-hide, and a handle is fastened with buffalo sinews. These hoes are used to dig earth, wild artichokes, and for scraping the hair off hides when tanning.

The most curious process was making files and rasps. To do this, an alderberry stick was taken and split in two. The pith was then scraped out, and in the grove thus formed, was poured glue, mixed with pounded flint. When dry, the particles of flint formed the teeth of the rasp, or file. If the file became dull, it was only necessary to wash it in hot water, when the glue and old, pieces of flint washed out and new teeth appeared. These files were very handy, and of vast use to the Indians. What steel is to iron, they are to the wood and stone used by the Indian. When ponies hoofs became too long, ox splintered, they were trimmed down by these rasps; also, ax handles, teepee poles, and iron, even, were rubbed down with them.

War clubs are made with handles three feet long. A sharp flint stone is found, and dressed oil into an oblong shape. A saplings then split, the stone heated and placed in the split. This is repeated until the crack is almost closed, when it is left to grow fast. It is then cut, the handle trimmed out, the whole, except the point of stone, covered with rawhide, and sewed with sinew, when it is beautifully painted and ornamented.

Spears are made of hard wood, and pointed with stone or iron. If an Indian can get an old bayonet, or sword-blade, he is delighted, as it makes a splendid head for his spear. If no iron can be obtained, the wood is charred in the fire; the burnt particles are then scraped off, leaving it very hard and sharp.

The butt end of the pole is always used for the head of the spear, and the whole length of the instrument is twelve to fifteen feet. The Sioux, Cheyennes, and a few other tribes still use these weapons, but they are fast disappearing.

They are clumsy, but very dangerous when skillfully handled, and can be thrown a great distance with considerable accuracy.

Hiding whips are made in great numbers by the Indians. They are of various kinds and curious patterns. Some are twisted out of horse-hair, and wrapped with fine sinew, to make them stiff and elastic; others are woven of buffalo fur, and others of grass or bark.

The regular Indian riding whip is made of leather, fastened to a wooden handle. A bone, or piece of round, hard wood, about six inches in length, is taken, and through each end a small hole is bored across the grain. Another longer hole is then bored in the end of the stick along the grain, until it intersects the first hole. The lash, with a loop on its end, is next inserted in the end of the whip, and a peg driven through the small hole and loop, to keep it from coming out. A loop, or wrist-strap, is then put in the other end of the handle, and the whip is ready for use. The lashes of these whips are two or three feet long and very heavy, being made generally of buckskin, elk, or buffalo hide. They are frequently not plaited, but knotted every five or six inches. These knots are called "bellies," and are intended to make the punishment more severe than it would otherwise be.

The elk-horn whip is very pretty, being usually beautifully carved and painted many colors. Sometimes the long prong of a blacktail deer is used, studded with brass tacks, or pieces of silver. Frequently, the handles are covered with fur, oi buckskin, which is ornamented with bead-work.

72

The Santees could make a rude knife when they could get hoop-iron, but nearly all the Indians have knives made by white men. These knives are branded Samson & Good now, J. Wilson, Clement & Hawks, though how these manufacturers got their knives among the Indians, I never could learn.

The Crow Indians are the only ones who make combs. They are very simple, and consist of a hedgehog's tail, the bristles serving as teeth. When the hog is killed, the tail is skinned off the bone, and a wooden handle inserted. When dry it is ready for use, and is by no means a bad substitute for the bone, or horn comb we use. A hedgehog comb is an indispensable article to every Indian girl, as it enables her to keep her long black hair in order.

THE CHEAPEST GOODS IN THE WORLD

THE robes used by the Indians in winter for wearing as protection against the weather, are made of the skins of small buffalo bulls or cows. The skin is dressed down or thinned by means of chipping and' scraping of the flesh side with an adze or hoe made of bone. When it is as thin as it can be cut with the adze, it is rubbed down to the right thickness with a sandstone. This done, the robe is well soaked in buffalo brains and grease, after which it is dried. It is then washed in clear water, and re-washed, until all the grease and brains are taken out. , The skin now only has to be rubbed dry, and the tanning process is complete.

Squaws and men all wear buffalo robes about their person in winter. They are always worn with the fur side inwards, or next the skin, and the flesh side is painted with stars, squares, stripes, or whatever strikes the fancy of the wearer. The paint is seared in with a hot iron, and is generally black, red, or blue, in color.

The robes made for trading purposes are entirely different from those worn by the Indians themselves. A private, of body-robe, as it is called, is worth a dozen trade-robes. The trade skins are never painted, but merely fleshed, brained, washed, and rubbed. Once in a while a painted robe finds its way into the market, but only as old family jewels find their way to the pawnbroker's shop among civilized people. An Indian will not part with his painted robe unless pressed with hunger, or to obtain powder and bullets. A new body-robe is seldom or never sold, and those seen in the East are 'mostly old robes, that the Indians have parted with' because they were about to get new ones.

The trade-robes, or bull-hides, usually cost at the tribe grounds from $1.25 to $4.00. The traders pack them in bales of ten robes each, and ship them East, where they are sold at $70 to $90 per bale. What it costs to transport them, I am unable to say; but it is fair to presume that the trader clears from $4 to $6 on each robe.

When I lived with the Santees it was not yet the trading season; but I have often seen the Crows and Pawnees trade on a large scale.

74

This is generally done in the fall; and not infrequently a single trader will secure as many as one thousand robes. These cost him only $1,250 in goods, and he can sell them in the East for $5,000 to $6,000 in cash. The Indians do not want money, but goods; and the trader keeps constantly on hand a large assortment of Indian traps. The articles generally sought for by the savages are the following:

Red, white, blue, black, and green Mackanaw blankets.

Red and blue "squaw-cloth" which is a flannel of various colors, and costs $4 per yard.

Red, white, blue, black, green, yellow, and purple worsted, in one pound skeins. This is used for making tassels and ribbons.

Cotton thread, flax thread, and needles.

Blue and striped bed-ticking, used by the squaws for making dresses.

Cotton and worsted shawls; very small, and worn over the shoulders, and around the neck.

Balmoral skirts of the most brilliant colors. I have also seen crinoline and hoop-skirts readily sold to the squaws.

Red, blue, and various colored handkerchiefs, both silk and cotton.

Lampblack, indigo, Chinese vermilion, green and yellow chrome, and all kinds of paints.

Gunpowder, bullet molds, bullets, and percussion caps.

Brass, copper, and iron wires.

Wire worms, for extracting charges from loaded guns.

Brass hawk-bells and brass tacks.

Brass finger-rings, jewelry, and buttons.

Butcher knives, lead, ax helves, handles, saws, files, and hatchets.

Pipes and stems of all kinds.

Silver and gold ear-rings.

Brass wristbands.

Sugar, tea, coffee, flour, tobacco, candy, raisins, and figs.

Chip hats, calico, paper collars, and whisky.

Wampum beads, a string, one yard long, being worth fifty cents. The trader both sells and receives them at that price, and they pass as currency among the Indians, the standard value being fifty cents per yard, if white or pink, and if purple, seventy-five cents per yard. A wampum moon, which is a small sea-shell, out of which the wampum beads are made, will sell for $1.

These are the principle articles found in every trader's store, and for them the Indians exchange buffalo robes, elk, deer, antelope, beaver, muskrat, mink, fox, bear, and many other kinds of skins.

The flesh or meat of the animals they kill is dried, put away in caches, for winter use, and the hides go into the traders' bales.

The average value of skins among the Indians is: for a buffalo robe, $1.25; for an elk skin, $1; deer and antelope skins, 75 cents each; beaver and otter, $1 each; wolf and coyote, 25 cents; muskrat, 10 cents; mink, $1.

At the time of this writing, $1.00 was worth about $17.50 in 2015 dollars.—Ed. 2015

Great labor and a vast deal of time is expended in tanning these skins, and I may safely say that, considering the amount if work put upon them, they are the cheapest articles of trade in the world. A squaw frequently toils a whole day on a skin that will only bring her husband ten cents worth of goods, which are really worth no more than five cents in cash.

PIPES AMD TOBACCO

WHERE and when did men first learn to smoke? The sacred Scriptures make no mention of this practice. Neither Abraham, Isaac, nor Jacob smoked, and none of the old fathers offered their guests the pipe, though the Old and New Testament make frequent mention of food entertainment. Job set a good table, but there is no evidence he smoked. God speaks of "a smoke in my nose," but this is the smell of meat offerings, and not tobacco or pipe fumes.

The tobacco plant belongs to North America, and has been used by the Aztecs and Indians, from time immemorial. It was a luxury in Powhatan's sylvan camp, in the days of Pocahontas. Sir Walter Raleigh first carried it from America to England, in 1588, and to the English belong the responsibility of introducing this weed to the civilized world.

As far back as we can trace the savage,, the pipe has been his pride, the solace of his leisure and weary hours, and the emblem of his friendship. The story-tellers of the Indians say, they first received the tobacco plant from an angel, sent by the Great Spirit. They smoked the leaves in their pipes, that the angels might smell the fumes and be pleased. It was also an oblation to the Great Spirit, and hence, the custom, to this day, of preceding all solemn occasions by much smoking.

The earliest Indian pipe was curved like an ox's horn, and bad no stem. There was a hole through it, and the tobacco was put in the large end.

In smoking this pipe, the Indian laid on his back. The next form of pipe used, was that of the body of a man, the stem of the pipe being placed in the small of the back. This design was got from the idols, which the Indians cut out of stone. The first attempt at ornamenting the pipe was, to make it in imitation of the snake. The tobacco was placed in the mouth of the reptile, the tail answered fora stem, and the body was carved to represent the scales. The highest art ever attained in carving an Indian pipe was to cut a rude imitation of a lizard on the front of the bowl.

The warrior's pipe, of the present day, is made of red clay, or soap-stone, which is found in nearly every part of the American continent. There are some stones that-are held in great estimation by the Indians, for making pipes. The quarry, four miles below the falls of Sioux River, between Dakota and the State of Iowa, is held in high repute. The soft red clay, or soap-stone, on the Iowa shore of the Missouri, and found on the Yellowstone Make, also makes beautiful pipes. This stone is soft when taken out, but rapidly becomes hard when exposed to the air.

Indians make their pipes with the common jack-knife. The bowl is long, deep, and eight square, or round. The shape of the pipe is' a rectangle, and the hole for the stem is bored with an iron rod, or sharp piece of stone. The pipes are of all sizes, some of them being very large, but all have the same elbow.

The stems are of various lengths and shapes, but those most commonly in use are made of a hollow stick, or one through which a hole has been drilled. They are fully three feet long, an inch in diameter, and ornamented with brass tacks, wire wrappings, and paintings.

The Santees, Ogallalas, and Yanktons use a flat stem, very long and very thick. They are sometimes three inches broad, and ornamented at both ends t with bright feathers. Rows of vermilion, green, duck, and gold-colored eagle quills, are split and fastened with glue, by their flat surfaces, to the stem of the pipe, and the ends are then wrapped with wire. Carvings of birds, beasts, fishes, and men, are cut on the bowls and stems, and filled with paint.

Besides the red-stone pipe, the Indians use the hammer a: tomahawk pipe, made of iron. Nearly all the tomahawks se in civilization are made by blacksmiths, employed by the go eminent, and sent out to the Indians. The friendly savage for whom they are manufactured, trade them to their warlike brethren, and thus they become scattered far and wide. These tomahawks, though often carried in their belts, are seldom used by Indians as weapons, and, notwithstanding they have passed into history as a deadly instrument, they are more for ornament than use. It frequently happens, however, that the tomahawks made at the agencies, for friendly tribes, are captured by hostile Indians, and these savages, in their contests with the whites, sometimes use their tomahawks to brain captives, hence, the dread of them, and the bloody name they bear.

The instrument generally used by Indians in killing captives, is the war-club, made of oak or iron wood, and fully described in another place. An oaken club of this kind was once shown me that had been used by the Indians, at the massacre of Fort Phil. Kearney, in the Powder River country, in [December 21,] 1866, to break the skulls of ninety-six soldiers and citizens. The club was a rough stick, and the knots and end were still clotted with blood, brains, and human hair. This deadly instrument was made of burr oak, was .three feet long, shaped like a bat for ball playing, and driven full of nails, some of which were bent over to form a loop, or hook.

To return to our subject, the Indian pipe is not valued by its possessor so much on account of the material it contains, as its history. Thus, a little, dirty-looking pipe, which I saw in the hands of a Santee squaw, was valued at three ponies, or one American horse, three squaws, or their equivalent, $150.00, because it had been owned by her grandfather, and her great-grandfather, who was a great medicine man.

The Sioux women smoke, though a young woman is seldom seen with a pipe, and most of the smoking is confined to the men. Warriors smoke as a part of their religious duty, and an acknowledgment of an all-wise Creator. All treaties and acts of friendship are preceded by smoking, which calls God to witness the sincerity of the Indian's heart. No important trade can be made, or message delivered, until the parties have smoked: and when Indians meet together, for pleasure or business, the first thing done is, to fill the pipe, hand it to the eldest man present, when another seizes a fire-brand, holds it to the bowl, and the father smokes. The Indian who holds the pipe in his mouth can seldom light it, on account of the great length of the stem, and hence he requires the aid of someone else. When the father has drawn in a mouthful of smoke, he forces it out through his nose, turning his face to the east, then the west, north, and south. He thus makes a smoke-offering to the

Great Spirit, and having done so, passes the pipe to the Indian next on his left. Each warrior takes but two or three whiffs, before passing the pipe to his neighbor. One pipe is sufficient for five or six smokes. And not only do five or six Indians smoke from the same pipe, but they inhale the smoke, and pass it through their noses, instead of blowing it away, as white men do. An Indian says a white man does not know now to enjoy a smoke. Indians do not talk while smoking, but chat gayly while others are passing the pipe. When the pipe is exhausted, it is refilled, and the first smoker of the new pipe always makes a smoke-offering to the deity.

The Indians make much of their wild tobacco, made from the bark of trees. The Sioux, Omahas, Winnebagoes, Cheyennes, Arrapahoes, and Ottoes, use willow bark. The squaws gather a bundle of the largest-sized shoots, and carry them to the teepee, where the wind does not blow, and there scrape off the bark with a knife. First the outside coating is taken off, which is thrown away; the soft inner bark is then scraped into a piece of rawhide, and left to dry. It is of a greenish color, and emits a pleasant smell. The fall of the year is the season for gathering the willow bark, as the sap is then going down, and the bark is mild and more pleasant to smell than if peeled in summer. When dry, the squaws grease their hands with buffalo fat, and then crush the bark until it is pulverized fine enough for the pipes. The grease adhering to the particles of bark makes it burn freely. Each squaw puts up several pounds of this bark, for the use of her warrior, and I have known Indiana to travel a hundred miles for the purpose of gathering cham-pa-sha.

The Pawnee Indians use the red leaves of the sumac bush for tobacco. It abounds on the plains, in the Rocky Mountains, and on many streams east of the Missouri. This kind of tobacco is called "Lup-pitch," and the Pawnees greatly prefer it to the "Lup-pa-hot," or "Cham-pa-sha," which is the Sioux Kinnc-kan-nick.

The Crows, or Absaracks, use a green leaf, which grows on a running vine, in the mountains. This' leaf is found above the perpetual snow line, and is called O-pe-sha by the Indians, and Lambre by the whites. The vine runs on the ground, has a pear-shaped leaf, and resembles the pig-weed of the north. It is an evergreen, blossoming in the winter, on beds of snow, and bears bright red berries, of the size of a pea. The berries are sour, Very hard, and always retain their color.

The O-pe-sha is mixed with tobacco, when the Indians can get it, and is smoked, half and half of each.

The Sioux have three substitutes for tobacco; first, the leaves of the wild rose bush; second, the leaves of a bushy weed, which grows in the cations, or valleys of the west; and third, the small curled leaf of the dwarf sumac. These leaves are rolled up like minute rolls of tobacco, and when crushed, it is impossible to tell them from cut and dry. Indians, whether alone or in company, always observe the solemnities of smoking. Never does a Sioux Indian light his pipe but he draws a great puff of smoke, and blows it out of his mouth toward the sky, ejaculating, How-wa-con-ton-ka, meaning, "I remember thee, O God," or "To thee, O Great Spirit," at the same time pointing with the stem of the pipe upward.

The Winnebagoes blow two puffs toward the sky, two to the east, two west, two south, and one down, following each with the stem of the pipe pointing in that direction. At the same time they mutter "O God, propitiate the winds of the east, the west, and south, and bless the earth."

The Crows blow a buff-of smoke to the sky, one east, and one west, meaning, "O Great strength, I remember thee, from the rising to the setting of the sun" (How-ba-tsa-ka). The Cheyennes make the same offering as the Sioux, but use a different speech. There is no set term, but generally such expressions as "O thou God, keep me." "God defend me from all harm." "O God, see me," are used. When on the war path, they pray; "God send us our enemies." The Arrapahoes blow a puff of smoke upward, and pointing with their pipes, say, "God, remember us on earth," or "God and us."

The tobacco for their pipes is carried by the Indians in pouches, or bags, made of the skins of wild animals, buckskin, or calico, ornamented with porcupine quills. The pouches are sometimes five inches wide, and eighteen to twenty inches long. They are carried with the mouth of the pouch under the belt, and hang down, generally having the tail dangling, if the bag is made of the skin of an animal.

Nearly all the pouches are ornamented with fringe, or bead pendants, four or five inches long. The value of a tobacco bag, of course, depends on its workmanship; a fine buckskin bag, ornamented with beads, and fifteen days' labor, is worth $3.00; a mink-skin pouch is worth $4.00; an elk-skin, worked with porcupine quills, $5.00, and an otter kitten as much as $6.00.

THE ART OF TRAPPING

STRANGE as it may seem, it is none the less true, that the Indians learned the art of trapping from white men. Long ago they stole along the banks of the creeks, and, hiding in the brush, waited patiently, for the beaver to show himself in the shallow water or on the banks, when they shot him. This process was very tedious, however, and they longed for some other manner of capturing the smooth-haired little animal, so it was with much satisfaction that they saw the white men go along the streams, and set a curious instrument in the ground, to which the beaver came, and which held him fast until the trapper saw fit to take him out.

Sly Indians watched the process from their bushy cover, and when the trapper had gone away, they stole the trap and carried it off to their camps. It was a long time before the Indians could set their traps, and not until the white men taught them, that they learned how to sit in the still moonlight and watch the beaver work; how to walk on the ice and see if there were beaver holes or houses, and then, when having ascertained the presence of the coy little fellow, how to put' the trap down, grease it with the oil of his own tail, and leave it to snare him.

A trap weighs about five pounds, and it is considered a good load to carry twelve. It will require a walk of ten or twelve miles, and all of one day, to set a dozen traps properly. If three beavers are caught each night for every dozen traps set the trapper considers he is doing a good business. The skins, untanned, are worth about one dollar each. During the winter season the hunter will average not over four beavers per week, for there are many days he cannot trap. I had one hundred traps worked hard for three months, often floundering through the ice, getting wet to my waist, and having to build fires to keep from perishing, and at the end of ninety days had but fifty beaver skins, worth fifty dollars, for my labor. Still there is something jolly about a trapper's life, a wild, roving excitement that strangely allures and fascinates one. Why it is I cannot tell, but most frontiersmen love trapping, and will pursue it, even though they take but a dozen beaver per month; just as I have seen sportsmen go, day after day, in the East, to angle in a little stream, when they knew there were not twenty trout from its mouth to its source.

The setting of the trap is a delicate job, and every trace of it must be concealed, or the cunning little animal will not fall into it. Each Indian saves the musk of all the beavers he takes, and with this rubs his traps; so that the beaver may smell them, come up, and fall a prey. When a beaver smells another, he has great curiosity to know where he is, and so runs about looking for him, until he treads on the fatal spring and is caught.

After an Indian has set his traps, he becomes very morose, and goes to his tent and smokes a great deal. He does not run about the village or talk, but sits alone, endeavoring to think of his traps all the time, for thereby he believes he will draw the beaver to them. When he lays down to sleep, he recalls all the battles and skirmishes in which he has been engaged, and tries to dream of them. If he dreams that he is victorious, then he rises and goes confidently to his traps, but if he sees a dead or live beaver in his dream, he will not visit his traps next day for he knows by his vision that there are no beaver in them Should he imagine he is fighting five men and whip them, there are five beavers in his traps, but if only two men, then there are but two beavers. Should he meet men who run away from him in his dreams, it is unlucky, for the beaver have run away with his traps into their holes.

The otter does not abound along the Missouri, in Nebraska, where I trapped, but sometimes we caught one in the traps set in the edge of the water for beaver. The otter's skin is much more valuable than that of the beaver. I never saw an Indian trapping for any other animal than the beaver, though they often shoot otter, mink, and muskrat with the bow. The arrow will generally prevent them from getting into their holes, being shot with sufficient force to pierce the animal.

The Crow Indians will neither trap nor hunt the bear. They believe it is bad luck to kill a bear, and will not touch the food. A party of hunter , who induced the Crow chief, Iron Bull, to eat bear meat by representing to him that it was roast beef, came near paying with their lives for the deception, for the old chief found out the trick that had been put upon him, became very wroth, and it took a present of several ponies to get the bad medicine out of him. The Crows say the bear has a spirit in him, and to kill it offends the great Wa-con Ton-ka. If a Crow meets a bear, when out hunting, he will go around him, and if the bear attacks him he will run away.

The Sioux both hunt and kill the bear, and are very fond of the meat. They use the skin for robes, and wear the claws strung around their necks as ornaments. What the Crows believe of the bear, the Sioux do of the, prairie dog. They will not kill or allow anyone to hurt this little animal, and if they see any person kill one, they run away lest it makes them have bad luck. The prairie dog is nothing more or less than a prairie squirrel, and runs on the ground instead of climbing trees, as does the black and gray squirrel of the North. I have often eaten the prairie dog, and his flesh is precisely like that of the squirrel. There is a prejudice against eating this little animal on account of its name, but in this case, unlike most others, everything is in the flame.

NO BALD HEADS IN HEAVEN

WHEN the Indians first began to scalp people, or where they got the idea of cutting off the scalp-lock, it is impossible to tell, but it has been practiced among all tribes ever since the discovery of America, in 1492. The savages believe that no one can make a respectable appearance in the spirit and baldheaded. It is remarkable, but I never saw a baldheaded Indian, nor did I ever hear of one. To scalp an Indian is to debar him from the happy hunting-grounds, and hence it is they scalp white people, believing they cannot get into heaven without their hair.

The Indians do not all scalp people alike; nor do they wear their own hair alike. The Sioux warrior has a three-strand braid or plait of hair taken up on the crown of his head, over a space of three inches in diameter and nine inches in circumference , and this it is that his enemies cut off when they capture him.

The Winnebagoes wear six or seven braids, and it is necessary to cut the skin around three or four inches on the crown, in order to get a full scalp. The Pawnees have but one braid, the Cheyennes one, the Crows one, and the Arrapahoes one. The Sioux part the hair in the middle of the forehead, and then down to the ear from the scalp-lock; this they wear with the hair behind, made into rolls, and tied with red flannel oi ribbon. I have seen the hair wound about strips of flannel or buckskin, and made into a roll as thick as one's wrist, and over three feet long.

Many of the Pawnees cut the hair close to the skull all around, leaving a ridge or shock of hair three inches wide running from front to rear over the top of the head. This strip of hair gradually lessens in width, until it reaches an edge in rear near the back of the neck. It gives the warriors a fierce and unnatural appearance. In the center of the ridge of hair grows the long scalp-lock, which is plaited and falls down the back. I speak now of the custom when the Pawnees were savages. Since they have become friendly, they seldom shave the head, but wear their hair long and unplaited. This is done, however, as much from policy as for any other reason, for they are still rascals and thieves; and they found wearing their hair unlike any other tribe on the plains caused them often to be detected in their depredations, when they might otherwise have escaped and avoided punishment.

The Crows, except the scalp-braid, wear their hair long, and hanging down. To keep it from blowing about their eyes, they take little balls of pitch, such as ooze out of the pine-tree, and stick it in their hair in belts an inch wide, until it is matted together all around their heads.

Nearly all Indians have black hair; the hair of the Cheyennes, Sioux, Snakes, Pawnees, Omahas, Arrapahoes, and Winnebagoes is jet black, and very coarse. The Crow Indians, however, have hair of every color; I have seen full-blooded Crows with auburn, red, gray, brown, and black hair. Many of their old men are white-headed, and their long hair gives them a very venerable appearance.

The Winnebagoes are the only Indians who can, at the present day, be distinguished by means of their scalp-locks. They still persist in wearing the six or seven long plaits around their heads.

Nearly all tribes wear some ornament in the scalp-lock next to the head. These are made of wood, copper, iron, brass, silver, and gold, but most generally of silver. I have seen a piece of thin German silver, as large as a man's hand, in the scalp-lock, the hair having been drawn through two holes in its center. It is also tied to the hair with strings, and not unfrequently has a long feather attached, called the scalp-feather. This feather can be taken off and put oh at pleasure; it is nearly always taken off at night, as the warrior would undoubtedly break or soil it in his sleep if left in the hair. In war times, if this feather is stolen or snatched off by an enemy, the warrior is irreparably disgraced.

Some wild Indians wear a steel or iron ring in the scalp-lock, the hair being plaited around the ring in such a way that it cannot be removed, unless the hair is unbraided or the scalp-look cut off. I have often removed the ring by taking off a piece pf the scalp, which is the simplest form of getting it.

To the ring the feather is tied with a buckskin string, so that it be removed at will.

The Sioux have long had the name of "long tails," a distinction given them by frontiersmen and emigrants, on account of their wearing a strap six, or even seven, feet long attached to their scalp-lock and hanging down their backs. This trails on the ground when they walk, or sails in the wind behind them when, they ride at full speed. The scalp-lock, as well as the strap, was generally covered with tin or silver plates, made round, and fastened on six or seven inches apart. Most of these circular-plates were made of silver dollars, beaten out thin.

A Sioux is very proud of his scalp-lock and tail; and I have seen as many as twenty dollars on the hair and strap. The whole weight of the tail is borne by the roots of their hair, and, as-it sometimes weighs several pounds, it must pull a little at first. To tramp on a Sioux's long tail, or pull it, would be a mortal offense, and demand the shedding of blood to wipe out such an insult. When one Sioux pulls another one's scalp-lock, it is equivalent to the sending of a challenge among white men.

Mr. Belden showed the editor of these papers a magnificent belt, made from the silver he had taken off a Sioux "long tail." The silver weighed one pound and the strap to which it had been fastened three-fourths of a pound. The whole weight had been sustained by a small wisp of hair in the top of a warrior's head.—Note in original.

PAINTING THE FACE

THE painting of the face and body is a very ancient custom among the Indians. The early discoverers of the continent found the Indians using paints, made of clay and stone, to beautify, as they thought, their persons; and none were more hideously painted than the Caribbean Indians, who were among the earliest savages known to Europeans. There is not, to my knowledge, a tribe in the West, however civilized, that does not yet use paints.

The Yanktons, Sioux, Santees, and Cheyennes use a great deal of paint. A Santee squaw paints her face the same as a white woman does, only with less taste. If she wishes to appear particularly taking, she draws a red streak, half an inch wide, from ear to ear, passing it over the eyes, the bridge of the nose, and along the middle of the cheek. When a warrior desires to be left alone, he takes black paint, or lamp-black, and smears his face; then he draws zig-zag lines from his hair to his chin, by scraping off the paint with his nails. This is a sign that he is trapping, is melancholy, or in love. There is, however, no general meaning attached to the painting of the head or body by many Indians—anymore than there is by white men parting their hair on the side, of the head, instead of in the middle. All Indians, both men and women, part their hair in the middle; the men paint red that part of the scalp exposed by parting the hair.

The sign paints used by the Indians are not numerous, but very significant. When the warriors return from the war-path, and have been successful in bringing back scalps, the squaws, as well as the men, paint with vermilion a semicircle in front of each ear. The bow of the arc is toward the nose, and the points of the half circle on the top and bottom of the ear; the eyes are then reddened, and all dance over the scalps.

A warrior who is courting a squaw, usually paints his eyes yellow and blue, and the squaw paints hers red. I have known squaws to go through the painful operation of reddening the eye-balls, that they might, appear particularly fascinating to the young men. A red stripe drawn horizontally from one eye to the other, means that the young warrior has seen a squaw he could love, if she would reciprocate his attachment. Of course such an advertisement naturally creates a flutter in the village, and sets every young feminine heart to aching, and tongue to inquiring, if its possessors the person meant. Some laughable mistakes have occurred with this paint, and many bitter disappointments. I once heard of a famous Indian belle, who loved a young warrior, and employed every feminine art known in savage love, to entrap his affections. One day the young man mounted the love paint, and the Indian girl was so sure her charms had been effective, that she told her friends she would soon be married, and even went so far as to hint the same to the young warrior. Imagine her chagrin and disappointment, when he politely and frankly informed her, that, not she, but a very plain girl in the village, was the person meant by his paint.

The Sioux have a paint with which they smear their faces, when about to pass sentence of death on anyone, but as this paint is put on in the council chamber, I have never been able to learn what it was like, or in what form it was used.

The Crow and Snake Indians paint their faces red, and leave them so for days, renewing the coloring as fast as it rubs or wears off. Every Indian who can get one, carries a small looking-glass, slung to the wrist by a buckskin strap. This, and the paint-bag, are inseparable companions of both Indian men and women. The girls often go to clear streams and lakes, for the purpose of looking at their reflections in the water. I once accidentally surprised a maiden entirely naked, gazing at her fair proportions in the lake and she could never afterward look at me without blushing.

INDIAN HEAD-DRESSES

THE head-dress is an indispensable article in the outfit of every first-class warrior. They wear them at all great feasts, dances, councils, and when on friendly visits of ceremony to neighboring tribes. They are generally made out of the skins of elk, deer, buffalo, or bear. Most of them are round skull-caps, ornamented with eagle, crow, or duck feathers Take the half cover of a ball, and you have the exact idea of an Indian warrior's cap. The feathers are fastened on in bunches with sinew, and the bunches are sewed close together. They are put on in rows or layers, the feathers all lying one way. Fasten a dozen feathers by their middles to a piece of leather, then break them, so that both the top and butt end will stand up, and put another bunch on beside it, and so on until the whole piece of leather is covered. Next trim off the feathers evenly, leaving them about three inches long, and you will have made an Indian head-dress. The butts of the quills must be cut out so they will not show; but the better way is to take only the tops or small ends of the quills, cut them off the right length, and then fasten them by the thick .end to the cap. These, when trimmed a little, will make a beautiful head-gear.

Most Indian caps have a long tail hanging down behind, which is ornamented with little bells and bright feathers. The bells rattle when the warrior dances, walks, or rides, and the feathers, being fastened loosely by their quill ends, swing about, giving him a picturesque appearance. At the end of the tail are fastened tufts of hair, colored blue, red, or yellow.

A very popular style of Indian cap is made of buffalo hide and horns. It consists of a piece of hide taken from across the forehead of a buffalo, over the top of his head along the back of the neck and down the spine, including the tail. The bone is taken out and the 'tail stuffed, when the piece is one unbroken strip from the head to the end of the tail. On each side of the head are set horns, and frequently horns are fastened along the strip hanging down the back. The head-dress of the Sioux chief, Standing Bull, recently killed by Lieut. Mason, near Fort McPherson, was over six feet long and carried twelve horns. As the whole horns would be very heavy, they are split from top to base by sawing, and the thick part so hollowed out as to make them comparatively light. The horns are highly polished and set six or seven inches apart. Besides the horns, a great deal of bead-work, and eight to ten bells are put on the head-dress. I have seen four or five large sleigh-bells fastened to the tail, and not unfrequently the tails are, as much as nine feet long.

When the warriors are en route to visit another tribe, or are on the war path, they carry their head-dresses with them, neatly done up in a cylindrical bandbox, made of buffalo skin or raw hide. These bandboxes are highly ornamented and fancifully painted. They are not so symmetrical and elegant as the hat and bandboxes of Eastern ladies and gentlemen, but resemble more exactly the old-fashioned churn, with the dash taken out.

To roll up an Indian head-dress, and put it in the drum so the feathers will not get broken or spoiled, requires as much skill as to pack away the wardrobe of a fashionable white woman. When traveling, the drum is strapped to the back of the saddle, and carried as the old-fashioned valise used to be. Before entering the village they are to visit, the warriors dismount, put on their head-dresses, paint their faces, and arrange their hair. When their toilet is complete, they remount and ride through the town. An Indian always tries to accomplish one of two things, either excite the admiration of the women or fear of the men.

The American bald eagle and the great black eagle are frequently found in the Rocky Mountains and on the plains, but they soar very high, and it is extremely difficult to kill them. Twelve leathers from the crown of a full-grown eagle will buy a good pony among the Indians. These birds are much sought after in all tribes, and their feathers are used to ornament various articles, as well as make head-dresses. It is exceedingly difficult to buy an eagle headdress from an Indian, and a good one can never be had for less than two hundred dollars ($3,500 in 2015 dollars).

The white feather of the eagle's tail is worn attached to the manes and tails of the war ponies. When returning from the war path, the warriors attach black feathers to the eagle feathers, and when riding through the village, everyone has only to count the black feathers to know how many scalps and by whom they have been taken, the black feathers indicating success are always tied in the pony's tail, near the crupper, and to the white eagle feathers. If the white eagle feathers are gone, and only a black feather there, it indicates that the warrior fell, but killed an enemy before dying. If the white feathers are there and no black feathers, it means the warrior still wears his own scalp, but has taken none from the enemy. When the expedition has failed and returns, the black feathers are worn in the forelocks of the ponies. These feathers, fluttering in the wind from the heads of the horses, can be seen at an astonishing distance, and often long before the warriors reach the village the ill-success of the enterprise is known.

The feather worn by Indians in their scalp-locks is usually very long and symmetrical. It is ornamented with small wrappings of porcupine quills at the butt end, and the edges of the feathers are sometimes painted green, red, and yellow, in bars or stripes, according to the fancy of the wearer.

FINE MOCCASINS

THE Indians are their own shoemakers, and, with the limited means at their command, manage to manufacture an excellent protection for the foot, that does away with all fear of such modern torments as corns and bunions. The moccasin is made to fit the foot, and not the foot to fit the moccasin, as is the practice among civilized shoemakers.

Indian shoes are made by the women and old men. The sole is first cut out of rawhide, and then the uppers are cut from buck, antelope or elk skin tanned very soft and smooth. Buckskin is preferred when the moccasin is to be ornamented with beads, and the upper is always worked before it is attached to the sole.

The uppers are sewed to the soles with a strong thread made of twisted buffalo sinew, and sometimes a double sole is sewed on to protect the thread. To the sides and back parts, flaps or ears are fastened, which come well up on the ankles, and are tied with strings. Frequently the flaps cover the calf of the leg, and are fastened at the top by two long strings, in the same manner as a woman ties her apron. This is done when the moccasin is made for hunting or performing long journeys in, as the high tops not only brace the leg, but prevent the moccasin from slipping on the foot, and keep out the dust, brambles, gravel, cold, and snow.

It is no very difficult job to make a moccasin, and a squaw will cut out and sew up a plain pair in half a day. If they are beaded, however, it takes a week or more to finish them, and those ornamented with porcupine quills require a month of patient labor.

In the winter season the moccasins are made of buffalo hide or the skins of fur-bearing animals, the hair being turned inward. The Indians never wear stockings, but leggings, which are an excellent substitute when one has fur shoes to cover the feet.

It will be observed that they are all different in shape, and will make a different track. An expert frontiersman can readily tell to what tribe Indians belong by seeing their tracks in the sand. Unlike their arrows, they seldom or never change their moccasins. The following will serve to show the imitative faculty and ingenuity of the Indians: One day, while in camp, I saw a Winnebago squaw weaving cloth in a kind of loom.

She had many threads strung to little sticks fastened in a frame, and through these threads she passed a string of beads, pressing the whole together compactly, after the manner of a weaver. The different colors of the beads were ingeniously arranged to give a brilliant effect. I examined a purse this girl had made for the trader in the Santee village, and it was really beautiful. Soon afterward I saw another purse in the trader's store made by her, and it had on the side "James Buchanan" neatly worked in many-colored beads. I asked if she could read, and she said no, but showed me a medal which had been given by President Buchanan to one of the tribe during his visit to Washington, and from the letters on the medal she had copied the name.

The Winnebagoes are the only Indians I have ever met with who have any knowledge of the manufacture of cloth, and they can only weave such things as garters, armlets, purses, leggings, and long, beautiful, white bead-bands, which the women wear around their hair.

The Winnebagoes are very light in complexion, and many of their women might be called beautiful, if they would keep themselves clean. These women are tall, well-formed, have bright black eyes, and long, shining black hair. They take great pride in plaiting up their hair, winding it in coils, and ornamenting it with bead-bands. These bands are often five or six feet long, and fringed with many-colored beads. They wind them about their heads in an ingenious way, and the effect among their jet-black hair is very charming.

The Sioux, unlike the Winnebagoes, never put up their hair, but always allow it to hang down. They sometimes tie the ends of the plaits with ribbon, or wind them with red flannel, but further than this they attempt no ornamentation of the hair. The Sioux, however, are passionately fond of ear-rings, and I have seen as many as a hundred; small rings in a Sioux ear, a slit being, cut the whole length of the ear to make, room for them. Many of their ear-rings are very heavy, being made of square or oblong pieces of California sea-shell, which is a regular article of trade among all the Rocky Mountain tribes of savages. The shells are about one-fifth of an inch in thickness, five or six inches long, and four inches broad. They are shaped like a saucer, and the outside is prismatic, the colors often merging into blue, green, pink, and gold. Near the edge the shell is very thin and delicate, but hard to break. The Indians saw the shell into pieces, some round, others square, oblong, or pendant, and these they string together by means of wire passed through little holes bored in the pieces. Brass beads are often strung on the wires, as a sort of washer between different parts of the ear-ring, and beads strung on sinew form the pendants. A large brass ring for the ear generally begins a Sioux ear ornament, and to this are hung five or six pendants made of beads strung on wire; to these pendants are attached a cross-piece of rawhide or wood: then another column of pendants, to which are hung one large and two small beads; then another cross-piece, and next three large wampum beads, beneath which is suspended the piece of shell that gives the ornament its value. A shell will make one pair of rings, and it generally costs two robes, or about six dollars in cash. It will be observed that the accompanying illustration represents only one-third the actual size of these ear ornaments. In fact, they are frequently eighteen inches in length and from three to four inches in breadth in the widest part. What the ears of the wearers are made of is a mystery, but pride and vanity tell the story with the untutored savage, as well as with the more cultivated, but no less proud and vain dweller in civilized communities.

The accompanying cut shows the prevailing style of dressing the head for state occasions among the Crows, and it must be acknowledged that it is much more light and airy and more sensible withal, than the immense chignon, and the frizzles and fruzzles of the pale faces. Once in-Produced among the ladies of fashion, I have no doubt of the immense popularity of the Crow I lead-dress, and I would seriously recommend it to their earnest consideration.

INDIAN WOMEN—PHYSICAL ENDURANCE

CHILD-BIRTH among Indians has long been supposed to be attended with less pain and danger than among other races. This is a mistake, for human nature is very much the same the world over, and the Indian women, in bringing forth their children, suffer no less than their white sisters. The same stoicism which enables the warrior to bear without complaining the torture of his enemies, enables the Indian mother to endure in silence her labor-pains. The education in this direction begins the moment a child is born. First, it is lashed to a board, and then left for days and days, being suckled without being untied. If it cries, no attention is paid to its murmurings further than to ascertain that it does not suffer from pain or hunger, and it, soon learns that crying does no good.

When it can walk, it is allowed to romp and indulge in the most violent exercise. If it lives to grow up, it is taught to bear heavy burdens, walk long distances, and brave summer's heat and winter's cold. In this way all the muscles are thoroughly developed, and the maiden becomes healthy and strong.

But besides a healthy frame capable of bearing suffering, the Indian woman is taught that to complain is weak and unwomanly. And again, menstruation and child-bearing are a matter of shame and not to be published to the world. Hence it is that the Indian woman, finding her time of labor come, will often leave her home and go into a swamp or woods, and there remain until her child is brought forth, and she is able to return to her lodge. With no eye save God's to pity her, and no hand save her own to help her, she endures the most terrible pain to which humanity is subjected.

The papoose in camp or on the march is always carried on a board. It is made of sufficient length to allow it to rest its head and feet, and the board is wide enough to wrap the child snugly, and have the strings press on the chest and legs instead of the sides. The bottom of the wrapping is stuffed so as to make a firm support for the feet, and prevent the child from slipping down and becoming wedged in, which would misshape its feet and legs.

The strings that hold it are fastened to the board, and are tied in bow knots on its breast and belly. Little or no compression is made of the lower limbs, they being loose in a sort of sack formed by the wrapping. The mother removes the child from the board as often as necessary for the purposes of nature, and no oftener. A willow is bent and fastened to the top of the board, which serves as a handle to lift it by, and also as a frame upon which to hang a cloth or skin to protect its face from the weather and flies. The mother carries the board on her back, it being held in its place by a band which passes from the top of the board over her forehead.

The practice of disfiguration prevails extensively among nearly all the western tribes. One day an Indian boy was thrown from his pony and dashed against a cottonwood-tree with such violence that he died next morning of his injuries. His mother and sisters, as a sign of their grief, cut off a finger each at the first joint. I have seen the Crows gash their arms, legs, bodies, and faces when their friends died. The women cut several gashes on the forehead near the roots of the hair, and the blood was allowed to remain until it dried and wore off.

To tie up a wound inflicted as a sign of grief is considered cowardly. It must not be noticed for at least twenty-four hours and then only to stop the blood. Many Indians bleed almost to death from their self-inflicted wounds, but it is considered justifiable to take any position to staunch the flow of blood, and Indians not unfrequently, after severing a finger, hold the hand above their heads, or stand all night holding to a pole until the twenty-four hours are up, when the wound may be tied up in rags.

It is said that at .the Fort Phil Kearney massacre, [December 21] 1866, over three hundred Indians were killed, and that hundreds of fingers were cut off and gashes innumerable made on their persons by the friends of the dead. A chief, two years after the massacre, said, in council, "The Sioux, Arrapahoes, and Cheyennes have not done mourning for our braves who fell at Phil Kearney."

*Eighty-one soldiers were killed, including Captain William J. Fetterman, for whom the fight is generally named by white historians.— Ed. 2015

When a warrior is killed, his pony is gashed in the sides and on the legs with knives, to make him feel sorry for the death of his master.

Travelers have often noticed the gashes in the ponies' sides and the missing fingers of Indians' hands, and attributed them to accident or war, but in nine cases' out of ten these disfigurations are traceable to the causes mentioned above.

INDIAN DOGS

DOGS and Indians are inseparable companions. Where you find an Indian you are pretty sure to find a dog; and, if you enter a village you will see hundreds on hundreds of these animals running about. The first question one asks himself, on arriving at an Indian town is, What can all these dogs be kept for? but a short residence will soon convince him that there are none too many.

The Indian dog resembles the coyote, or prairie-wolf, and his bark is so much like this animal's, it is often difficult to distinguish the two apart. There is no doubt but that the wild dog is a cross between the domestic, or house dog, and the wolf.

The flesh of the Indian dog is very fine, and resembles the flesh of a calf or antelope. There is none of that blackness, or coarseness, found in the meat of the domestic dog. Each Indian family keeps from six to sixteen dogs, and they are very useful for many purposes besides eating. They can be made to draw water, carry or haul wood, and when the village moves, they are put into little shafts and made to drag burdens of camp equipage. They are excellent watch dogs, and nothing can' approach the camp without their seeing, or hearing it. They are very cowardly, but always give the alarm by barking when a strange animal or man approaches. They are fierce looking brutes, and hundreds of them will run toward a stranger as though about to tear him to pieces, but a club shied among them will set them scampering in all directions. If you run from them they will bite, but if you rush at them, scores of them will take to flight, and never stop until safely ensconced in or near the teepees of their owners. Their terror, in times of attack, is extreme, and they are, undoubtedly, the most cowardly brutes in the world. They are ravenous, and will bite, or throw down a child to get a bone, or piece of meat out of its hand. They are constantly on the watch, and if you lay down any food for a moment, some villainous cur will be sure to snatch it and run away with it. The coyote is not more sneaking or treacherous in his disposition than a wild dog. What Indian dogs live on, no one can tell, for the Indians take no pains to feed them, unless it be a favorite that they wish to eat, and then he is tied up by the teepee to fatten. I have often seen them out hunting on the bottoms, and along the creeks for mice, prairie-squirrels, and rabbits, which they devour with avidity.

When any great event happens, such as a victory or successful hunt, the Indians make a great dog-feast, and old and young partake of the savory food. Dog meat is considered a great delicacy, and an old country woman in the East is not more proud and careful of her pullets, than is an Indian of his young dogs. I have often eaten dog, though I can't say I am partial to that kind of food now.

Soon after I joined the Indians, I was invited to two dog-feasts, and feeling that it would not be courteous to refuse, I went to one. I did not intend to eat any of the meat, but changed my mind, on being informed by a friend, that it would be downright ill-manners not to partake, at least, of the soup. The dog had been boiled well, and was fat, which did not help the matter or make the dish more palatable. I had a foolish notion that I could eat lean dog, but dog-fat-was positively repulsive to me. When I arrived at the feast, I was given a huge wooden bowl that would hold about three quarts, and invited to come up and have it filled. I went to the great kettle where the dog had been boiled, and was helped to the under-jaw and a part of the fore-quarter. The teeth of the jaw looked white and wolfish, and, as I imagined, gave me a grin when they came from the pot. Corn and wild artichokes had been boiled with the dog, and I was given two huge ladle-fulls of these vegetables. I retired to my place in the circle, and taking up my spoon of buffalo-horn, endeavored to keep up appearances. I pretended to scrape off some of the meat, but as it stuck tight to the bone, I took up some of the corn and soup, and tasted it. To my surprise, it was very palatable, and if I could have forgotten it was dog soup, it would really have been good. I was conscious that the Indians were watching me, and did the best I could to swallow as much soup as possible. .Unluckily, as I dipped down deep in the bowl for corn, I brought up a piece of meat which had become detached by the boiling. I wished to throw it back, but saw two Indians looking directly at me, and I boldly raised it to my mouth. As it passed between my lips, I felt an involuntary shudder seize me, as though I were cold, and I expected to be instantly nauseated, but as I masticated it, 1 found the meat sweet and savory. I tried some more, but despite my resolution, I could only eat sparingly. Candor compels me to say, however, that but for my prejudice, the food would have been pleasant and wholesome.

After this, I attended many dog-feasts, and soon learned to eat as Heartily as anyone. At one time, I had got so far along as to seriously think of trading for some dogs, that I might have a supply of the meat on hand for my use at all seasons, but I gave it up, more because I wished to appear respectable in my own eyes, and retain some semblance of civilization, than because I had any longer a repugnance to dog—soiled, roasted, stewed, or fried.

THE DELIVERANCE

THE summer was drawing to a close and the autumn days coming on when the annual hunt would begin. Before the fall hunt I determined to go on an adventure of my own, and, on communicating my intention to several of the Santees, they expressed a desire to accompany me. It was all soon arranged as to who would go, and we made preparations for a special hunt in the Big Horn country.

First, we were to fall down the river a distance of one oi two hundred miles, and having drawn as near the mountain? as possible, and supplied ourselves with buffalo meat, strike across the country.

Our trip along the Missouri was delightful, and our stock improved every day. We had all the game we needed, and at night camped in delightful spots by clear, running streams Fish, deer, and antelope abounded, and the weather was mild and refreshing. Nothing could have been more pleasant than this mode of traveling on the broad, wild-prairies of the West.

One evening, just as we were thinking about going into camp for the night, I spied a buffalo bull lying on a little hillside, and I determined at once to capture him. La Frombe, who was with me, and one of the Santee warriors, moved out so as to get on the wind side of him, and then we ran for the beast. On looking to the west, I saw-at a short distance a whole herd, and, leaving La Frombe and his companion to manage the bull, made for the herd. I was soon up with it, and, singling out a bull, fired a ball into him. The herd made off as fast as possible, the wounded buffalo following rapidly. In jumping a small ravine my pony fell, and so badly sprained his shoulder he was unable to keep up with the game. While I was chafing at my disappointment, and urging my little pony to do his utmost, La Frombe and the Santee came up with me, having finished their bull, and followed to see what had become of me. As soon as La Frombe noticed the condition of my horse, he cautioned me against going farther, and said it would be unsafe to attack a bull with the pony in his present disabled condition. Just then, however, a flue young bull separating from the herd, I called to La Frombe to head him, and as he turned give the buffalo a shot. La Frombe did as I desired, and then rejoined the chase after the herd. Having my game now going toward the camp, I rode along leisurely for some distance, and then dashed up and gave him another ball. Instantly, as it seemed to me, the beast wheeled, lowered his head, and charged. I spurred my pony sharply, and barely escaped his horns. In the surprise and excitement of the moment, I had dropped my gun while trying to reload it, and before I could recover it the buffalo was again upon me. I plunged the [spur's] rowels into the pony's flanks, and he dashed forward, but the bull kept close in his rear. I now saw that the animal was only enraged and not disabled by the shots I had given him, while my pony began to show evident signs of exhaustion.

On we went over the prairie, my pursuer with his head close to the ground, and intent on plunging his horns into the pony's flanks. I looked back as we were ascending a little slope, and the bull was within eight feet of me. When I reached the crest of the slope, I saw before me a steep descent, full of rocks and holes. I hesitated to risk my pony on such uneven ground, for he was not sure-footed, but the frightened little fellow plunged down the ridge, and I let him go. Suddenly I felt him sinking under me, and the next moment I rolled headlong among the rocks. I looked up, and saw the buffalo, with lowered head, plunging at me, and scarcely twenty feet distant. Every instant I expected to feel his sharp horns in my side or be trampled to death beneath his feet, and closed my eyes. While I lay waiting for my death, the sharp crack of a rifle rang out on the air, quickly followed by another shot. A sharp pain thrilled me, and I felt myself flying through the air. The confuted sound of voices nearby caused me to open my eyes, and there sat La Frombe and the Santee on their ponies.

They had followed me, and arrived just in time to give the bull two fatal shots as he was about to gore me to death. I was so sore from the effects of my wounds that I could not rise, but they dismounted and lifted me up, when I saw the bull lying dead scarcely a dozen feet distant. An examination showed that the beast had struck me with the side of his horn on the shoulder, and although he had sent me spinning like a top, the horn had not entered the flesh.

In a little while I was able to walk, and, with the assistance of La Frombe, to mount my pony, who had not been hurt by his fall, and was quietly grazing nearby. I rode slowly back to camp, fully resolved to be more careful in future when I hunted buffalo. It was many a day before I recovered from the effects of my bruises, and never, until the day of my death, shall I ever forget how I felt when I imagined that buffalo's horns driving through me.

WHAT FRIGHTENED THEM

WE now had all the buffalo meat we needed, and at once set out for the mountains. After reaching them, we skirted along their base, looking for deer and elk, and succeeded in capturing a number of fine animals.

A pleasant temporary camp was located, where we rested for a day or two, and then set out for any adventure that might come in our way. We had left the base of the mountain one morning, soon after daylight, and were" moving across the plain, when we noticed three objects going in the direction of a cañon a mile in advance. Whipping up our ponies ye were not long in coming upon three huge grizzly bears. In a moment all was excitement, and we dashed forward, endeavoring to head them off from the cañon, where we surmised they had a den. We knew that to attack them on the open plain would lessen the danger of the conflict greatly, so we rode hard, but despite our efforts they reached and entered the cañon ahead of us.

My horse had outstripped those of my companions, and seeing the bears about to escape, I spurred on until I passed the grizzlies, and then turning, fired a shot, hoping to turn them back or bring them to a halt. They, however, came steadily on toward me, and I rode to the side of the cañon and attempted to climb its steep bank. I succeeded, and for a time lost sight of the animals. I waited several moments, expecting to hear the guns of my friends in the conflict below, when I would ride down and join them. All remained quiet, however, and, becoming impatient, I dismounted, and leaving my horse, walked to the edge of the cañon. I could see nothing of the bears or horsemen, and ventured down the bank. I was straining my eyes in all directions, when I heard a noise above me, and, looking up, saw on the top of the ridge, not more than fifty yards from me, the three bears. They had followed me up the bank, and skirted along the crest, until they came near my horse. I heard the pony snorting and trying to break his lariat rope, and a moment afterward he was dashing along the ridge, dragging the rope behind him. I had hoped the bears would follow him, but, instead of doing so, they sat down to watch me. The hill-side was thickly strewn with shaggy little pines, blown down by the wind, and among these I took up my position. The bears, seeing me apparently moving off, followed and one came within forty feet before he saw me. Hoping to frighten off the brute as well as attract my friends, I fired my revolver in the air. The bear gave an angry growl, and came still nearer. Glancing up the cañon, and seeing nothing of my friends, I concluded to fire, and raising the hammer of my Henry rifle, I took a steady aim at the beast's heart, and pulled the trigger. With a roar that made the hill shake, she fell to the ground and rolled over. In a moment more she got up and, shaking herself, fixed her blood-red eyes upon me. My heart sank in my breast, for I saw I had missed the vitals of the animal, and only enraged by wounding her. The other two bears, which I now saw were large cubs, lay crouching near their mother, and apparently watching the battle. Seeing the old bear about to rush upon me, I hastily threw the exploded shell out of my Henry, and raising the hammer sent a ball at her, but, owing to her sudden change of position, missed her, and hit one of the cubs that was just behind her. The cub bellowed lustily, and the dam ran to him. This was most lucky for me, and I lost no time in putting three more shots into the old bear. Once more she came bounding toward me, and I plumped a shot into the cub that made him yell with agony. The old beast was within a few feet of me, when, unable to withstand the piteous cries of her cub, she turned and went to him. I now pumped the shot into her as fast as possible, but presently she came on again, when again I hit her cub, and sent her back to lick his wounds. She had received thirteen balls, when she made off, followed by the cubs, one of which was so lame he could hardly walk.

I was debating in my own mind, whether I should pursue and finish the bears or let well enough alone, when I perceived my companions coming riding down the cañon, and directly in front of the grizzlies. I hallooed to them to head off the bears and attack them in front, while I followed up my attack m the rear. I ran as fast as I could, and coming up to the hindmost cub, laid him out at one shot. I next shot the other cub, and fired twice at the old bear, but she was getting too far ahead for my balls to be effective. La Frombe and the Santee headed her, when she came running back to her dead cub, sat down, and howled most piteously. Then she took her paw and rolling him over and over, shook him as if to wake him. Smelling his nose, she seemed to understand he was dead, and cried as if her heart would break. Suddenly she saw me, and, standing on her hind feet, looked at her persecutor. She made no attempt to come at me, but seemed to be waiting for her death. Never did I see so magnificent a beast, as she stood there, with ears flattened against her head, her eyes blazing like coals of fire, her neck stretched out, and her mouth wide open, disclosing four rows of immense white teeth. I did not long keep her in suspense, but fired at her heart, and she fell down and rolled over, catching her cub, and seemingly trying to embrace it as she died.

This bear would certainly have weighed over one thousand pounds, and after my severe contest with her I had a desire to possess her skin. La Frombe helped me skin her, while the Santee went to hunt up my pony. We left on the claws and skin of the head. Just as we had finished our job, the Santee came back with my pony, and taking the entrails out of the smallest cub, we lifted him upon La Frombe's horse, and all set out to return to our camp.

We had gone but a mile or two, when we saw several horsemen riding furiously across the plain, apparently with the design of heading us off. It needed no second look to convince us they were hostile Crows, and, dropping the bear, we broke for the hills. It was a ride for life, as there were fully fifteen Indians in the other party, and we knew if we were caught they would burn us at the stake, for they were at war with the Sioux, and, what was worse for us, we were hunting game on their hunting-grounds.

Suddenly the Crows halted, and, apparently without any cause, put back as fast as they had come. On ascending a little knoll, we saw the cause of their alarm, for there stood our camp, half hid away among the trees. The Crows had seen the camp, and thinking our party, was strong, and that we were decoying them to the camp, they began their hasty retreat.

In a few moments not a Crow was to be seen, and we rode quietly into camp, laughing heartily at the needless alarm of our enemies.

After a hearty supper, we packed up, and, fearing the Crows would return and discover our weakness, when we should all be killed, we determined to move off at once. All night long we rode briskly forward, and when the sun rose, gilding the mountain peak with silver and gold, we were nearly fifty miles distant from where our camp had been.

We breakfasted on fresh antelope, and rested until noon, when we again set forward, and continued our journey for two days. Being now far in the mountains, we felt safe, and pitched our camp, intending to hunt for a season.

THE RETURN

WE had been at our new camp several days, and taken all the game we wanted when, one morning, I determined to climb the mountain peaks and have a hunt after the famous mountain sheep. My companions liked the idea of a dash at the "hard heads," and we all three set out together. The sun met us as we toiled up the steeps, and it was scarcely half an hour high, when La Frombe, who was in advance, halted, and pointing to a cliff half a mile distant, said, "There they are." We looked in the direction indicated, and saw a group of four sheep walking along the edge of the precipice. They had not yet discovered us, and we stood still until they passed out of sight behind some projecting rocks, and then ran as fast as we could along the mountain side until we were directly under where we had seen our game. Carefully ascending from crag to crag, we were not long in coming upon their fresh tracks, and now we crept along, looking carefully ahead at every turn. Presently, La Frombe pointed to the right, and there, standing on a rock, scarcely two hundred yards from us, were three large sheep. We each selected a sheep—La Frombe taking the one on the left, the Santee the one in the middle, and I the farthest on the right. At a signal from La Frombe, we fired together, and when the smoke cleared away saw one sheep lying on the rock. I ran as fast as I could up the rocks, and' arrived in time to see the other two big horns going around the bluff a quarter of a mile off. La Frombe had killed his game, but the Santee and I had missed our mark. I, however, noticed blood on the stones, and knowing that one of the other two was wounded, determined to follow them. Leaving La Frombe ana the Santee to skin and dress the dead animal, I climbed from ravine to ravine, and rock to rock, for nearly an hour, and had began to despair of seeing my game again, when I unexpectedly came upon some blood and tracks. I saw where the sheep had laid but a few moments before, and as there was some soft soil at this point so, I could follow the tracks, I crawled carefully along. I paused often to watch and listen, but could see nothing, and all was silent, as only the vast solitudes of a mountain can be. I had begun to descend a little, with a view of getting among some scrubby pines nearby, in order the better to shield myself from observation, and just as I reached them, I saw a stately-, ram walking slowly along a ledge of rocks, closely followed by a small ewe. I was as yet too far away to shoot with precision, and as they were moving slowly, and had not seen me, I stood still .until they turned the rock. They were moving parallel with me, and I now hastened, under cover of the pines, to get ahead of them, if possible. After getting one or two falls, and nearly breaking my gun and neck over the stones, I perceived the sheep nearly above me, and not over two hundred yards distant. I crawled to the edge of the rocks, and selecting an open spot, where I knew the sheep would pass, rested my gun. In a moment they appeared, and when the ram came opposite the end of my rifle, I fired. The old fellow dropped, rolled over, turned upon his horns, and fell over forty feet, lighting on his head. He was desperately wounded, but still able to rise. As he steadied himself for another jump; I put a third ball into him, and he lay down on-the rocks. I scrambled up to him, and when he saw me, he made desperate efforts to get upon his feet. He lay upon his side, his great red eyes rolling fiercely: When I went near him he bleated piteously, and struck with his-forefeet, at the same time tossing his great horns savagely about. I tried for some time to get hold of him, not wishing to shoot him again, as I had but two charges left in my gun, and I had left my ammunition-belt behind, in order to climb the better. Every time I approached, he struck at me, until finally, losing my patience, I pounced upon him from behind, and seizing hold of one of his horns, attempted to draw my hunting-knife across his throat. Throwing back his head with a strength that surprised me, he struck me with his horn on the knee and almost broke my leg. It was only after a severe struggle that I was able to drive my knife into his neck and finish him.

When I had killed the ram, I looked up, and there stood the doe, hardly fifty yards distant. She had been looking at the death of her mate, and now, even as I looked at her, bounded nimbly away over the rocks. I fired a shot after her, but it did not hit her, and I sat down perfectly satisfied with my ram.

I was not long in signaling my companions, and presently I heard the long "talla-ho!" of La Frombe, who was coming up the steeps below me.

I had my sheep skinned and dressed by the time they came up, and the pines affording a favorable place, we cut off some of the choice bits, roasted them on the coals, and dined.

We were all three very tired, and having bad enough of sheep-hunting for one day, we rested for a couple of hours, and then, packing our meat on our backs, began the descent. It was quite late when we reached our camp, and as we were weary and bruised by many a fall, received during the day, we soon went to bed.

DEATH OF THE BUFFALO

WE were now out of the buffalo range, but occasionally we met an old bull, who, having been driven away from the herd by the sharp horns of his younger brethren, had wandered far up into the mountains, to graze and live out the remnant of his days in peace.

These old fellows, disturbed by our presence, would, on being approached, throw up their heads defiantly, and then trot off to other pastures.

One day a desire seized me to have a battle with one of these monarchs of the prairies. Saddling my pony, I rode out, and was not long in coming upon an old soldier who was grazing in a little grassy valley. He was monarch of all he surveyed, but nevertheless thought it proper to acknowledge my superiority by shaking his head, as a sort of negative admission, and then gallop off toward the hills.

My little pony soon overtook him, however, and I gave the old fellow a shot that made him grunt, and set every nerve in him quivering. I did not desire to kill him at once, but exercise the agility of my pony and the skill of myself. Seeing him making for a ravine, I spurred by, and, swinging buffalo robe before his face, sought to turn him. He ran back at once, and when he was on the open prairie, I gave him a shot through the hams. This made him switch his tail and cut dirt for a mile, but he presently made signs of battle. This was precisely what I wanted, and I gave haste to shoot him again, this time in the neck. He now turned and charged upon me, but my little pony wheeled and was off like the wind. Away we went over the prairie, the pursuer and pursued. I zigzagged the pony, and, as the old buffalo could not turn on less than an acre of ground, he had to run more than twice as far as the little horse. It would take him some time to bring himself to bear upon us, but, having got himself in range, he would come on like a steam engine, sure that he had us, but only to be, zigzagged out of line again, and find he was charging the air. In a little time he gave it up and started for the ravine, near which we had been maneuvering. He had a good start before I perceived what his object was, and, although I rode hard, .1 could not head him in time to prevent him from entering it. I dashed down into the cañon, and, not seeing my game, was about to pull rein, when my horse, in turning the sharp butt of a little bluff that run into the ravine, came suddenly upon the buffalo lying down, and, before I could chock his speed, stumbled and fell headlong over-him. I rolled over and over on the ground, and was so stunned and bruised, that for several minutes I could neither rise to my feet nor collect my senses. An indistinct idea of danger thrilled me, and still, half blinded and choked with dust, I got upon my knees, and, feeling for my revolver, which was in the scabbard strapped to my waist, I drew and fired it twice at a black-looking mass before me. Whether it "was the smell of the powder or the noise of the explosion that brought back my recollection and sense, I cannot tell, but in a moment I saw the buffalo close by me, and attempting to rise to his feet. I aimed at his side and fired twice, and, to my inexpressible relief, saw the great brute roll over and die. I was still so dizzy I closed my eyes and laid down on the ground. Presently, by remaining still, I felt better, and, rising, I examined to see if any bones were broken. I was terribly bruised, but still whole, and I felt so delighted at this discovery, I walked, or rather hobbled, to the buffalo, and, cutting his throat with my great butcher-knife, sat down upon the carcass. It was fully half an hour before I could realize what had occurred, and then I found my poor little horse standing in a pocket of the cañon, and so lame he could hardly walk. My gun was broken and my hat lying near it, torn almost in two.

An examination proved that the buffalo had run into the cañon, and, thinking himself free from his tormentor, had laid down behind the butt, when a moment afterward I came along at full speed, and both rider and .horse tumbled over him. The collision had rolled the buffalo over, and the blow necessary to do this had nearly dislocated my horse's shoulder. I made haste to mount and work my way back to camp, where I arrived in sad plight, long after dark. My companions had become so uneasy about me that they were just starting out to hunt me up, when I came in and related to them my adventure and miraculous escape.

LEGEND OF CRAZY WOMAN

FRESH pony-tracks, seen in a gorge, warned us that the hostile Crows were about, and hastily packing up, we decamped to a more safe locality.

After many days travel, we came in sight of a broad, rolling stream, shaded by cottonwood, and pitched our camp on its bank. The valley along the river was wide and fertile, and flocks of prairie hens and ducks rose from the long grass and flew away in all directions. Deer, antelope, and elk, bounded over the hills, and far in the distance could be seen a drove of wild horses. I could not help wondering how soon this wild scene would be changed, and the smoke of the white man's cabin ascend all along the rich valley. Already, I saw, in imagination, corn growing on the slopes, farmhouses nestling among the trees, a village in the great bend of the stream, and I thought I could hear the tinkling of cow-bells, the laugh of children, and the solemn tolling of church-bells.

La Frombe said the stream was called Crazy Woman, and the valley had long been known to the Crows as Crazy Woman's Valley. I asked him how it could have obtained such a singular name, and he related the following story:

Many years ago, I visited this spot with a band of Crows, and one evening a venerable Indian told us this legend of Crazy Woman: Years ago, when my father was a little boy, there came among us a man who was half white. He said he wished to trade with our people for buffalo-robes, beaver, elk, and deer skins, and that he would give us much paint, and many blankets and pieces of cloth in exchange for furs. We liked him, and believed him very good, for he was rich, having many thousands of beads and hundreds of yards of ribbons. Our village was then built on the river, about twenty miles above where we now are, and game was very plentiful. This river did not at that time have the name of Crazy Woman, but was called "Big Beard," because a curious grass grows along its banks that has a big beard. What I am about to relate caused the name of the river to be changed.

The trader built a lodge of wood and stones, and near it a great, strong house, in which he kept all his immense wealth. It was not long until he had bought all the robes and furs for sale in the village, and then he packed them on ponies, and bidding us good-bye, said he was going far to the East, where the-paleface lives, but that he would soon come back, bring us many presents, and plenty of blankets, beads, and ribbons, which he would exchange as before for robes and furs. We were sorry to see him go, but, as he promised to return in a few moons, we were much consoled. It w-as not long until our spies reported something they could not understand coming into our country, and the whole village was, in a great state of alarm. Some of the boldest ventured out, and returned with the joyful intelligence, that the strange objects our young men had seen, was the trader and his people. All the village ran to meet him, and the sight was strange enough indeed. The Crows had in those days never seen a wagon-horse or ox, and the trader had brought all these things. The wagons they called teepees on rollers; the horses were giants, beside the little ponies, and the oxen, all believed were tame buffaloes. There, also, was a squaw who was perfectly white, and who could not understand anything that was said to her. She wore dresses down to her feet, of which she seemed to be ashamed, and our women said she tied cords tightly about her waist, so as to make it small. She had very long hair, and did not plait, but rolled it, and, instead of letting it hang down, wrapped it tightly about her head.

It was not long until-the trader had all his wagons unloaded, and his store open. He had brought all the women beads and ribbons, and the mem brass rings. Besides what he sold, he made many presents; so everybody loved him, for no one had ever before seen so rich and generous a man.

One day, he told the Big Chief to come into the back pail of the store and he would show him something wonderful. The chief went, wondering what it could be, and when they were alone, the trader drew out a very little barrel, and taking a wooden cup, poured out some black-looking water, which he told the chief to drink. The chief did as desired, and immediately felt so jolly he asked for more. The trader promised, if he would never tell anyone where he got the black water, he would give him all he wanted. The chief promised, and the trader gave him another cupful. Now the chief danced and sang, and went to his lodge, where he fell down in a deep sleep, and no one could wake him. He slept so long, the warriors gathered about the lodge wondering what could ail him, and they were about to go to the trader and demand to know what kind of medicine he had given the chief to make him behave so strangely, when the chief woke up and ordered them all to their lodges, and to ask no questions.

Next day the chief went to the trader, and said he had had great dreams; that he thought he had slain many of his enemies, and that the black medicine must be very good to make him have such pleasant visions. He begged, the trader to give him some more, and he did so. Thus the chief did every day, and all the village wondered, for they believed the trader had bewitched him. In former times the chief had been a quiet and very dignified man, but now he sang, danced in the streets, and publicly hugged the women, so everyone thought him crazy. The Crows disliked the conduct of the chief very much, and began to grumble against the trader, for they thought he was to blame for the great change that had come over their chief. Some said he was bewitched, others that the trader had an evil spirit in one of his boxes, and thus they talked, some believing one thing and some another, but all blaming him. One of the young warriors called a secret council, and the matter was discussed, and it was finally decided that the trader must leave or they would put him to death. A warrior, who was a great friend of the trader, was sent to tell him of the decision of the council, and when he did so the trader laughed, and said if he would come into the back of the store, and never tell anybody, he would show him what ailed the chief. The warrior went, and the trader gave him a ladle full of the black water to drink. Presently he began to sing and dance about, and then went out into the street and sang, which greatly surprised everyone, for he had never done so before. The young men gathered about him, and asked him what ailed him, but he only said, "Oh, go to the trader and get some of the black water!" So they went to the trader, and inquired what kind of black water he had that affected people so strangely; and the trader told them he had only the same kind of water they drank, and brought out his pail, that they all might drink. Each warrior took up the ladle and drank some, and made the trader drink some, and then they sat down to wait and see if it would affect them like the chief and their brother warrior; but it did not, and they rose up and said, "The trader or our brother lies, and we will see who is the liar." They went to the warrior's lodge, and found him sound asleep, nor could they wake him. Two remained to watch by him, and the others went to their teepees. When the sun was up, the warrior rose, and, seeing the others sitting in his tent, said, "Why are you here, my brothers?" And the eldest of the two warriors replied, "You have lied to us, for the trader has no black water." The warrior, recollecting his promise not to tell, said, "It is true that the trader has no black water, and who said he had?" They explained to Tim his conduct of the day before, at which he was greatly astonished, and he declared if such was the case he must have been very sick in his head and not known what he had said. Thereupon the warriors withdrew and reported all to their brethren. The warriors were greatly perplexed, and knew not what to do or think, but decided to wait and see.

The chief and warrior were now drunk every day, and the young chief called another council. It was long and stormy in its debate, all the wise men speaking, but no one giving such counsel as the others would accept. At last a young warrior rose and said that he had watched, and that it was true the trader had a black water which he gave the chief and warrior to drink, for he had made a hole in the wall of the trader's store, and through it saw them drinking the black water. He advised them to bring the trader and warrior before them, and he would accuse them to their face of what he had seen, and if they denied the truth he would fight them.

This speech was received with great satisfaction, and the young chief at once sent some warriors to fetch the trader and their brother.

When they wore come into the council and seated, the young warrior repeated all he had said, and asked if it were not true that they would fight him. The warrior who was first asked rose up and said the young warrior lied, and that he was ready to fight him; but

118

when the trader was told to stand up and answer, he, seeing there was no use in denying the matter, confessed all.

He said the black water was given him by the white people, a great many of whom drank it, and it made them behave as they had seen the chief and the warrior do. He also told them that after a man drank of it he felt happy, laughed and sang, and when he laid down he dreamed pleasant dreams and slew his enemies.

The curiosity of the warriors was greatly excited, and the young chief bade the trader go and bring some of his black water, that they might taste it. He was about to depart, when the young warrior, who had before spoken, rose and desired him to be seated, when he said:

"The warriors heard my speech, and it was good. The brother, however, when I asked him if he would tell the council the truth, said I lied; and he would fight me. "Let us now go out of the village and fight."

The young chief asked the drunkard if he had anything to say, when he arose and addressed the council as follows:

"Oh, my brethren, it is true that I have drank of the black water, and that I have lied. When the trader first gave it to me to drink, he made me promise I would never tell what it was or where I got it, and he has many times since said if I told anyone he would never give me anymore to drink. Oh, my brethren, the black water is most wonderful, and I have come to love it better than my life or the truth. The fear of never having any more of it to drink made me lie, and I have nothing more to say but that I am ready to fight."

Then the council adjourned, and everyone went out to see the warriors fight. They were both men of great skill and bravery, and the whole village came to see the battle. He who had drank the black water was the best spearsman in the tribe, and everyone expected to see the other warrior killed.

The spears were brought, and when they were given to the combatants it was seen that the hand of him who had lied shook so he could hardly hold his spear. At this his friends rallied him, and asked him if he was afraid. He replied that his heart was brave, but that his hand trembled, though not with fear, for it had shook so for many days.

Then the battle began, and at the second throw of the spears, he with the trembling hand was clove through the heart, and killed instantly, while the other warrior did not even receive a wound.

After the fight was over, the warriors all went to the trader's lodge, and he brought out in a pail more than a quart of the black water, which he gave in small quantities to each warrior. When they had swallowed it, they began to dance and sing and many lay down on the ground and slept as though they were dead.

Next day they came again and asked for more black water; and so they came each day, dancing and singing, for more than a week.

One morning the trader said he would give them no more black water unless, they paid him for it, and this they did. The price was at first one robe for each sup sufficient to make them sleep, but, as the black water became scarce, two robes, and finally three were paid for a sleep. Then the trader said he had no more except a little for himself, and this he would not sell; but the warriors begged so hard for some he gave them a sleep for many robes. Even the body robes were soon in the hands of the trader, and the warriors were very poor, but still they begged for more black water, giving a pony in exchange for each sleep. The trader took all the ponies, and then the warriors offered their squaws, but there was no more black water, and the trader said he would go and fetch some.

He packed all the robes on the ponies, and was about to set out, when a warrior made a speech, saying that now that he had all their robes and ponies, and they were very poor, the trader was going away and would never return, for they had nothing more to give him. So the warriors said he should not depart, and ordered him to unpack the ponies. The trader told them he would soon return with plenty of black water, and give it to them as he did at first. Many of the warriors were willing he should depart, but others said no, and one declared that he had plenty of black water still left, and was going off to trade with their enemies, the Sioux. This created great excitement, and the trader's store and all his packs were searched, but no black water found. Still the warrior asserted he had it, and that it was hidden away. The warriors declared that they would kill him unless he instantly told them where he had hid it, and upon his not being able to do so, they rushed into his lodge and murdered him before the eyes of his squaw, tearing off his scalp and stamping upon his body. This so alarmed the white squaw she attempted to run out of the lodge, and, as she came to the door, a warrior struck her on the head with his tomahawk, and she fell down as though she were dead.

The chief made a great speech, saying that now, as the trader was dead, they would burn his lodge and take back all their robes and ponies. So the lodge was fired, and as it burned a Crow squaw saw by its light the white squaw lying before the door, and that she was not dead, and she took her to her lodge, sewed up her wounds, and gave her something to eat. The squaw lived and got well, but she was crazy, and could not bear the sight of a warrior, believing everyone who came near her was going to kill her.

One day the white squaw was missing, and the whole village turned out to look for her. They followed her tracks far down the river, but could not find her. Some women out gathering berries a few days afterward, said the white squaw came to them and asked for food, showing them, at the same time, where she was hiding in the bluffs nearby. She begged them not to tell the warriors where she was, or they would come and kill her. The squaws tried to dissuade her from a notion so foolish, but they could not get her to return to the village.

Every day the squaws went and took her food, and she lived for many months, no one 'knowing where she was but the women. When the warriors came about she hid away, and would not stir out until they were gone.

One day, however, a warrior out hunting antelope came suddenly upon her, and she fled away, but he followed her, wishing to bring her to the village. All day she ran over the hills, and at night the warrior came back being unable to catch her. She was never seen again, and what became of her is not known, although it is likely she died of hunger, or that the wild beasts destroyed her.

Ever after, when the Indians came here to camp, they told the story of the crazy woman, and the place became known as "the place of the crazy woman," and the name of "Big Beard" was almost entirely forgotten.

The moral pointed in this tale, and the language that adorns it, are, in my judgment, both admirable. The story is probably entirely true, and an actual occurrence. The "Big Beard" grass mentioned still grows in the valley, and the stream, though yet far beyond the most remote cabin of the white man, is known to all frontiersmen, and is laid down on all maps as "Crazy Woman."

The conduct of the chief and warriors after drinking the black water, the fate of him of the "unsteady hand," and the death of the trader, are all thrillingly told by Mr. Belden, and with a naturalness and adherence to truth that is quite surprising in an Indian tale.—Note in original

FIGHTING THE INDIANS

BEFoRE returning home, I made up my mind to steal some ponies from our enemies, who had given us so much annoyance. Nelson, whose name I have not before mentioned, was a white man, and had accompanied us for the purpose of hunting, and having a share in such adventures as might fall to the lot of our party. He had a Sioux wife and two children, but was a roving, reckless, dare-devil sort of fellow, who always needed to be led, and who could never be intrusted to lead in any expedition, on account of his rashness and indiscretion.

Nelson and I set out alone to steal some ponies from our Indian foes, little caring whether they were Pawnees, Cheyennes, Arrapahoes, or Sioux, so we got their horses. We rode on for several days, and finally halted one evening by a clear running stream. While I fixed up the camp, Nelson took a jog down the creek to see that all was clear, and, if possible, shoot a deer for our supper. He soon returned with plenty of game, remarking he had seen no Indian signs, but thought he had, from the top of a hill beyond the stream, discovered smoke rising, tar down to the east. We made but little fire, and, then putting it out after supper, circled around the adjacent hills once, and seeing nothing, returned and lay down to rest."

I was up before daylight, for I felt uneasy, and rousing Nelson, told him to go out on the hills and keep a lookout while I kindled the fire and cooked breakfast. He soon disappeared over the bluff with his pony, and I hurried to prepare the morning repast of fresh antelope, broiled over the coals. The breakfast was ready, but no Nelson was there. I ate heartily, and waited for him an hour, but still he did not come, and I was preparing to mount my pony and follow his trail when, just as the first rays of the sun were streaming over the hilltops, he came riding leisurely into camp, and reported that he had gone over to the hill from which he thought he saw smoke the night before, and sure enough, he saw it again rising distinctly against the sky, not more than three miles distant. He rode down the creek-bottom, and was soon able to discover a large party of Indians preparing their breakfast; and, leaving them to enjoy their meal in peace, he had returned to tell me all about it, and get his own breakfast. The coolness of the fellow nettled me not a little. One would have thought, to have looked at him, that he was dining in a first-class restaurant in a peaceful town, instead of eating within a few miles of a band of hostile Indians, who might at any moment dash down upon us and put a stop to our ever eating again. I said to him, "Hurry up, Nelson, and let us get out of this, for a straggling Indian may, at any moment, discover our camp, and lead the whole band down upon us." "Well, Squire," he replied, as was his custom to call me, "I reckon you wouldn't turn a fellow out to such hot work as we are likely to have, without givin' him a square meal, would ye?" I bade him again hurry, but was forced to wait until he gorged himself to his heart's content. Then we rode out into the hills to reconnoiter, and consult what was best to be done.

We crawled along behind the bluffs, until we got sight of the Indian encampment. It was quite large, and evidently perfectly at rest. All day we lay in the bluffs, keenly scrutinizing every party of warriors that left the camp. Once a party struck out in a direction that we knew must cross our trail, and we felt much anxiety, but as hour after hour wore away, and we heard nothing of them, we concluded they must have crossed without observing it. During the day, we discovered that the encampment was a temporary one, and that from the scarcity of men, most of the warriors were out hunting, or on the warpath; intelligence not a little gratifying to us, and favorable to our design. From the signs, we also concluded, the village was composed of the families of warriors, and that they had been left behind with a very small guard.

As soon as it was dark, Nelson and I crept down from the bluffs and crawled to the village. This we did early, to prevent the dogs from noticing us, for it is a peculiarity of Indian dogs, that they seldom become vigilant until some hours after dark. We lay for some time, and then began to move about among the ponies. Nelson went to the right and I to the left. Several times warriors passed and repassed, but whenever they came near me, I wrapped my blanket closely about me, and pretended I was asleep, when, no doubt thinking I was one of the warriors who had been out hunting all day, and was tired, they passed on, leaving me to my repose. Every opportunity I got, I cut a lariat, or hopple, and after working industriously for an hour with my butcher-knife, I had loosened some twenty ponies. Nelson had, meantime, been busy, and having a side of the town that was not subject to interruptions from strolling warriors or squaws, he had succeeded in severing some, forty horses from their pickets. We were succeeding admirably, when an old squaw came out to change the grazing-ground of her pony and found him gone. She ran to the picket-stake, and picking up the end of the rope, felt it, and finding it had been cut, set up a howl, that brought the warriors tumbling from their lodges. Nelson gave me the signal to "run," and springing on a little black pony that, stood near me, I swung my blanket around my head, flirted it in the faces of the ponies, and shouting, "Hoo-yah-hoo!" at the top of my lungs, started some twenty of them toward the bluffs. Nelson was equally lucky, and in the confusion that, ensued in the village, we managed to get together. All was noise and excitement throughout the town; children screamed, women shouted, men whooped, while the dogs set up a dismal howling. Shots fell thick and fast around us, hut we succeeded in reaching the bluffs unhurt with all our ponies.

We pushed along smartly for a mile or two, each moment getting deeper into the hills. Turning now to the right, then to the left, we kept very quiet, hoping in the darkness to throw the pursuers off our trail, and before daylight be far to the eastward. Just as we began to hope we were not to be followed, we heard the Indians directly behind us, and, judging by the clatter of the ponies' hoofs, the party was a strong one. They, however, approached with great caution, not knowing our strength, and fearing an ambush. Twice they made ineffectual attempts to stampede the herd by sending warriors ahead and concealing them on the line of our march, but the extreme cowardice of the savages caused them to run away almost as soon as they shouted at the ponies. So we jogged along until near daylight, hoping each moment that our pursuers would turn back, for we did Not wish them to know our weakness and it was evident the first streaks of morning would disclose to them our numbers. Having kept remarkably quiet for nearly an hour, the Indians had become quite bold, when suddenly Nelson and I turned and charged them. They were in a gulch at the time, and, believing they were cut off, rode furiously for the mouth of the gorge) nearly a mile in 'their rear. We did not pursue them, but returned to the herd, leaving them to continue their flight until their fears should subside. We had not gone far, however, until we heard them coming on again close behind us. Nelson said he knew of some timber not far to the north, and we drove hard, hoping to reach it before day would break, but as we were crossing, the prairie, streaks of red shot up the eastern sky, and soon objects were distinguishable all around us. We saw we had lost many of the ponies in the darkness during the night, but still had some twenty left. Telling Nelson to drive these on, I halted on a rise in the prairie to wait for our enemies to come up. They soon appeared over a bluff, and I saw they numbered twelve by actual count. The odds were fearful, but I felt relieved, for I had thought not less than twenty were in the pursuit, and I now sincerely regretted Nelson and I had not ambushed them during the night. They continued to follow cautiously, until, seeing there were but two of us, they set up a great shout, and came on whooping and howling like demons. I dismounted behind a little hill, and hiking deliberate aim with my Henry rifle, as the foremost Indian came around the turn of the hill, I dropped him from his pony. I now pumped the shot at them as fast as I could, until I had nearly emptied the chamber of my gun, and had the satisfaction of seeing them turn back, carrying two of their wounded companions with them.

Rejoining Nelson, we pushed on for the timber, which was now only a few miles distant, and had nearly succeeded in reaching it when the Indians charged down upon us again. There were but eight left in the pursuit, and, taking my shotgun, I loaded each barrel with a powerful charge of powder and nine buckshot; then, waiting until the Indians were quite close, and as much together as possible, I wheeled and fired both barrels at them. The shot raked them like grape and canister, and I could see three or four of them were slightly wounded. They could not understand where so many balls had come from when they saw but one man fire, and so became more cautious than ever. At sunrise we reached the friendly shelter of the grove, and driving in the tired ponies, left them to graze, while

Nelson and I sallied out, and, boldly attacking the Indians, chased them over the plain, firing as rapidly as we could with our Henry's. We succeeded in wounding one fellow, but Nelson got a ball through the arm, nearly disabling him, and we returned to the grove.

We lay all day in the woods resting, but saw nothing more of the Indians. Nelson's wound was quite painful, but not dangerous, and we dressed it with green leaves and cold water.

As soon as it was dark we set out again, and drove along cautiously, fearing the Indians were up to some devilment, as they had been so quiet all day. The night wore away, however, and we began to feel assured there would be no attack, when, while we were driving along a narrow cañon, a shouting arose in front, followed by a few rapid shots, and the terrified ponies, turning suddenly, nearly ran over us. We succeeded in keeping seven in the cañon, but the rest escaped to the open prairie, where we saw the Indians driving them off. We made no attempt to pursue them, contenting ourselves with the seven we had left, and finding it all we could do to keep them, as the little fellows were disposed to escape and follow the rest of the herd.

We now drove rapidly to the east, hoping the Indians would be satisfied with what they had got, and leave us to pursue our way in peace; but, elated by their success, they came on again, and charged the herd, apparently determined to get the remaining seven. My blood was now up, for I thought they were acting a piggish part in wanting all, and riding over a little rise in the prairie, I dropped from my pony, and as the first Indian came on the crest of the divide, I shot him dead as a door nail. His companions ran to him, and I gave them a round dozen of Henry balls, causing them to dodge and scatter in all directions. After this they came on again several times, but when I turned and presented my Henry, as much as to say, "Keep off," they would run fit to break their necks. All day the red devils followed us, but at sundown gave up the chase, and in the twilight we saw them galloping over the hills far to our rear on their return to the village. We were not again disturbed, and on the evening of the seventh day entered our own village, bringing in safely all our seven ponies, and finding our friends, whom we had left on the "Crazy Woman," at home to welcome us.

BATTLE WITH THE WHITE BUFFALO

DURING-the dull days we lay in camp, waiting for the buffalo season to begin. I heard many curious tales and legends related by the Indians, and some of these I will repeat.

Once there lived on the Big Horn River, at the place where Fort Smith was afterward built, a Crow chief who had a most beautiful daughter. Many of the young men in the tribe courted her and were anxious to marry her, but her father would not part with her unless he received a hundred ponies; and, as no warrior was able to give so much for a wife, she was obliged to remain single. A young chief, who loved the maiden dearly, and desired to possess her, urged the old chief, tier father, to reduce the number of ponies, but he only became more morose, and finally declared no one should marry his daughter unless he had a hundred ponies that had been captured in battle. As such a thing was impossible, the young warrior despaired, and shut himself up-in his tent and refused to eat. The girl, who loved him dearly, sent him word to be of good heart and persevere, for she would be faithful to him, and die rather than marry any other warrior. Greatly encouraged by this message, the young man ate again, and all went along smoothly for several months.

The lodge of the maiden was pitched close beside that of her father's, and occupied by her alone. Often at night the wily old chief thought he heard strange noises in his daughter's lodge, but, when questioned, she always denied that she had heard any noise, or that anything unusual had occurred.

One day, however, she could no longer conceal her shame from her mother, and confessed that she was about to bear a child. When the old chief heard of it he was greatly enraged, and assembled his council, that measures might be taken for putting her to death, and thus wiping out the disgrace of his family.

When the council was assembled, the girl was brought before it, and her father sternly commanded her to explain the cause of her disgrace. To the astonishment of everyone, she came not as a guilty wretch, but with head erect, and a clear, flashing eye. When any of the old men questioned her, she looked disdainfully at them, and bade them hold their peace, for she was a chief's daughter, and would answer only to her august father. Her conduct greatly pleased the chief, and he said, aside, that whatever might be her fault she was a real Crow, and fit to be his daughter. When commanded by her father to relate all that had happened to her, she arose and said: "Venerable fathers, and you, my noble chief, some moons ago, one night, a strange thing happened to me, such as perhaps never happened before to any maid in the world. I was sleeping m my lodge, by the side of my noble father there, when suddenly I heard a most peculiar noise as of hoofs and some animal walking. I became conscious of something being in my teepee, and, being greatly frightened, I lay still. Presently I heard the coals being scraped together on the hearth, and blown into a flame. When it was light I looked, expecting to see a man, when I would have called my father, but, strange to relate, I saw, not a man, but a white buffalo. He walked upon his hind feet, and I was so terrified I could neither speak nor move. He came to my bed and sat down, and I fainted away. When I awoke, he was gone. So he came every night to see me, and each time I was as much frightened as before, and entirely unable to call out for help. The animal was very careful not to hurt me with his hoofs or horns, and how it came about I cannot tell, but in a few months I found myself in the condition you now see me, and I have no one to blame for my misfortune but the white buffalo."

The chiefs had listened to this harangue with great patience, and when she had done, the chief asked her when the white buffalo had last visited her, and she replied, "When the moon was full, and that he would come again the first full moon." When her story was finished, she was conducted back to her lodge, and the old men fell to debating about the matter. Most of the chiefs did not believe the story, for they said that such a thing as a white buffalo they had never seen in all their lives. An old man rose, however, and said there, was once a white buffalo on the plains, and that he did strange things, often being seen in the clouds and walking on water. This statement greatly confused the council, and they fell to debating anew At last a chief, who was very old and wise, said that it must be possible for a woman to bear children without being with a man, for many years ago, when he went to see the Great Father at Washington, the whites took him to hear their great medicine man, and the medicine man told of a woman who had brought forth a child without lying with any man, and this all the white people believed. The child was not only born, but had lived many years, and became a very great medicine man.

At last it came the turn of the young warrior, who had wished to marry the girl, and he rose and said:

"I do not doubt the story of the girl, nor question her chastity. Undoubtedly a most extraordinary thing has happened, but all things are possible to the Great Spirit, and if he came and visited our daughter in the form of a white buffalo, it is no more than was related by our brother about the daughter of the white chief."

This speech was received by all with much favor, and the great chief, who had not spoken a word, adjourned the council, stating he would call them together at some future day, to talk further concerning the matter.

The next council had little talk, and almost unanimously agreed the young girl should be put to death when the young chief, "her lover, rose and said, as it was near, the full of the moon, when the white buffalo would come again, he begged that the execution of the sentence of the council might be delayed until after the full moon, when, if nothing occurred to corroborate the girl's story, she should die. This was readily agreed to, and the pipe was passed all-round, to see in whose hands it would go out, that he might be selected to mount guard over the girl's teepee, and watch for the white buffalo. The pipe went out in the young chief's hands, and the council adjourned.

When the moon was at its full, the chief took up his position. He could see the door of the girl's lodge, but could not be seen himself. Ho also instructed her, if she saw the buffalo, to call out, and he would immediately rush to her assistance. On the third night of the watch, he heard her scream, and rushed into the lodge with his, battle-ax, when, sure enough, there was a white buffalo standing on his hind legs. As the chief came up, the beast raised its forefoot to strike him, but the chief brought his ax down with such force that it completely severed the hoof from the leg. The next moment however, the chief was struck senseless by the other forehoof, and when he recovered his senses the buffalo was gone. The old chief, who had heard the noise of the conflict, had risen and was dressed, when the young chief, who was still suffering from the blow he had received, came to him, and said that the white buffalo had indeed appeared, and that he had fought with him, and cut off one of his hoofs, which was produced, and an examination of the maiden's teepee showed a pool of blood, where the buffalo had bled from the effect of his wound. Great excitement spread in the village when the news was made known, and nearly all remained up, being afraid to sleep.

Early next morning the old chief assembled the council, and the debate began. The father of the girl was greatly exasperated, and pronounced the whole affair a lie, a fraud, and swindle. He said he had examined the ground around his daughter's lodge, but could find no footprints of a buffalo, yet everyone must know that, if so heavy an animal as a buffalo had passed that way, he must have left deep hoof-marks in the soft soil. It was also absurd that the buffalo could have got into the girl's lodge without being seen by the young chief, in his opinion, both the girl and the chief were a lying pair, and he more than hinted that the young chief was himself the white buffalo. He recommended, that both the girl and the chief be shot to death with arrows, at sunrise in the morning.

This speech had great effect, and the council almost unanimously voted to put the girl and her supposed paramour to death. They were led away, placed under a guard, and bade prepare for their fate on the morrow v

Now it so happened, that there was a warrior in the village who had been very sick, and many feared he would die. This warrior was greatly admired and feared, on account of his bravery and prowess. No other warrior in the village had slain so many of the enemy, no one was so strong, and none so willing to go to battle. His sickness excited much talk in the tribe, for all hated to lose so valuable a defender. He would not tell what ailed him, but lay all the day long, his hands placed under his robe, and apparently suffering great pain. On the morning of the execution, a girl of the village passed by the sick warrior's lodge, and stopped in to tell him about the fate of the chief's daughter and the young chief. She found the warrior asleep, and his hands lying on top of the robe. The bandages had fallen off, and to her surprise, she saw he had but one hand, the other being gone. Quickly it flashed through her mind, that the warrior had something to do with the affair of the white buffalo, and she ran with all her might toward the hill beyond the village, where the execution was to take place. As she drew near the hill, she feared she would be too late, for she saw the crowd part, the prisoners led out, and the bowmen take their places. When she came up, the young chief was making his last speech, and the bowmen, with arrows on their strings, were ready to, fire as soon as he should conclude. The girl rushed up to the great medicine man, who was conducting the execution, and whispered something in his ear, at which he was greatly astonished. Then he listened, and the girl repeated what she had said. When she had done speaking, the medicine man walked between the condemned prisoners and the bowmen, and, raising his hands, bade them put up their arrows. He then told the crowd, bowmen, prisoners, and all, to follow him, and see what they should do. He walked down to the village, and entering the, sick warrior's lodge, bade him hold up his hands. At first he refused to do so, but seeing he was found out, he held up his arms, and exhibited one hand and a bloody stump. The medicine man asked where the hoof of the white buffalo was, and being told it was at the old chief's' lodge, he bade them go and fetch it. When it was brought, he took his knife, and, splitting open the skin of the hoof, to the surprise of everyone, drew forth a human hand, which had been neatly sewed up in the hoof. Holding it up, so all could see it, he placed it on the stump beside the warrior's other hand, and it fitted exactly everyone now knew who was the white buffalo, and all cried out, "Kill him! kill him!" The old chief hastily assembled an informal council, and the young warrior was at once condemned to death. So the bowmen who were to shoot .the young chief and the girl, shot him as he lay in his tent.

The old chief was so pleased when he knew his daughter had told him the truth, that he conferred her in marriage on her defender, the young chief. The child of the white buffalo was born and strangled, after which the young chief and his wife lived many years happily together, and raised a large family of handsome daughters and brave young men.

BIRTH OF THE STORM

MANY years ago, there was a great famine among the Indians who lived along the eastern slope of the Big Horn Mountains. The fall hunt of the Crows had proved unsuccessful, and they knew not what to do. A winter of terrible severity came down upon them, and starvation stared them in the face. They were at last reduced to great extremity, and runners were sent out in all directions to find game. One of them returned one day with the joyful intelligence that he had found a locality in which game of all kinds abounded. The village was hastily packed up, and all left the Big Horn, and journeying for several days under the guidance of the young warrior, they at length came to a thickly-wooded country full of bears, deer, elk, and antelope. The encampment was pitched on a plain by a stream, and soon the teepees were filled with meat. For a time, all went well, but presently the game, being hunted so much, began to move off, and the Crows saw starvation again before them. They determined to make a big hunt, and, V possible, take enough game to last them through the cold weather. Men, women, and children turned out, and surrounding a vast extent of forest, they drove the game toward a common center, where it was to be slaughtered. The hunt was very successful, and much game had been taken, when suddenly it began to blow; then black clouds gathered, the thunder rolled, and the lightnings flashed overhead, while strange noises were heard in the earth. The Crows were greatly frightened, for they never had heard it thunder before in midwinter, and from the rocking and trembling of the earth, they thought it was about to fall to pieces and swallow them up. Presently an inky, black cloud covered the peak of the mountain where they had driven the game, and after resting on the earth a few moments, it rose and hung over the mountain top. Then, two long arms were seen to reach out of the cloud and lay something on the earth, after which the cloud rose in the air and drifted swiftly away. The sky cleared off, the sun shone again brightly, and the killing of the game went on. When all the elk, deer, antelope, and bears were slaughtered, two warriors went up to where the cloud had been seen to lay something on the earth, and there, resting on a flat rock, they discovered a young female child, perfectly green in color. They called up several squaws, but none of them could be induced to touch it; on the other hand, they begged the warriors to come away and leave it. When no one would take it up, one of the warriors said, "I will care for it;" and lifting it in his arms, he carried it down the mountain and toward the village. As he was crossing the plain, and when quite near the encampment, all heard a great noise, and looking up, they saw the black cloud coming back and rapidly approaching the warrior; again the thunder rolled, the lightnings flashed, and the earth shook. Suddenly the warrior was enveloped in a bright flame and fell to the ground; then, the two hands were seen to reach out of the cloud and grasp the child, which disappeared in the vapor, and the whole, lifting into the sky, drifted away to the eastward. The warrior was found quite dead, and his skin as black as the cloud that had enveloped him. He was taken to the village, and the next day buried.

While the warrior was being enveloped in the cloud, an old squaw, who had not borne children for years, stood looking at him. No sooner did she see the child disappear in the vapor, than she felt herself seized with violent labor-pains. All night she suffered, and, in the morning, was delivered of a female child, perfectly green, like live grass. The Indians all said it was the same child that had been in the cloud, and that the mysterious hands had no sooner taken it from the warrior than they transferred it to the woman. The squaw persisted that it was not the child of a man, though she had a husband. In token of its strange birth, the Indians named the infant "A-pa-ka-her-ra-ris!" the one who dwells in the clouds, or, "The Storm-Child." The pappoose lived and grew finely, and, in course of time, became a woman, married, and had a large family.

Mr. Belden says, "I often saw the squaw named 'The Storm-Child,' and truth compels me to say, that I have seen few uglier Indian women."

Note.—This story originated in a natural phenomenon. There was a storm, and a squaw, frightened by it, gave premature birth to a child. The warrior was killed by lightning, and the color of the child, and the hand seen in the clouds, are purely Indian exaggerations. It frequently thunders in the Rocky Mountains in the winter time, though seldom so far north as the lands of the Crows. The "Storm-Child" is still living, and greatly feared and respected by her tribe, on account of her supposed mysterious birth.—Note in original

INTELLIGENCE OF THE INDIANS

THE day was very warm, and I had been lying down in my teepee, sleeping most of the time, for want of something to do, or for lack of energy to do anything, if I had it to do.

I had seen but few of the Indians out of their teepees that day, and, though the squaws worked incessantly in warm as well as cold weather, their liege lords and masters took the warm weather to be too much for even their warm natures; so they stretched themselves out on the grass-rush mats of their teepee floors, and went to sleep till eating time should come round again (which meant whenever they got hungry), and were compelled to undergo the cruel exertion of raising themselves to a sitting posture, and be waited upon by their squaws, who handed each one a wooden bowl of boiled meat and corn. No coffee or tea was used, nothing but the beverage provided by nature, cold water, and at that season the water was not very cold, as it was procured from the Missouri River.

1 had been awakened by a jabbering outside my teepee door, and, raising the bottom of the teepee cloth, I saw five men, and some two or three squaws, seated under my shade (some forks stuck up in front of the teepee door, over which was laid a, quantity of green willow brush to answer the wants of a porch), busily engaged in gambling for silver earrings and bead necklaces with plum-stone dice. I lay still and watched them for a little while, when, finding sleep impossible, and not wishing to affront the company by ordering them to keep quiet, I got up and crawled out to where they were, and, declining to accept their invitation to join the game, contented myself in quietly watching and learning it.

They used a kind of dice made of the stones of the wild plum, which grew very plentifully in the deep ravines and cañons a mile or two back from the Missouri River at this point. These stones were first dried hard, then polished by scraping them with a knife. Six were used for the game, four of them being spotted on one side, and blank on the opposite, and the other two striped or checked on one side, and left blank on the other. These spots and stripes were made on the stones by means of a small iron instrument which they used to paint buffalo robes with. The iron was heated, and the spots and stripes then seared or burned in the stone. The Indians used a wooden bowl, small and light, for shaking the dice, and never threw them out of the bowl. To play the game, they sat on the ground in a circle, and a blanket, or robe, was doubled up and placed in the middle of the ring—the bowl containing six dice, being placed on the folded blanket. The stakes usually were two or four silver earrings, put up by those who engaged in the game, and the sport commenced by someone of the players seizing the edge of the bowl with his thumb outside and the ends of his forefingers inside the rim, and, raising it an inch or so, bumped it down on the folded blanket three or four times, causing the light plum-stones to jump around in the most lively manner. After the player had shaken the bowl thoroughly, he sat down and allowed the stones to settle on the bottom, and then they were counted, thus: if all the spotted and striped sides were uppermost, the player won, unless someone else tied him. If he threw four spotted ones, it was the same as four aces in cards, in the game of bluff; but if he threw three spotted and two striped ones, it was equivalent to a full hand of bluff, and so on, the only difference being, that when all the spotted and striped sides were turned up, it showed a higher hand than four aces, and when all the blank sides were turned up it showed a flush that ranked next to the highest hand, and above the four aces.

During the game there was considerable quarreling between a couple of old men, who were proverbial throughout the village for their cross, crabbed natures, but, aside from using their tongues very freely in ridiculing and maligning each other, nothing more serious occurred. Each repeatedly referred to me as a responsible arbitrator in the cause at dispute, but I pleaded utter ignorance of the game, and, therefore, inability of judging. For this, I did not fail to get my share of their abuse, for having lived so long among as respectable a tribe as the Santee Sioux, and not knowing the celebrated plum-stone game. I took all their abuse good-naturedly, as I knew no one in the village ever minded anything these two old boobies said. While they played dice, the squaws sat by smoking and laughing at each one's losses. Presently, all but one were dead broke; the game stopped, and good nature being once more restored, all joined in a smoke. As the day advanced, and evening came on, the atmosphere became more endurable, and conversation became lively. One of the young men asked me to tell a story, and all joined in the request, urging so hard, that I agreed to do so, provided one of the old men would, in return, favor us by telling some old story of the San-tees who had lived before the present generation. I knew the old men in almost every tribe were full of such stories, and they were always agreeable. I inquired what I should tell them, whether of some other Indian, tribe, or of the white people? "Of the whites," they all at once replied. My supper was now ready, and, inviting those present to join with me in eating a limited number of dishes, I ordered served some coffee, dried elk meat and corn, boiled together, for which I had to thank the good missionary of the tribe. The invitation was accepted by all, and supper was brought outside the teepee where we, were sitting. After the meal was finished, and another smoke indulged in, one of the young men said, "Now for the story." I seated myself, and, in as concise a manner as possible, related to my auditors the history of the discovery of America; the sailing of Columbus; his trials and reverses; his landing in triumph; his meeting with the first Indians ok the Atlantic coast, and the growth of the present nation; winding up with a description of Washington, his battles, and the success of the struggle for independence. When I had concluded, I read the interest betrayed in my narrative by the upturned faces of my audience, which had augmented in numbers to some fifteen or twenty persons, and among whom was the old medicine man of the tribe. The pompous old fool, to show his wisdom, said, as soon as I had done, "Me know him, Washi'ton; me see him, Washi'ton, heap o' times. Him good man, Washi'ton. No tell um lie. One little lie no tell um!" All acquiesced in this statement, and "How'd" in an assenting manner at the end of each sentence. I then told them of Washington's boyhood; the old story of the apple tree; the heroic truthfulness of the young first President, and his father's pride in his honest boy. To all this the Indian repeatedly assented, by saying, "How!" as if they all knew of the circumstances quite as well as I did. I soon found, however, a solution of this enigma, by learning from the missionary that he had brought several Sabbath-school books up with him, among them a condensed history of George Washington. He occasionally loaned these books to such as took care of them, and he said that several Santees could speak, read, and write English in a very good manner. To these persons he loaned books, and the contents were, very naturally, told to the balance of the tribe by the fortunate readers. They always listened with avidity to the tales of the readers. When I had finished my story, night had fallen over us, and the stars were coming out, one by one, illuminating the sky with their tiny spangles of diamonds. A large circle of dusky, quiet, red men were seated in front of my lodge, waiting to catch the words of the old man, who was about to begin his story. It was an expectant crowd, and every noise was hushed save the soughing of the night winds among the tops of the stately cottonwoods that overshadowed our camp. The 'quick rush of the Missouri broke with a hollow sound on the shore, as it sped toward the south to meet the Mississippi, and bear up the great white trafficking ships of the white men. Here, far away from the haunts of civilization, the river's waters were as clear as crystal, and no noise or bustle disturbed the calm and tranquil scene.

THE OLD MAN'S STORY

THE fire had gone out, and the ashes were knocked from the bowl; leaving the sacred pipe lying upon his blanket which he had folded and laid upon the ground, the old, gray headed warrior got upon his feet, in the center of the circle, and began his story. I managed to get as near to him as possible, in order that I might not lose a word of what he said. The old man seemed to feel sorrowful, as he looked at the ground near his feet for a few moments, evidently trying to recall to memory events of many years gone by. Then, raising his head, and looking around upon his hearers, he

"Many years ago, many moons, many winter's snows, and summer's grasses have come and gone, and many a Santee warrior has come into the world, and, after a brilliant and noble life, left it again. Many a parent and child have been carried to the grave, since the men lived of whom my father's father told me when I was boy, and of whom I will now tell you. You see my hair is gray, but it was not so when my father's father told me this story, of things that happened when he was young. In those days the Sioux all lived together, and were a large and powerful tribe. They were then one nation of brave warriors, feared by all the tribes, who sought their favor, and neglected no opportunity to cement a friendship with the most powerful band, that owned hunting-grounds for hundreds and hundreds of miles in every direction. No tribe ever dared to insult or provoke them to battle; no other tribe dared to trespass on their hunting-grounds; no other tribe ever owned such beautiful and accomplished women, such upright and brave warriors, as the Dakotas. They were rich in ponies and silver earrings, their herds covered 'the valleys of the great rivers, their teepees were as white and numerous as the snow-flakes in winter, and every stream and grove was peopled by them. If any other tribe had occasion to go to war with their neighbors, they first courted the countenance and favor of the Dakotas, and if they obtained it, they were sure of winning a victory, sometimes without any-apparent resistance from their enemies, who had been informed that the Dakotas favored the other side. Times then were not as they now are. When a foreign chief's embassy called upon the Dakotas, to ask for permission to fight on their grounds, or to ask for assistance in the battle they premeditated, their speeches were heard by upright and honest men, who would never recognize a war for plunder or gain, and who never refused assistance to the injured or oppressed of other nations. Thus they were loved, feared, and respected by all, and the decision of the Sioux chiefs, in every case, was irrevocable law.

So there was but little war, and year after year the tribes increased in numbers, and the warriors lived to great old age, and died, some over a hundred years old. Time went on, and one day a stranger was brought into the village, whose face was white, his hair brown, and his eyes the color of his hair. This man's whole body was white, and he could not understand us when we spoke to him, nor could we understand him, though he talked and made a noise with his mouth, and sometimes laughed. He had been found on the high prairies, walking alone, and had a bow without any strings to it, and the arrows he used were very little, but heavy and round. He fired off his bow, and it so frightened our people that several squaws dropped to the earth, stunned by the noise which the arrow made in the air. This bow would shoot one of the little arrows many steps distant, and send it through the stoutest shields of buffalo hide that our warriors owned. The white warrior could also shoot very straight, and never missed what he aimed at. So, many of our people revered this white man, who they believed had been sent to show them how to make and shoot with the strange bows that made a noise. Some, however, said he was a bad man, and used the Great Spirit's thunder in his bow, that he had no right to do so, and if the man was to be allowed to live in the village among our people, we would be visited by great calamities. These were for immediately driving him away from our teepees, and not allowing him to return. The council-house drum was beaten and the chiefs called to deliberate the question whether we would keep the white man or send him away. After a whole day and night's consultation, it was decided that the man should stay in the village, and so it was. He had been called in during the council, and laid his bow down on the ground, when it was with great fear and reluctance taken up and examined by one of the boldest of the warriors, who said it was made of iron, and was very heavy, and not a bow, but a hollow rod The chief then motioned to the man to fix it ready to fire, but not to fire it. He did so, and all saw, what they had not before observed, that the white warrior first put some black, shining sand in the iron, and then put a little iron ball in the end of the rod, which he forced down with a long stick. This stick he drew out of a case under the hollow iron, and put one end of it on the ball and then pressed with all his might on the other, until the ball was pushed to the lower end of the hollow. Next he withdrew the stick, and put it back in the ease, and then he took up the iron and put some of the black sand in a little cup on the side of it, and covered up the sand with a flat, crooked piece, which was fast to the iron. Just behind this crooked iron was another one, in which was fastened a flat piece of stone, which was made to strike fire when the man pulled on a little-wire under the hollow iron. Whenever this stone made fire, the same noise was heard, and fire and smoke came out of the end of the iron. None could see the little iron ball as it went to the mark, and some who watched, said that the ball struck the tree before the fire came out of the iron.

"So the man stayed and was given a teepee, and he soon married a squaw, and was suffered to live with us for several moons, until the hunting moons came, when the tribes were to go out to kill and dry their winter's meat. The buffalo ranged all around, near at hand, and every season yielded the necessary amount of food for the great tribe on whose hunting-grounds the buffalo could not be counted, so great was their number.

A day's journey from the village always took our people into the midst of the buffalo country, and, pitching their teepees, men and women set to work, and in a few days' time had prepared sufficient fat and buffalo to last them until the next season came.

"The hunting moon was now at hand, and all the village was active, preparing to go out upon the hunt. Among others was the white man, with his hollow iron. He had learned to talk our language, and could now speak and understand everything. He was also well liked by nearly everyone, and was especially a favorite with the young women, who constantly envied the white man's squaw her position. Some of those who had predicted calamities if the white man was permitted to live among them, though they never abused him, never had anything to do with him, but held themselves aloof and kept their peace, though they did not like him.

"So all went to the hunting-grounds, and there it was observed that the white man's hollow iron would bring down a buffalo at the distance of two arrow flights, twice as far oft as the best warrior of the tribe could shoot an arrow, and where s sometimes it took a dozen arrows to kill a buffalo, the white man always shot but once and killed him dead in his tracks. In two days' time a sufficient number of buffalo had been killed to last the tribe the season, and many of our people now thought the white man and his hollow iron were gifts from the Great Spirit, sent to make them more powerful as a tribe, and render them invincible in war against other nations.,

"All the following year the white man lived with the Dakotas, but when the buffalo season came again, and the tribe made preparations to go out upon the annual hunt, the parties of warriors who had always been sent out in advance a day or two, to see where the buffalo cows were feeding (because they are better and more tender meat than the bulls); came back and brought tidings that, no buffalo could be found. When this was made known in the village, the warriors were derided and scoffed at, as being lazy, good-for-nothing fellows, who had not taken the trouble to go far enough, and they were sent back again by the chief, together with several other young men. After several days' absence, they returned, and brought back the same intelligence. Great was now the consternation in the village, and starvation stared all in the face. It was remembered, that when the white man had shot his hollow iron, the buffalo jumped and bounded with surprise and fear at the thunder of the noise, and immediately ran away. But a short time was necessary to convince everyone that the white man's hollow iron had driven off all the buffalo, which had always before been easily found. Now, also, were the predictions of calamity remembered, and the council was again called. While the chiefs were debating in the council-house, the warriors and women of the tribe rent the air with their lamentations, so that their shrieks reached the ears of the-chiefs in the council-house, and urged them to prompt action. It was determined that the white man was an evil spirit, who had used the Great Spirit's thunder to scare away the buffalo. All knew they did not fear a mounted warrior of the Dakotas, but turned and fought with hoof and horn, while arrows in great numbers pierced their sides, but when the white man fired his gun they made off. It was, therefore, solemnly declared, that the Great Spirit was offended at the killing of buffalo with stolen thunder, and the council decided that the white man's blood should be offered up as an atonement for the sin of the tribe in eating the meat which had been killed by the hollow iron.

"The white man sat in his lodge apparently unconscious of what was going on without, until he heard voices crying, 'White man! White man! come out!' He then got up, and came to the door, when, as soon as he was observed, a dozen arrows were fired at him. Just as the bows were bent to send the arrows again, the white man's squaw, 'An-pe-tu-Sa-pa-U-we-a' (black day woman), threw herself before him, and fell pierced by a dozen shafts. The white man ran inside the teepee, got his hollow iron, and coming back to the door, shot at the medicine man, who stood way off by the council-house, and he immediately fell dead, not even uttering a single word. The white man then pushed down another ball, and called out to the warriors, 'Go away! or I will have to kill you all! Go away!' Most of the warriors went away, and presently the white man came outside, carrying the hollow iron in his hand. His face was white as snow, and he said he was very angry. He took up the body of the dead squaw, and putting her face close to his, held it there several moments, then placing her body on his shoulder, he started toward the river bank. He walked fast, occasionally turning around to see if anyone followed him. When he had gone some distance, no one thinking of running to certain death by following him, the leader of those who had predicted evil from the white man, raised his voice and demanded his death. 'Do you not see him going off? He has killed the old medicine man! He is carrying off one of our women! Why do you stand staring at him? after him, all of you! Kill him!' he cried. 'Yes, kill him!' all shouted, as they ran after the white man, who saw them coming, and made every effort to gain the water's edge, where he had a canoe hidden in the willows, and in which he hoped to escape, if he could but reach it unharmed. His pursuers, however, were too numerous and swift. They were not loaded down with a burden as he was, and so ran faster. Soon they neared him, when he gently laid the squaw on the grass, and raising his hollow iron, pointed it at the crowd. He held the iron aimed, but did not fire. Many ran away, and all stopped and stood looking at him, when he said: "Why do you follow me? Have I stolen your ponies, or taken anything from you, that you should seek my life?" "Yes, you are a thief, though you never stole from us answered the chief, who disliked him, "you have not stolen from us, but you have stolen from the Great Spirit, and for this you must die!" "What is it I have stolen from the Great Spirit?" inquired the white man. "You have stolen his thunder, and used it to scare away our game." replied the chief. The white man laughed, but suddenly becoming serious, said, "You are all a pack of fools, and I swear by the Great Spirit, that I have never done what you accuse me of. Do you see this poor girl? She was of your people, and I loved her with all my heart, yet you have killed her. For this, the-Great Spirit will one day thin your tribe; he will punish you with diseases, hunger, and degradation. Your tribe will decline in glory day by day, and my people will take away your hunting-grounds, and drive your game beyond the setting sun; then you will be poor in numbers, and weak-hearted.' Now, let me go back to my people, and before I go, let me bury the poor girl, who has given up her life for me, and when I have done it, I will leave you, and never come near you anymore When he had spoken, the chief urged the warriors to shoot together, and fill him with arrows; at the same time declaring his words were lies, intended to frighten them from doing their duty. No one obeyed him and the chief, becoming angry, snatched a bow and arrow from the nearest warrior, saying. 'I will kill him!' and immediately placed an arrow upon the bow-string, but as he sought to bend it, a loud noise came from the hollow iron, and the bow dropped from his hands, the chief fell forward on his face and died without uttering so much as a groan. In an instant twenty arrows were shot at the white man, and several of them struck him, and stuck in his flesh. But he did not mind them, and, stooping, picked up the dead girl, and ran toward the river. He soon disappeared from sight under the bank, and in a few minutes more was seen jumping from stone to stone, at the very edge of the great falls. He had dropped the hollow iron over the falls, and now carried the dead girl in his arms. He leaped along until he suddenly came to a wide gorge, over which the water had washed for many centuries, wearing a passage in the solid rocks. Could he but once get upon the other side of this gorge, the white man knew he would be out of reach of the arrows of his pursuers. He looked first at the water, then at the angry crowd on the shore, and holding up the body of the dead girl, cried out, 'You see her? She and I will come to see you again, and you will know us, when your spirit is broken, and your hearts fail you under great oppression. Then disease and death will appall you, and you will die.' So saying, he threw the girl in the river, and immediately jumped in after her. For a few moments he was seen to struggle, and then floated down and passed over the falls. The Indians searched for the bodies, but they never were found.

"After this, the tribe sent out runners in every direction to see if they could find game, but all were unsuccessful. All in the village were in a starving condition, when an old chief, assembling his band, started in search of new hunting-grounds, saying, if he found game he would send back word to the rest, and they might come and join him. Accordingly, he left the village with his party and traveled to the westward, toward the mountains. For many days no tidings reached the village of the chief and his party, and the small game and corn beginning to give out, it was determined to send another party to find the first. This was done, and the village rested, until the time came when the last party should-return, or send tidings of their success. Days and weeks passed, and as no messenger reached the village, all began to mourn the absent as lost.

"The tribe at length moved farther west to the great river, and here, finding game, built a village and remained.

"A year passed, and there were still no tidings of the two lost bands. At the end of another year, fears of starvation having subsided, and prosperity being restored in the village, it was determined to send out a third party to try, if possible, and obtain tidings of the absent bands. They were accordingly sent, and returned at the end of half a year, with the intelligence, that they could not find or even hear of them.

"For many years the tribe lived along the river, hunting and warring with other nations, who were angry, because the Sioux had come to their country to live, without so much as asking their permission. The small-pox broke out in the tribe, and carried off many of the people. Then, it had hardly left them, before the warriors quarreled among themselves upon the subject of moving to the mountains, and the tribe dividing, half of them went to the mountains, and the other half remained.

"So the white man's prediction came true; disease, quarrels, and starvation had split and divided the nation, until its numbers and strength were so reduced, the warriors had no heart to go to war.

"After many years, the tribe was visited by many white men, who all came armed with hollow-irons, killed our people, and drove away our game. From them we learned to use the hollow iron, and our young men traded for some to hunt with, as well as to use in war. But since the day the white man was drowned, the tribe has slowly been decreasing in power and glory, until now, it is but the wreck of what it once was.

"The lost tribes were, after a long time, heard from; they had learned to speak another language, and though we could understand them, yet our languages were very different.

"The first party, after leaving the village, had gone toward the setting sun, and meeting with no considerable quantities of game, had traveled on until they came to the mountains; they learned from a tribe they found there, that on the west side they would find plenty of game, and accordingly they started to cross the chain. The women and children could not travel very fast, and by the time they reached the middle of the mountains, they found so much time had been consumed on the road that their provisions would soon run out. They pushed along, however, through snow and ice, and at length their eyes were gladdened by coming upon a deep-seated, green, and fertile plain, where streams meandered through pleasant rales, and where the deer and elk were in numerous herds. Here they pitched their village, and lived for a long time, none being so hardy as to feel inclined to risk finding their way back through the mountains. So the tribe grew up, and, in course of time, began imperceptibly to make changes in the language they spoke.

"The second band traveled toward the mountains, but did not attempt to cross them, having kept to the southward along their foot, until they came to a broad stream, very shallow, and full of treacherous sands, and they saw great herds of buffalo feeding upon its banks. Here the tribe stopped, and, as the first party had done, built a village, and finding everything conducive to their comfort, contented themselves to live in peace, and the band was raised from the small numbers to a great multitude.'

"Their language was also changed in the course of time, and was different from either the original tongue, or that spoken by the band which had gone across the mountains.

"The half of the tribe which had moved to the mountains, after the small-pox had decimated the village, were also compelled to change their language.

"All these bands, though once strong, powerful tribes, through division and contentions, disease, and the white man's poisons, have become suddenly weak, and are constantly at war to defend themselves, or gain sufficient ground upon which to live and hunt.

"Thus the white man's prediction has been fulfilled, and hunger and disease have made us weak as women. We have often looked to see if the white man and the dead girl were beside us but though we have never seen them, we have seen the effects of what he of the hollow iron, prophesied. We murdered a woman of our own race, and then murdered him who came to aid us; so none of his people, who have come among, us since, have been kind, but all are angry, and avenge his death.

"This was my father's father's story, as he told it to me, and when he had done telling it, he cautioned me to try and be friendly with the white men, for they were powerful, and could do me and my people much harm."

The old man ended his tale, and sat down for a moment, with his head between his hands; then silently taking up his pipe and blanket, he moved away toward his teepee, and the rest of his audience, one by one, followed his example without saying a word.

It was very late, and I went into my lodge, and rolling myself in my blankets, lay down to sleep and dream of the four bands that had become so separated and divided. I followed them over again, through their superstitions and wanderings, and saw clearly their reasons for attacking the white man. Though my sleep was not refreshing, to my delight I awoke, in the morning, to find my squaw had not been filled with arrows on my account, but had cooked a kettle of elk and corn, upon which she was regaling herself, and I soon joined her.

I have since discovered that the party which went over the mountains, were the Brule Sioux—those who went to seek them, and built a village on the Platte River, the Ogallalla Sioux—the band that disagreed and went to the mountains, the Santee Sioux, and the other half of the band, that remained on the river, the Yankton Sioux. These four bands comprise the four great divisions of the Dakota, or Sioux nation, as it is now known.

THE TRICK SUCCESSFULLY PERFORMED

WHILE in the Indian camp, I witnessed many strange feats of strength and dexterity practiced by the young warriors, who, when not engaged in the chase or on the 'war path, were constantly exercising their muscles.

In a large circle of squaws, children, and old men, were seated about twenty warriors, witnessing the performances of four young men. First, let me tell you, that any tricks of a marvelous nature, such as practiced by mountebanks or jugglers, tire always very attractive to Indians, who will sit for hours quietly, wondering how this or that thing is done. One of the young men presently took a single-barreled shot-gun, of the flint-lock pattern, and, pouring down powder, held up a bullet, and, apparently, placed it in the muzzle; then, with a-rammer, pushed the ball down, as it seemed, to the bottom of the barrel; he next primed it, and gave it to a bystander, who was known to be a good shot, and requested him to shoot at his breast. The warrior at first hesitated, saying he might kill him, but; on being urged, the man suddenly jumped up, seized the gun, and fired it at the juggler's breast. All expected to see hint fall, but he stood perfectly still, as he did before the shot was fired, and very coolly took the bullet out of his mouth, saying, as he showed it to all around him, "You are a poor shot, my friend; you see I have caught it." This feat brought forth loud cheers of approval from his audience, much to the chagrin of the warrior who had failed to hit the juggler.

I said, "That is well done; but why do you use powder?" He inquired, "Can you do as I have done without using powder?" "Of course," I replied. He immediately handed me the gun, and I stepped into the ring, and gave it to several old men to examine, and see if it was loaded. They blew down the barrel, thoroughly testing the emptiness of the arm. While they were examining it, I took the opportunity to pour a little powder into my left hand, over which I closed my fingers tightly, and, as the gun was handed back, I seized it by the muzzle with my left hand, allowing the powder to run down unperceived, while, at the same time, I stooped to the ground, and called their attention to my right hand, with which, 'having first opened the fingers, I seized a handful of ashes that laid on the ground where an old fire had gone out. I then held the ashes to the muzzle, and slowly poured the whole down the barrel. "Shoot that if you can," said the juggler, in an exultant manner. I struck the gun several hard blows near the lock, to jolt some powder into the pan, and, raising ".the hammer, pulled the trigger, when a loud report followed, throwing a cloud of ashes all .around.. The surprise of the savages was very great, and, bowing, I retired as a juggler while my credit was good. The juggler then performed several very good feats with bullets, successfully shifting them from one to the other of three or four moccasins placed about a foot apart. This was well done, no one seeing how it could possibly be accomplished without detection. Several young men next carried each other around the circle by a small belt placed about the waist, and which they seized with their teeth One powerful warrior, who wore a small belt, took a heavily-built man in his arms, and lifted him off the ground, holding him thus while a third Indian seized the belt in his mouth, and carried both men around the ring. This brought forth loud applause from the spectators, and, indeed, it was merited. Presently, a little pony, stout and sturdy, was led into the ring, and its owner offered to give him to anyone who would throw him down and hold him long enough to put on the bridle. This, I thought, was a chance for me, and I walked into the ring to try if I could throw him. I tried hard several times, but was finally compelled to give it up and retire, amid loud cheers and laughter from the lookers-on. Two or three warriors attempted to throw the pony, the little fellow standing quiet all the time, and never biting or kicking, as I had at first expected he would do. The owner of the animal, a light, active Indian, then came forward and said he would throw him, and actually did so, by seizing him by the fore legs, and raising his fore parts as high as three feet from the ground, then pulled him suddenly forward, and, quickly pushing him backward with a sidling motion, he fell on his back, and was instantly pinned to the ground by the agile Indian, who placed his knee on the animal's neck, and held him quiet until the bridle was put on and adjusted. He then allowed him to rise to his feet, and, leaping nimbly on his back, he galloped off. This ended the performances for one day.

TEACHING THE CHILDREN

I WAS invited to visit the missionary, and upon going up to the Mission House, was cordially welcomed by the good man, who took-me to his rude study, where we conversed for several hours. The burthen of his discourse seemed to be the expression of a desire that I should renounce my Indian mode of living, and either go back to my people again, or go into some business which would have for its object, the conversion of the savages to white men's ways. I pleaded my inability to handle such affairs as they should be, and stated, my present object in living among them was, to learn their language, manners, habits, and customs, as well as to have some little experience of wild life. He finally dropped the subject, and presently asked, if I would like to visit the natives' school.

I eagerly accepted his offer, and together we went to the banks of the creek, near which was a rude corral, with a shed over part of it, under which were seated, on the ground, some twenty little Indian boys and girls. In their midst stood a tall young Indian with a book in his hand, and I noticed that all the children had books. When recitation began, none of the children got up to their feet, but remained sitting, the teacher walking slowly around among his pupils, asking questions of this one, and that one, indiscriminately. Their books were printed in Washington, by the Indian Bureau, and the letters were in Roman type, on ordinary printing paper. But all the words were spelled in the original Sioux language, and no English words were used at all. The recitations were altogether in Sioux. This surprised me very much, and I inquired, why they did not teach the children English? and what was the object of teaching them what every child of any Indian tribe learns from infancy, by hearing it from its parents? The missionary explained, that they quickly learned to read and pronounce words of their own language, and that religious books were printed in the Sioux tongue, which were intended to be read by these same pupils, who were now just taught the meaning of these Roman hieroglyphics, that they might know them when they were again seen in religious works. This was one of the plans, he said, for conversion of the Indians.

After listening to the proceedings of a Sioux school for over an hour, we walked back to the village, and while passing by the trader's store, I was warmly censured for neglecting of late my visits to the good man. Leaving the missionary to go to his home, I talked a little while with the trader, whom I had found to be quite an intelligent man, who knew many legends, and had had many adventures among the Sioux, which he said he would "trade," or exchange, for some narrations of mine. The proposition pleased me, and I-said I would come down in the evening when he had closed the store, and we would have a talk in the back room, where we often sat.

The trader acquiesced, and asked me to bring the old man along who had been talking in front of my lodge the night before, "for," said he, "as I was coming up from the river, heard part of his story, which was very interesting, but could not stay to hear it out." I promised I would bring the old man, and hurried home as fast as I could, for it was growing late, and I was very hungry.

After supper, I went to the old man's teepee, but he would not then go with me to the trader's store, promising, however, he would be over by and by. So I walked over alone.

I was shown into the back room, where many bales of beaver skins were stacked against the walls, and in a corner was spread a thick bed of buffalo robes. Throwing down a couple of beaver bales for seats, I sat down upon one of them and explained the cause of the old Indian's absence. My friend Pete (or French Pete), as the trader was called, had a good-looking squaw, who came to him, and he told her something in an undertone, when she left the room, and presently returned with a bottle of ginger wine—"medicine," as Pete called it—and we both took a dram. Then, as my friend cut off some tobacco, to mix with willow-bark for a,, smoke, he asked me to tell him how I came to live with the Santees, and where I had come from. I complied with his request; told him of my history and of the Pawnee raid; after which, I lit my pipe, and settled myself to hear the trader's story.

THE TRADER'S STORY

"I WAS living up in St. Paul (Minnesota); about six years ago," he began, "and the Indians having gone elsewhere to do their trading that season, business was very dull.

"St. Paul, at that time, was only a big trading post, and but few settlers had moved there. The Indian trade was the life of the place, and one season's failure in this trade caused quite a panic among the traders, many of whom had put every cent of cash they could get into large stocks of goods, on which they expected to double their money. Their disappointment was very great, therefore, and several of them boxed up their stores and moved back east, while others sold out for what they could get, fully believing that the Indian trade at St. Paul was at an end. Whole stocks of goods were sacrificed at small figures, and I concluded to give up my situation as clerk in a trader's store, and with what cash I had saved up, buy some goods and go where the Indians lived. This I did, and having three ponies already, I purchased another, to be paid for when I returned, and loading my stock of blankets, squaw-cloth, beads, paint, looking-glasses, hawk-bells, wampum, necklaces, shells, brass wire, and sheet silver, started for the Missouri River country. I got along well enough until I reached the Yankton village (near where Fort Randall now stands), and "did a little trading there, after which I started up the river, when I met, on the second day's journey, two of the La Frombe boys, and as L knew them both well, when they were with their brother, Frank La Frombe, a trader at St. Paul, I was, of course, glad to meet them, and they were ,also glad to see me again. They were going down to Sioux City, on no particular business, and I tried to get them to go along with me, but they said that the Sioux and they were not on very good Terms, and they had concluded to stay away from them, lest they might have trouble. I endeavored to ascertain the cause of the ill-feeling between the boys and the Sioux, but both of them kept very mum, and would not tell me. Presently, I changed the subject, and began asking them for information which might enable me to easily find the Indian villages. By the time we got through talking, it was getting on toward night, and Baptiste, one of the boys, said we had better go back for about a mile and a half, on the road they had just come, where we should find an old log shanty, built by a man named Bremer, some two or three years before, and in which we could all pass the night. I would find, they said, four wails to inclose my ponies for safety, and a good fire-place to cook in. So Baptiste, Louis, and myself, moved leisurely along the road, conversing all the way, until we reached the old house. By this time it was dark so dark, that if the boys had not known exactly where the house stood, we might have passed within a few feet of it and I not seen it.

"I tied my ponies' lariats all together, and allowed them to feed just outside the building. The boys hunted around for sticks to build a fire with, and had soon raked together an arm-load of weeds and brush. We found no fire-place, however, and had to tramp down the weeds for three or four feet inside the house to make sufficient room to build our fire.

"Soon a bright blaze rewarded our efforts, and leading the ponies up to the door, one at a time, I unloaded them, and laid my packs down inside the house. Then hoppling their feet, I let them get some more grass before tying them up for the night. I now went inside to get something to eat, and found the La Frombe boys had the hind-quarter of an antelope on one of their saddles, and as I had some coffee, a little sugar, and some Indian bread, we soon-made a hearty meal. I ate fast and got through as quickly as I could. The La Frombes were but half done eating when I finished, and then sat waiting for the bone of one of the antelope quarters to roast a little more for Baptiste. Presently, as I was busy untying the hopples, and bringing my own and the boys' ponies inside, I thought I heard someone talking out on the prairie, a hundred or a hundred and fifty yards distant. I was just untying the hopples on the last pony, when I again heard voices distinctly, and I raised up to my feet and listened, but hearing nothing more, concluded I had been mistaken, and went into the house with the ponies. I did not say anything to the boys about having heard the voices, for fear it might turn out to be a false .alarm, and I would get laughed at. Lighting my pipe, I drew the buckle of my belt a little tighter, and went to the opening, which had once been a door-place, and, leaning against the wall, smoked and listened the La Frombes were still eating and conversing to each other, and I began to think of what harm could attend us, even if Indians were in the vicinity, for they were not at war with the whites, and I had heard lately of no depredations being committed by them. 'P'shaw! there was nothing to fear after all,' I said to myself, 'but might they not be around trying to steal stock?'

"Here was food for my thoughts, and I was busily turning the matter over, when I noticed a sudden cessation of the, conversation between the La Frombe boys. Each sat by the fire, their mouths open, their eyes half closed, and apparently listening to sounds outside. In a moment more, Louis La Frombe got up very cautiously, and carefully avoiding to break any of the tall weeds as he stepped, went to the corner farthest from the fire, where all our rifles were, and quietly removing his own from the stack, came back to the fire, and spoke a few words to Baptiste, who got up and went for his rifle. I now had my suspicions aroused, and motioned for Baptiste to bring my gun with him, which he did. When he got to the door, where I was still standing, my ears stretched to catch any sound that might betray the existence of an enemy outside. Baptiste whispered to me, and asked if I had heard it. 'Heard what?' I inquired. 'someone talking outside the wall, on the side opposite the door,' Baptiste replied. 'Louis heard it,' he added, 'but when I listened, I couldn't hear anything but the sucking of your pipe.' I led Baptiste over to where Louis was, and told both of them what I had heard myself. 'They've followed us, Baptiste!' said Louis, 'let us put something in the doorway, for they've found us, sure as we live, and we must fight.' In a few minutes, we had arranged my packs, and the saddles, so as to form a tolerable barricade in the door, and each of us arranged our arms and ammunition so as to have them at hand in case of sudden need. Then we waited in silence for something to transpire. After we had been quietly watching and listening for a long time, and the fire had gone down until the blaze died out, and the coals only, remained gleaming in the ashes, I began to feel more easy, and to believe that the night breeze which rustled the tall weeds around the old house, had made the noise imagined by all of us to be human voices. So I took out my pipe, cut some tobacco, and filling it, went to the fire to get a light. Going back to the boys, who sat leaning against the wall, their guns in their hands, I said, 'Louis, what did you mean, when you said awhile ago, that the Indians had found you out, and had followed you?' 'We had a little difficulty with some Santees about two days ago, and Baptiste killed a girl by accident, while shooting at a warrior, who was the Brother of Baptiste's squaw,' he replied. He then said, 'The warrior and Baptiste had a quarrel about a pony trade, and the wind-up of the affair was, each tried to killed the other, the Indian firing first, missed Baptiste, who, instead of taking steady aim, as he had plenty of time to do, jerked up his gun, and fired at the fellow, missing him, and hitting a girl in the throat, killing her almost instantly.' 'That's the whole of it, and the cause of our traveling eastward added Baptiste.'

"'The confounded brutes are after us, or I thought they were only a little while ago,' said Louis.

"'Well, it's a tough piece of business, boys,' said I, 'and I am surprised at Baptiste using his rifle to settle a quarrel about such an affair as a pony trade.'

"'Oh, this is not the first time his hot-headedness has got us both into trouble,' said Louis; 'he had to get on a bender down at Sioux City last fall, when we went with the Sioux to do some trading, and Baptiste quarreled with a white man, and drew his revolver and shot him four times, killing him dead. The man also shot Baptiste through the leg, and he was laid up for two months from it

"'Boys said I, 'one thing is clear: you and I have been mistaken about hearing voices outside, for if there had been any Indians close, we would have heard from them an hour ago. Let us spread out our blankets and lie down, then we can listen, and all stay awake as long as we want, or take turns in watching This was readily agreed to, and still keeping our guns with us, laid down .on our backs, with our coats doubled up under our heads for pillows. We lay thus for over an hour, when suddenly, I thought I saw something like a bunch of grass waving near the corner of the hall, on the side of the house opposite the door. There was no roof on the house, only the walls being left standing. So we laid under the sky. I watched the corner very closely, where I thought I had seen the grass move, and in a minute saw the, same thing again; this time I made it out against the sky to be a bunch of feathers. Slowly it rose above the wall, and then a head covered with long, black, shining hair, appeared, peering cautiously down inside the old house to see if we were there.

"After a moment's survey of our quarters, the head as slowly and silently withdrew. 'Did you see that?' I whispered to Baptiste, who laid near me. 'Yes,' he replied, 'only let it come up there again!' He raised the muzzle of his rifle, for the purpose of having it ready for instant use, when the head should appear; but Louis seized the barrel, and told Baptiste

V to hold up, and not to shoot too quickly, or he might repent it.

I told the boys that 'as we are now positive our fears are not without foundation, and that, beyond a doubt, the Indians are around us in large numbers, as they would not start on the trail of two such men as the La Frombe brothers; without having superior numbers and arms, so as to ensure their success, I will go outside and try to find out what they are after, and see if talking cannot send them o8?

"'It will be of no use, I can tell you said Baptiste, 'they are after me, and will do their utmost to get me. All your ponies and stock would not tempt them to leave us alone u 11 will try it anyhow I said, 'only I want you to promise not to use your rifle until I first see what can be done Louis and Baptiste both agreed to this, and, leaning my rifle against the door within easy reach, I put my two revolvers in my belt, and jumping over the barricade, I called out:

"'Sioux! my friends.'

"'What is it?' answered two voices.

"'I wish to-talk with you in peace, and find out why you are here, and what you want; I have left my gun in the house and do not want to shoot you, or have you shoot me. Will you talk with me?'

"'We do not know you. You have a strange voice; yet, you speak our language. What do they call you?'

161

"'I am a trader from the big trading place in Minnesota, and am on my way to visit your people to trade with them. I have four ponies loaded with fine goods I-replied.

"'We are your friends; and, if you are ours, you must pack up your ponies and go on your road to the village, which is only two days' travel. We want you to leave the men inside of the house, for we have been hunting them for two, days, and have now just found them.'

"'I am an old friend of theirs and their brother, and would wish to know why you are after them.'

"'They killed one of our tribe, and we come for revenge. We must kill them; will you go on toward the village tonight, or remain with them and be killed? If you start now, you will be safe; but, if you stay, you will die, for there are twenty-two of us, and we declare we will kill all we find in the house, after the fight begins

"'If I give you a blanket apiece, and some presents, will you leave us and go away?' I asked.

"'No, we want the men, and do not care for ponies or presents' the speaker replied.

"'Don't talk with the durned skunks any longer, Pete said Baptiste, 'come inside, or what would be better for you, tell them you will go on to their village to-night, and go. Louis and I can either clean them out, or get away from them before morning.' I refused to entertain the proposition of going on, and leaving them to fight their enemies alone, and immediately told the Sioux, that 'I had traveled a long way to visit, them, and had always been friendly with all other branches of their tribe, but I could not think of leaving my own countrymen to fight such an unequal battle, when I might aid them by remaining.' I said, 'I would rather lose everything I possessed, than shoot one Indian, yet, if they would attack the two men, I would stay and assist them. I had just concluded this reply, when crash went a rifle inside the building, and I heard the heavy thud of a body dropping on the ground, below the corner where I had seen the head peering over the wall. Quickly I leaped over the barricade, and gained the inside of the building, where Baptiste was engaged hastily reloading his rifle, having just added one more to his long list of notches on the stick. I seized my trusty rifle, and placed myself beside Louis, who was guarding the door. There was now a great jabbering among the Indians, who were carrying away their dead comrade; then, after a few moments' silence, the most unearthly yells, which ever met human ears, arose in the still midnight.

RENEWAL OF THE BATTLE

A MOMENT of painful silence succeeded the yell of tin savages, and then we could hear their suppressed breathing, as the red devils crawled under the old walls of the shanty. I held a position on the left of the doorway, where I could have an opportunity of seeing anyone who approached from the right, and Louis remained on the right side, where he could command the left of the doorway. While we were straining our eyes and ears to hear every sound, Baptiste suddenly fired, and shot another Indian from the top of the old wall, where he had climbed. We heard the body drop with a thud outside, where the first had fallen. The noise of voices; all talking together, and much excited, as on the previous occasion, was heard, and we felt that a great struggle was at hand.

"For about a minute not a sound was heard, not even the breathing of the villains outside the walls. Suddenly the sky grew red with the light of burning prairie grass, which had been heaped up around the old building, not with the intention of roasting us out, for that was impossible, but to make a light, so the savages could see where to attack to the best advantage. They also wished to prevent us from seeing where they kept themselves outside the blazing circle. Had they not attacked us immediately, the fire would have been to our advantage, for we could see and have time to strengthen the barricade.

"With a small hatchet, which I carried with me for camp use, md a butcher-knife, I dug up sufficient earth to fill one of the racks in the door, and had almost done working at it, when a shower of arrows came rattling over the top of the barricade into the shanty, several of which struck the ponies, causing quite a panic among them. We had no time to trouble about the ponies, however, for, while I watched the door, Baptiste tied a piece of calico around Louis's leg, an arrow having slightly wounded him, just below the knee. His wound was not dangerous or painful, but bled profusely. While Baptiste was tying on the bandage, I saw several savages leap over the smoldering fire near the building, and rush in a body at our barricade. I quickly called to the boys to come on, and we raised our guns, and, taking deliberate aim—Baptiste at those on the left, Louis at those on the right, and myself at the center of the yelling mass—we fired. The boys each got his man, and my old double-barreled rifle knocked down one Indian dead, and badly wounded two more. I still had a load in reserve, but not long, for, believing our guns to be empty, they came yelling on with bows and hatchets in their hands. I quickly fired again, and five of them were badly wounded by my second shot. In alarm and astonishment, they gave way, evidently having never seen or felt the effects of a double barreled gun before.

"They were now so weak in force, and so badly demoralized, that they waved a blanket, and called out: 'No fire again—little while.' This was a truce we were not sorry to accept, hoping they .would, in a short time, go away. I told the boys to grant their request, and soon saw the dark shadows busily engaged dragging off the dead and wounded, who lay in front of the building. I called out, and asked them to tell us when they were ready to begin again, that we were now impatient to have a good fight, and wished them to hurry, as it was only amusement for us. The answer to my request was, that they would notify us when they were ready, or, as they expressed it, 'Good! tell you by and by The dusky forms were seen flitting now and then in front of us, and stealthily moving over the ground, as if searching for some article they had dropped during the advance upon the building. While we were quietly watching these shadow's, one of them called out, 'Ready?' 'Yes!' I answered. 'Well, all right' he said and just as we laid our guns over the barricade to repulse them from the front, where the speaker stood, a dozen big savages dropped from the top of the wall into the house, and rushed upon us before we had time to take our rifles off the barricade. Smash! crash! bang! went the heavy rifle butts, and over rolled the warriors, one after another, until five laid on the ground, where the frightened ponies kicked and tramped them so badly that two were killed outright. The rest of the party, who were outside, now dashed over the door barricade, and then someone from behind knocked me down with a hatchet. I must have been unconscious for several hours, for, when I recovered, the moon was up very high; and it had not yet begun to rise when the fight was going on. I found myself lying on a buffalo robe outside the old building, and several Indians squatting on the ground about ten feet distant, dividing my goods and trinkets, which they had found inside the ranch. One of the Indians saw me turn over, or, perhaps, heard me groan, as I endeavored to turn my head in the direction they were, for he said: "Merican man, he awake; what shall we do now?' A low conversation was held among them, which I could not hear, when presently a warrior came to me, and said: 'Brother, you have acted very foolishly in helping those two bad men against us. You have been nearly killed, and would have been killed outright, only that we knew the two bad men had cast a spell on you, and you could not help doing what you did. Are you very sick?'

"'No I replied; 'where are the Frombes?'

"'There is one of them said the warrior, pointing to poor Baptiste, whose body dangled from the wall, over which he had been hung with his own lariat. His head looked white on the top, in the moonlight, and I. knew it was because the scalp had been removed. 'The other one got away' continued the warrior, 'but he cannot escape, for good hunters are after him; and we are waiting here until they return. He was badly wounded before he got on his pony, so badly, that if anyone had noticed him in time, we could have caught him before he mounted.'

"'What are you going to do with me?" I inquired.

"'You told us you were going to our village he answered; "and you can go with us."

"But what is the use of my going to the village, when you have taken away all my goods?"

"'If you will join our tribe, and help us fight our enemies, we will give you back everything we have taken."

"I will do it I said, "if you do not ask me to fight my own people."

"We will not ask that of you." the warrior answered, as he brought me my ponies, and assisted me to pack my things on the saddles. Then, bringing me my double-barreled gun, he stooped down and tied up my head with a piece of tanned elk-skin, and bound some cooling leaves over the wound, which made me feel quite comfortable.

"In about half an hour we heard a shout, apparently a long distance to the westward, and the Indians with whom I had been conversing answered it, and then hurriedly directed me to 'mount and come on All jumped on their ponies, and, getting behind my pack animals, whipped them into a fast pace t

We soon came upon the party who had been pursuing Louis, and I saw that the leader, a petty chief, held in his hand Louis's rifle. I was sure he had killed him, but could not account for be absence of the pony he had rode. My fears were soon set at rest, however, by the chief telling my Indian friend that Louis had swam the river on his pony, and had shot at them just before he went into the water's edge, and then dropped his rifle, which they had fished out. They said they fired some twenty arrows at Louis as he swam beside his pony, but they could not tell whether he was struck or not, as they did not see anyone coming out on the other bank of the river, but admitted it was too dark to see him, even if he had emerged.

"I felt thankful for Louis's escape, but discreetly said nothing. We now tramped along about a mile further, and then halted and encamped for the night. While we were lying around the fire, and I was asleep, an Indian came and shook me, and said: 'Why do you groan and make such a noise?' I told him I did not know I had done so, as I was asleep, and that my wounded head was probably the cause of it. He said, 'Your wounds are nothing—look at those six warriors over there! they are everyone worse hurt than yourself, yet they do not groan or make such a fuss; we cannot sleep.' I got up and went to one of the Indians who was awake, and who was the same one I had hurt with the buckshot of my double-barreled gun. Presently all awoke, and I asked one of them if I could do anything for him. He said he wanted water, and I immediately brought him some. They all drank prodigiously, their wounds making them feverish and thirsty.

"Next morning we moved out early, and by night reached the village. I bought a teepee, and put my goods up for trade, and, in a short time, sold out, at good prices, all I had. I f then went to Sioux

City, where I got on a steamboat, and hurried to St. Louis for more goods. I found Indian trading very profitable, and ever since then I have engaged in it, more or less, among the different tribes.

"About a year ago, while at old Port Pierre, on the west side of the Missouri, I met Louis La From be, and found him well and hearty. He said he had been badly wounded, and, after fording the river, in which he received an arrow in the shoulder, the shaft remaining in for two days, he had lain down on the opposite bank, utterly exhausted and helpless He fell asleep, and his pony strayed off a mile or two, putting him to a great deal of trouble to find him; but he finally succeeded, and moved up the river to the fort, where the traders had extracted the arrow and attended him until his wounds were healed. They had to keep him concealed all the time, however, for fear the Sioux, who came there occasionally, would find him."

Thus ended the trader's story, with which I was much pleased; and, after tasting the "medicine" again, and having a little conversation about his goods,' prospects in trade, and other matters, we parted for the night.

THE SIOUX NATION—TOLD BY THEMSELVES

THAT evening I had a long conversation with some old men of the tribe, during which the missionary was present, about the Sioux and Santees. I learned that they had, as far back as the oldest warrior could remember, been a separate band. Their forefathers had told them they originally lived in Minnesota; but they could not tell me anything beyond that, and believed they had always lived there. This idea has some foundation in the word Minnesota, which is a Sioux word, meaning "minne," water, "sota," bleared or turbid, turbid water. This I readily ascertained from knowing' that the word "blear-eyed," or, as the Sioux call it, "an eye with troubled water," is, in their language, "ees-ta" (eye) "so-to" (bleared or turbid), that is, "blear-eyed."

The Sioux never call themselves Sioux, but Da-ko-ta. The term Sioux is a mere nickname given them many years ago by the first white men that came among them, who were Frenchmen. The language they speak is called "La-co-ta," a word

The name of Sioux that we give to these Indians is entirely of our own making, or, rather, it is the last two syllables of the name Nadoues-sioux, as many nations call them.—(Extract from letter of Charlevoix, 10 1721. See Neill's History of Minnesota, page 51.) of their own the "la" being substituted for "da" to distinguish the word man from language. The word Da-ko-ta) which they prefer to be called, signifies "allied or joined together in love," and is the same as our motto, E pluribus Unum. A writer of a mission history, published, over two hundred years ago, says: "For sixty leagues from the extremity of the upper lake, toward sunset, and, as it were, in the center of the western nations, they have all united their forces by a general league."

The Da-ko-tas, as far back as we have any record of them up to the present time, are called Soos, Scioux, and Sioux. For many hundred years the Indians of Lake Superior were at war with the Dakotas, and when they speak of them they call them the Na-do-way Sioux, which, in Ojiboway language, means "enemy." From this we have the derivation for Sioux.

169

I also learned from the missionary, who had made the origin and early life of the Sioux nation his study, that from a very early period the tribe had been divided into three great nations or bands—the I-san-ya-ti, or the Ts-sa-ti, the name of one of the lakes where they lived. The principal band of the Is-sa-tis was the M'de-wa-kan-ton-wan, pronounced "Meddy-waw-kawn-twawn." The second great band was the "I-hank-ton-wan," or Yankton. They formerly lived north of the Minnesota Liver, and are now on the eastern banks of the Missouri River, near Fort Randall, D. T. The third band was the "Ti-ton-wans," who lived farther west than the I-hank-ton-wans. This tribe was sometimes called the "Tin-ton-wans," a corruption of the original name. The pronunciation of the name is Tee-twawons. In the last great band is embraced the bands known as Santees, Ogallalas, and Brules, who never appear in sight of emigrants wagons on the prairies, but their hearts fill with painful apprehensions.

North of the Dakotas, on Lake of the Woods, which is connected with Lake Superior, are the Assiniboines. They were once a band of the Sioux nation, and, speak the language at this day. An old Santee said he remembered a story, which had been handed down for many generations in his tribe, relating to the Assiniboines. According to this tradition, they are Sioux, and had always been, but the whites called them by another name. The following was given as the cause Assiniboine Warrior of their separation from the main Sioux tribe:

A young warrior loved the wife of another warrior, and whenever the latter was absent from home the young man went to the warrior's teepee, and talked to his squaw. She began to like him; and they enjoyed each other's company for many days, till at last the warrior, having noticed unmistakable signs of the faithlessness of his wife, threatened her with instant death unless she dismissed her lover. He then went to the council house; and, as soon as he had gone, the guilty woman hurried to her lover's lodge, and acquainted him with all that had passed. While she still talked to him the husband came into the tent for his squaw; and a quarrel ensued between the young man and the warrior. They came to blows; which were soon exchanged for weapons; and the husband met his death at the hands of the young man. The husband's relations, among whom was his aged lather, went to get the body of the warrior, which still lay in the young man's lodge, where it had fallen; and, on the way to the teepee, the father's party were met by some friends of the young man, and a fight ensued, in which three of the guilty man's friends were killed. The father then went back, and raised a party of sixty warriors, who declared war against the seducer and his friends. Several battles were fought; and the whole tribe finally joined in the war, the sides being almost equal in numbers. The affair ended in a revolt upon the part of the seducer and his adherents, who in time became a separate people, and are now called the Assiniboines.' So ended the tradition, which is the story of another woman who caused a war.

TO BE KILLED OR CURED

ON many occasions, when traveling over the Indian country, I found old deserted camps, in nearly every one of which, where the Indians had staid any time, were the skeleton or bent poles of the sweat lodges. These were not peculiar to any tribe, but alike in the camps of Arrapahoes, Cheyennes, Pawnees, and Sioux. A description of this curious institution will not be out of place. Unlike any other teepee, it is made of stout willows, two and three inches in thickness, which are bent, and both ends pushed into the ground firmly. When all the poles are thus set, they are in the shape of a large wire rat-trap. This lodge is only about four feet high, and is covered with good elk or buffalo hide, devoid of holes or open seams. The circumference of the lodge at its base is usually eighteen feet. When the canvas or hide covering is well stretched over it, the edges next the ground are firmly held to the earth by large heavy stones. On the inside of the lodge the ground is smoothed, and in the center a hole is dug for a fire-place, in which some ten or twelve large stones are always kept in readiness should any person need a sudden sweat.

If the science of medicine is not known, or there is no medicine man present with the band, the Indians are very solicitous and superstitious about their sick. The Sioux are well versed in anatomy, but the great secret of the causes and effects of circulation of the blood is not known among any of these Indians. All they know is that it is essential to life that the blood should be kept in the body. This they have discovered from simple causes, such as seeing persons bleed to death from wounds, or becoming weak from some slight accident, causing little or no pain. They know that when they kill an enemy, unless he is shot through the heart or brain, he generally lives till his blood is all gone, when he dies, but why, they cannot tell.

The young people who get sick are well taken care of, in nearly every instance, but the old men-and women are often neglected, because, whenever they have anything ailing them, the people of the tribe think it is sinful to try and cure them. They say whenever the Great Spirit calls for an aged person, "whose days have been long on

172

the earth, they should go." So they allow nature, in such cases, k, take its course. If the aged person gets well, it is all right, but if he dies, it is all the same. To effect a cure for many maladies, the Indians practice what is known as the "steaming process." The sick person is stripped, taken into the tent just described, and the opening or door firmly closed, to exclude all air. A fire is then built in the middle of the lodge, and a dozen stones heated as hot as they can be made. Water is next poured on these stones, which creates a great deal of vapor. The sick person is kept in the lodge until the vapor subsides, when he is taken out completely exhausted, and repeatedly plunged into cold water. This is done as quickly as possible after taking the patient from the sweat-house. The sweat-house is always built near the banks of a body of cold water, so that the patient may not be subjected to the air but a moment or two before being soused.

I became very unwell, one day, from the effects of the hot weather and tepid water we always had to drink, having been used to the water of the Missouri River, which is tolerably cold. I kept in my teepee all day, and ate but little. But the following night .1 had a violent attack of pain in my stomach, and I sent my squaw, about one o'clock in the morning, to the missionary's, to see if he had any laudanum or cathartics. She returned with a small phial of laudanum, of which I took pretty large doses. My pain was relieved for about an hour, but returned again. All the next day I experienced violent pains, and I suppose they would have killed me had not my solicitous squaw gone over to the old medicine man and told him of my condition. He came into the teepee with the squaw, and, not heeding my remonstrances, they gathered up the corners of the robe I was lying on and started off with me.

I abused the squaw and medicine man outrageously, and promised the squaw a good thrashing when I should get well; but the old medicine man, who seemed to be used to cross patients, only said, "He very sick; he be better by and by. We sweat him heap." So, not minding my ravings and abuse, they carried me to the sweat-lodge and laid me down on the ground, when the squaw left me and went into a teepee, and brought out a burning stick, which she carried into the little house built close under the banks of the river. I saw smoke issuing from the crevices, and presently the medicine man was told all was in readiness. The squaw then went with a sheet-iron kettle to the river, and returned with it full of water. She set the bucket down by the little house, and, at the direction of the old man brought a long lariat, which he tied around my body under the arms. After this, he and the squaw completely stripped me and, holding to the lariat, the old man said, "Get up now, if you can."

I tried, but I was too weak to rise. He and the squaw then pulled me to my feet, and, lifting me off the ground, carried me into the sweat-house. Here they placed me on my feet again, the old man holding me up while the squaw spread out a buffalo robe on the ground. I was next laid down on the robe, close by the fire, and as soon as this was accomplished, the old man received the kettle of cold water from the squaw, and poured it on the hot stones, which hissed and fumed until a dense vapor and smoke filled the place.

The old man hastily retired, and the opening in the lodge by which I had entered was securely closed from the outside. The hissing and sputtering of the water upon the stones was anything but pleasant to me, and in a little while I could scarcely breathe, so dense was the steam and the great drops of perspiration oozed from every pore; then my whole body began to grow clammy with moisture, and I called out to the old man, whom I heard walking around the outside of the lodge, shaking a couple of rattling gourds, that I had enough of it, and to take me out or I should die. He paid no attention to my cries, and I began to believe I really should die, so I called the squaw to help me, but she would not answer me. Then I lost all consciousness, for how long I know not, but I was revived by experiencing a drowning sensation, and in a moment felt myself raised to the surface of the water by means of the rope around my body, one end of which the old man, who was standing on the trunk of a cottonwood tree, held in his hands.

With wonderful rapidity I felt myself reviving and my former strength returning, and, after receiving one or two extra douches, I struck out for the shore. I was seized at the bank by 'the old fellow, who helped me out, and he and the squaw began a series of heavy

174

rubbing with a buffalo-skin towel, which almost curried the hide off my back and ribs. After being completely dried, I put on my limited wardrobe, and, singularly enough, felt all right; in fact, as well as if I had never experienced a day's sickness in my whole life.

I have many times since seen the sweat remedy employed for nearly all the diseases the Indians have, and in most instances it relieved the sufferer. The exceptions where the sweat-bath is not used, is where the person is dying, or a warrior has been wounded in battle.

THE INDIAN GIRL

IF you strolled through an Indian village at night, you would be sure to hear the unearthly chanting of the medicine man endeavoring to exorcise some spirit from a sick man; or you would see a group lounging about, whiffing, out of their sacred red-stone pipes, the smoke of red willow bark.

A common sight, too, is that of young men sneaking around a lodge, and waiting for the lodge fire to cease blazing before they perpetrate some deed of mischief. You would also hear a low, wild drumming, and observe a group of men naked, with the exception of a girdle about their loins, and daubed with vermilion, engaged in some of the grotesque and exciting dances of the nation, and others, again, praying for the success of the expedition which they proposed making on the morrow.

Again would be seen and heard the groups of story tellers, and the occasional song sung by the hearers at the end of each narrative.

The Sioux are the greatest people in the world for storytelling, and their attention, when others are telling stories, is quite as remarkable as their colloquial powers. Some of their tales and legends are very beautiful) and many of them are marvelous. I shall find occasion to repeat a few of them in another part of this work.

As before related, the manner in which historical events and traditionary legends are preserved among the Indians, is by their old men retaining the facts in their memory; and occasionally in the cool evenings of summer, when the people are lying around their villages, without having any hunt-ting or warfare on their hands, telling them to listening groups.

The Indians are possessed of peculiarly retentive memories, and are always respectful and attentive listeners to the narratives of their old men. A tale once heard is remembered by the hearers for years, and, in like manner, is handed down by them to another generation. Thus, events of many centuries are transmitted to posterity, and all the facts are remarkably well preserved, and, what is still more wonderful, are narrated without comparatively any change from the original version.

As Neil, the historian, says, "You might enter a Dakota village at midnight, and you would be almost sure to see some few huddled around the fire of a teepee, listening to the tale of an old warrior who has often been engaged in bloody conflicts with their old and present enemies, the whites;" or you might hear some legendary tale of deeds and events of the forefathers of the nation, who lived several hundred years before white men' were known to flu Indians.

The earliest songs to which an Indian boy listens are those of war, and his delight is in hearing, during the long summer evenings, stories of bloodshed, and the deeds his forefathers did before he was born.

As soon as the child begins to walk about, if a male, he is, as has already been said, furnished with a little bow and some blunt-headed arrows, which are the only playthings he is allowed.

The little girls are early instructed in the art of painting their faces, ornamenting their ears with rings, their necks with beads, and their little moccasins with porcupine quills. They soon become adepts in the art of coquetry, and cause many a bashful youth to rue the day of his birth.

The days of her childhood are the only happy or pleasant days the Indian girl ever knows. As soon as she is wedded to a warrior, her life of toil and drudgery begins, which ends only at her grave. This subject will be treated of more fully in a subsequent chapter. With the boy it is quite different.

The first thing he is taught, as being truly noble and manly, s taking a scalp, and he is eager until it is done. At the age of sixteen he is frequently on the war path. When his friends think he has arrived at the proper age to go to war, he is presented with weapons, one giving him a bow, another arrows, another a knife, and still another a horse. He makes his own war-club. He then consecrates certain animals, or parts of animals, which he vows never to eat until he has slain an enemy. After he has killed one enemy, he is at liberty to eat a certain portion of the animal from which he agreed to abstain. If he kills another enemy, the prohibition is taken off another part, until finally, by deeds of bravery, he has emancipated himself from his oath.

Before young men go out on a war party, they endeavor to propitiate their patron deity by a feast, music, and dancing. During the night, before they are to start, they perform the u Shield Dance," and follow the wild performance by feasting, drumming, dancing, and singing, interspersed with fierce shrieks and yells.

A SIOUX DOCTOR

UNTIL the past few years, the Sioux, whenever any sickness happened, believed they were possessed by the spirit of some snake, bird, or animal. The Crow story of the superstitions of that tribe, as narrated in this book, shows that, if the Sioux have in time come to banish such erroneous beliefs about animals, insects, and reptiles, taking possession of people's bodies, the Crows still hang to it, and hence, their superstition about "tails" of animals, which are said, and believed, to inhabit the stomach.

The medicine men of the Sioux are supposed to have unlimited strength and suction power, of the mouth, so that by sucking, alone, they can draw away the evil spirit from" the sick man, and thus Cure him.

Before going any farther, it will, however, be best to explain what kind of fellow the Sioux medicine man is anything mysterious and wonderful, or for which he cannot account, is always called Wa-can, or Wa-kah, (medicine). The early French explorers called a doctor "medicin" and all Indians have thereby called their doctors "medicine men" or Wa-ka, Pa-zhir-ta, We-cha-sa (spirit medicine man). "A medicine man" means, then, in the broadest Indian sense, "a doctor" who calls to his aid charms and incantations to cure the sick. The medicine men are divided into conjurers, or spirit doctors, and war prophets. These latter are greatly feared by all the tribes.

They have some very curious customs and ceremonies, which to me seemed ridiculous, but my good sense and knowledge of what was best for me, never allowed me to witness any of their freaks of foolishness, except with a grave countenance, and apparent respect and confidence in the power and ability of the medicine man to do whatever he wished. I have seen several cases of sickness under the hands of medicine men, and a description here of the general mode of procedure may not be uninteresting.

The doctor is always to be found seated in the medicine lodge, unless attending a feast, or dance, or when out of an evening walking for his health. As he never sends around his "bills for professional services," he must receive his fees in advance someone is sent to notify him that he is wanted, and the request is accompanied by a present of a pony, blanket, or something useful and valuable, for dress or ornament. The messenger sometimes has a gourd-rattle, which he shakes at the medicine man's door till he comes out; again he takes a pipe, lights it, goes into the medicine man's lodge, and hands him the pipe; then sits down in front of him, and rocking backward and forward, cries and groans, as though he were sick. Again, the messenger strips himself to his breech-cloth and moccasins, and carries the gourd-rattle in his hand. On entering the lodge, he shakes the rattle vigorously, walks up to the medicine man, and unceremoniously kicks him. He then jumps for the door, and having gained the outside, shakes his rattle and runs for the sick person's teepee as fast as he can—the medicine man following close after him. If the medicine-man overtakes the messenger in his chase, and kicks him, the doctor is at liberty to return to his teepee without having seen the sick person, even if the messenger is overtaken within a few feet of the sick man's door. The sick person then sends another messenger, and so keeps on sending runners, with presents, until one is fast enough to outrun the medicine man and reach the sick lodge first. As soon as the messenger beats the doctor to the sick man's teepee the physician enters, but, before going into the teepee, he strips himself, and wears only his breech-cloth and moccasins. He now sends to his lodge, where, in front of the doorway outside, hangs a large rattle of the kind just mentioned, only this one is covered with painted hieroglyphics, and ornamented with eagle's feathers at the handle. The rattle, or gourd, with the drum, medicine shield, and box containing roots, teeth, bear's and other animal's claws, hangs on a pole outside the door of every medicine lodge in an Indian village. The rattle is brought to the sick man's teepee, and the doctor begins to shake it, and sing it in a wiki, chanting voice. This he continues for a few minutes, when he gets down on his hands and knees and crawls up to the patient. He hangs over the breast of the patient a moment or two, and then rises to his feet, gags and makes ugly faces, as if he was sick at his stomach and trying to vomit. Presently he goes to a bowl of water and puts his whole face into it, and, by blowing, causes bubbles to rise thick around his face. He makes all believe (for it is their business to believe) that he has blown into the bowl of water the spirit which has been troubling the patient. The doctor next carefully examines the water while carrying on a slow and almost inaudible chant, and at length decides what species of animal has possessed the patient. He now makes out of bark an image of the animal he has discerned in the bowl, and plunges it in a kettle of water, set outside the door of the teepee. The animal of bark is to be shot, and two or three Indians are in waiting, with loaded guns, ready to kill it, whenever the doctor tells them to do so. To make sure that the conjuring has the desired effect, a woman must stand astride the kettle, with her dress raised as high as the knees. The executioners are instructed how to act by the doctor, and as soon as he makes his appearance out of the lodge, they all fire into the kettle, and blow the little bark image to pieces. The woman then steps aside, and the doctor goes to the bowl on his hands and knees, and commences blubbering in the water as he did in the teepee. While this is going on, the woman has to jump on the doctor's back with her feet, and stand there for a moment; when she gets off, and as soon as he has finished his incantations, the woman takes him by the hair of the head and pulls him back into the sick man's lodge. If there are any pieces of the little bark image left, after it is shot, they are buried under ground.

If this does not cure the patient, a similar ceremony is performed; but some other animal is shaped out, each time, until the patient gets well or dies; and if he dies, the conclusion is arrived at, that the Great Spirit, or Wa-kan Ton-ka, was the inhabiting one in the patient, and, of course, could not be cast out.

There is another class of Indian medicine men I have as yet barely mentioned, called prophets, or priests, who, by relating stories of dreams they have had, or pretended to have had, and by making exciting speeches or exhortations, endeavor to incite the tribes to war against each other.

If a party is successful in securing scalps, they generally paint their faces black and come home wild with delight. As they approach the town or village, the people run out to meet them and hear the news. They then conduct the warriors to the council house, when the war prophet, or medicine man, meets them at the door. He assumes great importance, and seems to say, "Didn't I tell you so? I brought you all this good fortune, and the credit is mine." The scalps are then prepared for exhibition, by being stretched on a small willow hoop or ring, and painted red on the flesh side. They are next tied to the top of a long pole, and set in the ground on some open space, suitable for accommodating a dance, in which the whole tribe can engage. If the scalp is a man's, they fasten an angle's feather to the hair; but if it is a woman's, no ornament of any kind is attached to it. The warriors who were on the expedition, in which the scalp was taken, form a large or small circle around the pole, and dance. If any of their party have been killed, an equal number of other warriors who remained at home, are selected for the dance, and their faces painted black from the eyes to the edge of the hair. They are then placed nearest to the pole, and do not dance, but stand perfectly still. They represent, the Indians say, the dead men who fell in the battle where the scalps were taken. The war party now form a circle outside of the representatives of the dead, and the villagers form another circle outside of the war party. Then the squaws, in two circles, are outside of the warriors—the oldest squaws forming the inner circle. The members of the war party have each a gourd-rattle, or a small drum, which they shake and play incessantly, singing all the time the scalp song, which varies in almost every tribe. I have heard three or four different scalp songs among the Sioux, and believe there are several which I have never heard. Some writer has stated, that "if a scalp is taken in the summer, the Indians dance, and celebrate the event until the leaves fall, and if it is taken in winter, they dance until the leaves come in spring." This may be so with the Pawnees, but it is not the case among the Sioux. The scalp is danced for only three days and nights, the Indians stopping to feast and rest, a few at a time for some moments, and then renewing the dance. At the end of three days, the scalp is taken down and claimed by the warrior who took it from the wearer's head. The owner hangs it up in his teepee as a proof of his bravery, and often wears it attached to his belt, or, if he has one there already, hangs one on each side of his body.

An eagle's feather, with a red spot painted on it, worn by a warrior in the village, denotes, that on the last war-path he killed an enemy, and for every additional enemy he has slain, he carries another feather, painted with an additional red spot about the size of a silver quarter.

A red hand painted on a warrior's blanket, denotes that he has been wounded by the enemy, and a black one, that he has been unfortunate in some way.

The medicine men, in the M'dewankantonwan tribe, have a sort of freemasonry among them, of which they are the founders, and this tribe is the only one of all the many tribes that can initiate, a warrior to the mysteries, superstitions, beliefs, and rites, which all real medicine men are supposed to possess.

In addition to their many other secret ceremonies, the M'dewankantonkas initiate a candidate for the honors of "M. D ." as follows: The candidate is first introduced to the chief medicine men by participating in "the medicine dance." This dance is said to have been instituted by Oanktahee, the patron of all medicine men. The editor of the "Dakota Friend," says truly, in his description of the dance: "When a member is to be received into this society, it is his duty to take a hot bath, four days in succession." In the meantime, some of the elders of the society instruct him in the mysteries of the medicine and Wam-noo-hah (shell in the throat). He is also provided with a dish (Wajate) and spoon. On the side of the dish, is sometimes carved the head of some voracious animal, in which resides the spirit of "Eo-yah" (an abbreviation for "Glutton God"). This-dish is always carried by its owner to the medicine feast, and it is his duty, ordinarily, to eat all which is served up in it. "Gray Iron" (a noted chief of former times), had a dish, which was given him at the time of his initiation, on the bottom of which was carved a bear, complete. The candidate is instructed with what paints, and in what manner, he shall paint himself, which must always be the same, when he appeal's in the dance. There is supernatural Virtue in this paint, and the manner in which it is applied; and those who have not been furnished with a bettor, by the regular war prophets, wear it into battle as a life-preserver. The bag contains, besides the claws of animals, the "Toanwan" (influence or power), with which they can, it is believed, inflict painful diseases and death on whomsoever they choose.

The candidate being thus duly prepared for initiation, and having made the necessary offerings for the benefit of-the institution, on the evening of the day previous to the dance, a lodge is prepared, and from ten to twenty of its more substantial members pass the night in singing, dancing, and feasting. In the morning, the tent is opened for the dance. After a few-appropriate ceremonies, preliminary to the grand operation, the candidate takes his place on a pile of blankets which he has contributed for the occasion, and is naked, except the breech-cloth and moccasins, duly painted and prepared for the mysterious operation.

An elder having been stationed in the rear of the novice, the master of the ceremonies, with his knee and hip-joints bent to an angle of about forty-five degrees, advances, in an unsteady, unnatural step, with his bag (containing medicine) in his hand, uttering, "Heen! Heen! Heen!" with great energy, and raising the bag near a painted spot on the breast of the candidate, gives the discharge, the person stationed in the rear gives him a push forward at the same instant, and as he falls headlong, throws the blankets over him. Then, while the dancers gather around him and chant, the master throws off the covering, and, chewing a piece of the bone of the Oanktahee, spirts over him, and he revives and resumes a sitting posture. All then return to their seats except the master; he approaches, and, making indescribable noises, pats upon the breast of the novice, till the latter, in agonizing throes, throws up the wamha (or shell), which falls from his mouth upon the bag which had been previously spread before him for that purpose. Life being now completely restored, and with the mysterious shell in his open hand, the new-made member passes around and exhibits it to all the members and to the wondering bystanders, and the ceremonies of .the initiation are closed. The dance continues, interspersed with harmlessly shooting each other, smoking, and refreshments, till they have danced to the music of four sets of singers. Besides vocal music, they make use of the drum and gourd-shell rattle.

The medicine-bag is made of the skin of an otter, fox, or some other animal of long shape—sometimes a skunk skin, containing certain articles held sacred.

RASCALITY OF WHITE MEN

AS, no doubt, nearly all the readers of these pages are ignorant of the modus operandi by which an Indian sale or transfer of land is made, and as I have been at considerable trouble to collect everything novel or entertaining about Indians for this book, I will here insert some verbatim copies of deeds made long ago by the savages to certain white persons. That rare old historian, Neill, has given us much that is curious, but he has by no means covered the ground; and what I give will at least have the merit of being new.

The following is a true copy of the great Carver deed, over which Congress wrangled for months in 1806, and which they finally decided to be a valid conveyance:

CARVER DEED

To Jonathan Carver, a chief under the most mighty and potent George the Third, King of the English, and other nations, the fame of whose courageous warriors has reached our ears, and has been more fully told us by our good brother Jonathan aforesaid, whom we rejoice to see come among us and bring us good news from his country, We, chiefs of the Nandowissies, who have hereto set our seals, do, by these presents, for ourselves and heirs forever, in return for the many presents, and other good services done by the said Jonathan to ourselves and allies, give, grant, and convey to him, the said Jonathan, and to his heirs and assigns forever, the whole of a certain tract or territory of land bounded as follows (viz.): From the Fall of St. Anthony, running on the east banks of the Mississippi, nearly south-east, as far as the south end of Lake Pepin, where the Chippeway River joins the Mississippi, and from thence eastward five days' travel, accounting twenty English miles per day, and from thence north six days' travel, at twenty English miles per day, and from thence again to the Falls of St. Anthony, on a direct, straight line. We do, for ourselves, heirs, and assigns forever, give unto the said Jonathan, his heirs and assigns forever, all the said lands, with all the trees, rocks, and rivers therein, reserving for ourselves and heirs the sole liberty of hunting and fishing on land not planted or improved by the said Jonathan, his heirs and assigns; to which we have affixed our respective seals, at the Great Cave, May the first, one thousand seven hundred and sixty-seven.

In order to show in what way, and for what consideration or price, Indian titles and claims were procured by the early French traders and settlers in the north-west of Wisconsin, the following extract is made from the records of Brown County, of that State (Record-book By pp. 110, 111):

[Translation of the Deeds and Entries.]

(No. 1.)

In one thousand seven hundred and ninety-three, are found present Wabisipine and the Black Tobacco, who have voluntarily given up and ceded to Mr. Dominique Ducharme from the head of the portage of Kakalin to the end of the prairie below, by forty arpens in depth; and on the other side...opposite the said portage, four arpens wide, by thirty in depth. The said vendors are contented and satisfied for two barrels of Rum. In faith of which, they have made their marks. The old Wabisipine being blind, the witnesses have made his mark for him.

J. Harrison,

Lambert Macaulay

Mark of the Wabisipine of the attribute of the Eagle. Mark of the Black Tobacco.

(No. 2.).

The undersigned, having claimed a right which they also have in the portage, have also sold their claims, and warranted from all troubles. They have accepted, for their part, five gallons of Rum, with which they find themselves content and satisfied. In faith of which, they have made their marks.

J. Harrison, Witness.

THE EAGLE.
PE CA MES.
HIS SON.
CHE MES.
BITTE.
THE EAGLET.

THE BEAVER,

(No. 3.)'

Ratified at the Portage of the Kakalin, in the year of our Lord one thousand seven hundred and ninety-six; the 31st day of July, in one thousand seven hundred and ninety-seven, on account of the portage, one barrel of rum.

August 8.

In one thousand seven hundred and ninety-eight, one barrel of rum, mixed, to content the sons subscribing.

July 16.

And in ninety-nine, one barrel of rum, mixed & me sines, to settle the difference between them, with which they find themselves content and satisfied

THE EAGLE.
THE BLACK TOBACCO.
D. DUCHARME.
WACHITTE.
THE BEAVER.
WABISIPINE.
THE DRINKER.

Land was cheap in those days, and the Indians of the Sioux tribe often sold theirs for a mere trifle—such as a keg of powder, or a few gallons of whisky. These swindles afterward caused great dissatisfaction, and the rascality of the whites was remembered against them even to the third and fourth generation. So well has the history of these transactions been preserved, that the Sioux yet know all about them, and to this day, speak bitterly of the folly of their fathers in allowing the white men to cheat them out of their ancient hunting-grounds. It is this that causes the Sioux to be suspicious of the whites, and to always sign treaties with the greatest reluctance.

EATING THE MOON UP

THE Indians compute their time very much as white men do, only they use moons instead of months to designate the seasons, each moon answering to some month in our calendar. The word "we" in the Indian tongue always means "moon," though it is often transposed in their sentences.

The Indians believe that when the moon is full evil spirits begin nibbling at it, to put out its light, and eat a portion each night until it is all gone. Then the Great Spirit, who will not permit them to take advantage of the darkness and go about the earth doing mischief, makes a new moon, working on it every night until it is completed, when he leaves it and goes to sleep. No sooner is he gone than the bad spirits return and eat it up again. The savages think all evil deeds are committed in the dark of the moon, and that it is a good time to go upon any prowling or stealing expedition. They generally will not start on the war path in the dark of the moon, but time their departure so as to arrive in the country of the enemy between moons.

I will here introduce brief accounts of two curious ceremonies, called respectively the Dog Dance and the Fish Dance.

The dog dance is seldom performed, most Indians thinking too much of their dogs to give them up for a feast. The dance begins as on ordinary occasions, when suddenly someone throws a dog into the middle of the crowd of dancers, and before the unfortunate animal can make his escape, he is tomahawked, cut open, his liver and heart taken out and tied to the pole round which the Indians dance.

The dancers now hop around very lively, the mouth of each watering for a bite of the delicious morsel hanging against the pole. After three circles have been accomplished about the pole, the highest in authority among the dancers steps up to it, and, without touching the body with his hands, seizes a mouthful of the liver and then takes his place in the circle.

After the dancers have described another round, the next warrior in rank comes up, and in like manner takes his mouthful of dog, and so on until all have had a bite of liver, when the squaws come in for the heart, which they eat in the same manner. Should any person be generous enough to throw in another dog, the operation is repeated.

There is no special meaning or importance attached to this feast on ordinary occasions, but it is often performed at weddings, and when unexpected arrivals occur. The people then dance to demonstrate their high esteem for the new comers, or to show good-will for the warrior and his bride. The bride groom, or the person in whose honor the dance is held, is expected to contribute two or three dogs for the feast, and the darning is kept up as long as tin; supply lasts. The capacity of an Indian stomach for dog meat is as infinite as it is wonderful.

The Fish Dance.—A Sioux chief was very sick, and the medicine men could not cure him, when one night, while the hot-wind (fever) was upon him, he dreamed that a spirit told him, if he would make a feast of raw fish, he would live until the young cranes were grown. So he summoned his warriors, related to them what had happened, and they all agreed to make a ceremony and assist the chief in eating his raw fish.

After one or two days spent in the sweat-house and in dancing the "Shield Dance," a tent .was prepared, with the door set toward the east. A long fence of willow bushes was then built from one side of the door, around a considerable space to the other side of the door, and within the inclosure was planted a bush for each person who was to participate in the dance. Nests were next built in the bushes, and early in the morning of the day on which the feast was to take place, the master informed two warriors where the fish were to be caught, how many, and of what kind. These persons went out, and as the chief desired, brought in two pike, each about one foot in length, which they had speared in the river.

The chief then painted the pike with vermilion, and ornamented their bellies and lower jaws with strips of wild-goose down dyed red, and when complete they were laid on some willows in the center of the inclosure, where they were left to dry. Near the fish were a number of birch-bark dishes filled with sweetened water, and the implements of war belonging to the participators were placed in the tent. When all was in readiness, the dancers, who were almost naked, fantastically painted, and ornamented with down dyed red, yellow, black, and white, formed in four ranks, and commenced to sing, each rank in its turn accompanying the song with drum and rattles.

The drums are used by only the fourth rank, the first, second, and third ranks being singers. The dancers rest when each rank has had a turn and ceased singing. Presently the fourth, rank begins to sing, the drums beat furiously, the dancers leap, yell, and make frightful contortions of the face and body, acting as much like demons as possible. Suddenly the music changes, the dancers dash at the fish, and tear them with their teeth, eating the head, body, and entrails. Then they swallow some mouthfuls of the sweetened water, and each, taking one of the large bones of the fish which are left, deposit them in the nests made in the bushes, and the feast is ended.

The Indians allege that the chief in whose honor this dance was instituted lived until the cranes had become full-grown birds, and then he died. Since then this feast is only prepared for a chief who cannot be cured of his sickness by the medicine men. A medicine man, however, if he is a chief also, may have the benefit of a fish dance, but no one else except chiefs are entitled to so great an honor.

The feasts and dances of the Indians are so near alike that I do not deem it necessary to repeat the same details for each, and will hereafter only describe them generally, when I have occasion to refer to them at all.

MAKE ME A SADDLE

HAPPENING into the teepee of Ma-to-sca (White Bear), one day, I saw one of his squaws working on a piece of red cloth; garnishing it in a most tasteful manner with cut-glass beads of different colors. Not knowing what the cloth could be used for, being of a different shape from anything I had before seen, I inquired, and was told it was a saddle skirt. The squaw had almost completed it,, and I asked her who it was for, when she told me it was a present for her husband. She promised to bring it to my teepee when it was completed, and let me see it, and three days afterward she brought it for my inspection. The Indian saddle was made of buckskin, having no frame, but being simply a pad of doubled soft leather, stuffed with antelope hair. The skirts were long, very beautiful, and ornamented with fringe. This saddle was only used for riding on important occasions, and was fastened to the pony's back Ma-to-sca's Saddle by a girth or band of rawhide three inches broad, which was attached to the buckskin pad. No buckles were used. A strong buckskin string fastened the girth to the pads. There were no stirrups, but-soft loops for the feet, a I tried to purchase this beautiful horse gear of White Bear, but, he said, as it was a present from his squaw, he did not like to part with it... I asked my squaws if they thought they could make me one like it, and offered to give them each a new dress of squaw cloth if they would do so; but they told me frankly it was "heap o' work," and they did not know how to lay off the patterns. Each of them, however, made me a present of a pair of dancing moccasins, finely beaded, with little brass hawk bells attached to the instep, and a magnificent pair of beaded leggings, so I felt compelled to give them the new dresses.'

White Bear's saddle had a crupper made of buffalo hide tanned soft, over which was laid blue squaw cloth handsomely beaded and embroidered, and to the end of' which was attached long buckskin fringe. His bridle was made much in the same fashion as those used by the .whites, only that, in place of being leather it was rawhide covered with red cloth, and ornamented with diamond-shaped silver pieces, two of which were placed on each "side of the cheek pieces, and two on the brow and nose-band.

There was no throat-latch, and I believe I have never seen any used by the Indians. The bit was a straight-armed curb of Spanish pattern, and ornamented at the extremities of the curb by pendant chains about rive inches long, to which was attached a silver plate. This swung back and forth, glittering in the sun as the pony galloped. The bridle alone was valued at thirty dollars, and, together with the saddle, would have cost sixty-five dollars.

White Bear was fifty-five years of age, and a great dandy, and very vain of his dress and ornaments. Though maimed, he was always anxious to appear to advantage in the eyes of the women.

He carried a gun of great length, and seemed to think a deal of it. This gun was protected from rain and dampness by a gaudy cover made of tanned elk hide, gorgeously beaded, and ornamented with fringe cut from buckskin.

He always carried his gun across the pummel of the saddle when riding, and the fringe was so long it hung down on each side in front of the rider's knees. These gun cases I have seen-many times among the Sioux, but had never seen as fine a one as Ma-to-sca's.

WHAT THE SQUAW SAID ABOUT HIM

I HAD often observed in the teepee of a good-natured old squaw, whom I used to visit almost every day, a warrior, whose hair was silvery white, and who was so old that no one in the village knew his age. Several of the Indians told me he was more than a hundred years old, and I would have guessed him to be over that age, so venerable was his appearance. He was a paralytic, and always lay in the same position when I entered the teepee. He never looked at me or any person in the lodge, and seemed barely alive. He could not so much as move a finger, and always lay stretched out on his back, being fed and attended by his daughter, who was the old squaw I have just mentioned.

No one seemed to pay any attention to him, everyone making the casual inquiry of "How is the old man to-day?" and the answer invariably was, "About as yesterday." Nothing could disturb the poor old fellow. Young, boisterous girls and squaws would laugh, scream, and cut up pranks in the lodge, but the old man never heeded them. He was very tall, over six feet high, I should think, but was a mere skeleton, his skin and bones being yellow and transparent. He eagerly sucked at a pipe whenever any of the company were good enough to present the end of the stem to his withered lips; but he never spoke or thanked them for what he seemed to relish so much; indeed, I believe he was never heard to speak, though he could talk when he wished to do so.

One evening some four or five girls and a couple of young warriors were with me at the old woman's lodge, and all were laughing and enjoying themselves; some of the girls quizzing the young men as to whom they liked best among the females of the village, and the warriors retorting by joking the girls. All were noisy and boisterous, never heeding the old man, who lay in one corner of the lodge. They had been laughing heartily at a remark made by the old woman, when I happened to look over to where the old man was lying, and taking pity on him, I turned to one of the young men, and asked him to let me have his pipe and kinnikinnick, and I would give the old fellow a smoke. He handed me the pipe and tobacco, and while I was cutting off some to fill the bowl,.one of the young men remarked, "I gave him a 'smoke a few minutes ago, and he cannot be very bad off." The old woman spoke up hastily, and said: "He'd smoke all the time if someone would hold a pipe, bother on him!" I filled the pipe and passed it to the young men to give-them a few puffs first, as courtesy demanded, then held it to the old man's lips, saying: "Father, here is the pipe, smoke in peace." He deigned no reply, but drew in one or two long puffs, and I saw his lips moving as if he was praying. I smoked the pipe a little to keep it lit, and put it to the old man's lips again and again, but noticed that he did not press the stem, nor draw away the smoke. Supposing he did not want to smoke anymore I went back to the company, and remarked, "We will have to finish this pipe, for the old man does not seem to want anymore." The old woman said: "You put the stem in his lips and he'll smoke any time." I replied he had smoked at first, but the last time I offered him the pipe he did not draw away any smoke. I also told them of his moving his lips as if in prayer; and, having aroused the curiosity of all, we went over to the old man's bed, and his daughter, lifting up his hand, said: "He is dead." He was, indeed, dead, having passed away without a struggle while he had been smoking.

This singular as well as unfortunate man was much reverenced in the village; and the old woman told me he had been lying as I saw him for fifteen years, having apparently lost the use of his limbs through age. She put his year at one hundred and eight.

AN ACCOMPLISHED INDIAN WIFE

AS before stated in these pages, the happy days of a Sioux woman is her childhood. When she arrives at the age of puberty she is sold to a warrior for his wife, and then her life of hardship commences. No matter how kind or loving her husband may be, his quality as a warrior, and his superiority as a man, will not permit him to depart from the old rules of the tribe, which marks the weaker, sex as the hewers of wood and drawers of water. All that is unusual for a white woman to do, the Indian wife must do. She cuts wood, butchers, dries meat, and waits on her liege lord.

The Sioux are notorious polygamists, and a warrior obtains his wife—or, more generally, another wife—by a practice as old as the Book of Genesis, that of purchase. When a young man courts a girl, and (which he seldom does) gets her to love him, he then obtains her consent, and buys her from her parents.

As a rule, when a warrior wants a wife, or an additional wife, he announces the fact to his friends, and begs them to use their influence to procure him one. When she is found, he is notified of the fact, and he then goes[t to her lodge to see her, the girl, in most cases, being ignorant of the object of his visit. She generally, however, has a suspicion, for every girl, after arriving at the age of maturity, is constantly expecting someone to come for her. After the warrior has seen his future wife, he leaves the lodge, and, if he is satisfied with her, takes an early opportunity to consult her parents, when the price to be paid for her is agreed upon. If all is satisfactory, the girl is then notified she has been sold, and is, thereafter, to be considered the wife of so and so. She immediately packs up her little keepsakes and trinkets, and, without exhibiting any emotion, such as is common to white girls, leaves her home, and goes to the lodge of her master. On entering his teepee, where he is waiting for her, he orders her to sit down on a blanket, folded up for a seat and laid on the floor, and, if she obeys, she thereby acknowledges him as her husband, and henceforth becomes his willing slave. I have read somewhere that the ancestors of many of the first families of Virginia purchased their wives from a London company for one hundred and twenty pounds of tobacco; but the Sioux pays a higher price for his wives, and takes more of them.

The usual price for an Indian girl is an American horse, or its equivalent, two ponies, four or eight blankets—indeed, anything amounting in value to one hundred dollars. A warrior sometimes falls in love with several sisters, and, in that case, buys the whole family. I once know a young man who had about a dozen horses he had captured at different times from the enemy, and who fell desperately in love with a girl of nineteen. She loved him in return, but said she could not bear to leave her tribe, and go to the Santee village, unless her two sisters, aged respectively fifteen and seventeen, went with her.

Determined to have his sweetheart, the next time the warrior visited the Yankton village he took several ponies with him, and bought all three of the girls from their parents, giving five ponies for them. A squaw wife can be sold by her husband to anyone who wishes to buy her, but at a greatly reduced price. Thirty or forty dollars is considered a large sum for a second-hand wife. The squaws are valued by the middle-aged men only for their strength and ability to work, and no account whatever is taken of personal beauty. The girls are always adepts in the art of beading and porcupine-quill embroidering, and this is often of great assistance in selling them, as most Indians like to have accomplished wives. Well indeed does the Sioux woman deserve the sympathy of every tender heart, for, from the day of her marriage until her death, she leads a most wretched life. They are more than the hewers of wood and drawers of water, for they are the servants of servants. On a winter day the Sioux mother is often obliged to travel eight or ten miles, and carry her lodge, camp-kettle, ax, child, and several small dogs on her back and head. Arriving late in the afternoon at the appointed place of camping, she clears the snow off the ground where the teepee is to be erected, and then, in the nearest grove, cuts down some poles twelve or fourteen feet in length, which she forms into a skeleton, or frame-work, for the teepee cover; she next unstraps her packs, unfolds the teepee, and brings the bottom part to the base of the poles, where she pins it fast to the earth with little wooden pins cut for the purpose.

She next obtains a long pole, fastens the small end of the young puppies are treated as tenderly as children, and, in fact, often inhabit the same wicker baskets with the children teepee cloth to it, then raises it up around the poles, pushing it to the top, and-stretching the cloth as tight as possible without pulling the pins out at the bottom. The two edges of the teepee cloth are then drawn around the poles until they meet, when a seam is formed by sewing it with little wooden pins.

This seam extends from the bottom to the top of the cover. She next goes inside the teepee, takes each pole in turn, and, raising it, pushes the butt end out as far toward the center of the lodge as the cloth will admit. When it is perfectly taut, she makes a small opening at the top for smoke to escape. This done, she rolls her baby in a robe, and leaves it in the teepee while she goes to the timber for wood. Presently she returns with about one-fourth of a cord on her back, builds a fire, and then goes for water. The camp-kettle is put on, and while it boils she cuts the meat and prepares supper. By the time the meat is done her husband arrives, jumps off his pony, goes in and sits down to rest or eat, while his wife takes off the pony's saddle and bridle, and pickets him out to graze. When supper is over she gets an ax and cuts a bundle of wood for the night. This done, if she receives no further orders from her husband, she nourishes her child, and sits down silent and tried to doze away an hour or two until her master goes to sleep, when, having assured herself that he is asleep, she folds her babe to her bosom, and, drawing her blankets around her, lies down for a few hours' repose, only to wake to repeat her round of toil on the morrow.

The Sioux wife is subject to all the whims and caprices of her husband, and woe be to her if he is a bad-tempered man. So severe is their treatment of women, a happy female face is hardly ever seen in the Sioux nation, and the few met with belong to single women.

Often they become callous, and take a beating much as a horse or ox does; but sometimes one of the more spirited women rebels against the cruel treatment of her husband, and resorts to suicide to put an end to her sufferings. An incident occurred some years ago at a lodge which was pitched at the mouth of the St. Croix River, which will serve to show the desperation to which Indian women are sometimes driven.

A warrior was continually drunk whenever he could get any liquor, and he was seldom without it, often keeping a keg in his lodge. Whenever he drank he was very abusive to his wife, often beating her and her children unmercifully. One day he went hunting, and, while he was gone, the poor woman hid the keg of liquor, and upon his return he could not find it. He demanded to know where it was, but she refused to tell him, when he beat her cruelly, and so distressed was she that she went to a grove of timber nearby and hung herself with a lariat rope.

Suicide is very common among Indian women, and considering the treatment they receive, it is a wonder there is not more of it.

THE FIRST NEBRASKA CAVALRY—COL. BROWN'S EXPEDITION

WE had heard occasionally of the great war being waged for the Union, but had received no very definite information until one evening, an Indian, who had been far down the Missouri, at one of the forts, came into camp, and brought the intelligence that the rebels were gaining victory after victory, and that all the soldiers were leaving the plains and going east to help fight the rebels. The Indian also said the Government was going to raise volunteer troops on the border to replace the regular soldiers who were going east, and many Omaha, Winnebago, and Pawnee Indians were joining the whites at the forts. I cannot describe how these tidings affected me. I could not sleep, and all night long walked up and down the camp. Next morning my mind was thoroughly made up to return to the east and help fight for the Union. Ordering my squaws to pack up the lodge, we at once set out down the Missouri. After many days patient journeying we arrived at Fort Randall, and there, bidding my squaws good-by, I left them to make their way with my property to their tribe, which was not far distant, while I continued my journey alone to Omaha.

On arriving at Omaha I learned a mounted regiment was being fitted out for service on the frontier, and presenting myself, was duly enrolled a soldier of the United States army in the First Nebraska Cavalry.* The Indians, under the celebrated Sioux chief, Spotted Tail, had become very troublesome, and our regiment was ordered to join the expedition of Col. Brown, then rendezvousing near North Platte, on the Platte River; The expedition consisted of the First Nebraska Cavalry, Twelfth Missouri Cavalry, and a detachment of the Second United States, and Seventh Iowa Cavalry—Col. Brown, the senior officer, commanding the whole force.

Records show Belden serving with the First and Second Nebraska Cavalry.—Ed. 2015

The snow was quite deep on the plains, and knowing that the hostile Indians, who were then encamped on the Republican River, were encumbered by their villages, women, and children, it was thought to be a favorable time to strike them a severe blow. There were many Indians in our command, among others a large body of Pawnee scouts. Early in January the expedition left the Platte River, and marched southward toward the Republican. When we reached the river a depot of supplies was established and named "Camp Wheaton," after the general then commanding the department of the Platte. This done, the scouting began, and we were ready for war. Nor were we long kept waiting, for Lieut. James Murie, who marched out to Short Nose Creek with a party of scouts, was suddenly attacked by a large body of Sioux, and six of his men wounded. Col. Brown considered this an unfortunate affair, inasmuch as the Indians, having learned by it the presence of troops in their country, would be on the alert, and, in all probability, at once clear out with their villages. He determined, if it were possible, still to surprise them, and ordered the command immediately into the saddle. We pushed hard for Solomon's Fork, a great resort for the savages, but arrived only in time to find their camps deserted and the Indians all gone.

One evening, as we were encamped on the banks of the Solomon, a huge buffalo bull suddenly appeared on the bluff overlooking the camp, and gazed in wonder at a sight so unusual to his eyes. In a moment a dozen guns were ready to fire, but as the beast came down the narrow ravine washed by the rains in the bluff, all waited until he should emerge on the open plain near the river. Then a lively skirmish was opened on him, and he turned and quickly disappeared again in the gulch. Several of the soldiers ran up one of the narrow watercourses, hoping to get a shot at him as he emerged on the open prairie. What was their surprise to meet him coming down. He ran up one ravine, and being half crazed by his wounds, had, on reaching the prairie, turned into the one in which the soldiers were. As soon as he saw him, the soldier in front called out to those behind him to run, but they, not under-standing the nature of the danger, continued to block up the passage. The bull could barely force his great body between the high and narrow banks; but before all the soldiers could get out of the ravine, he was upon them, and trampled two of them under his feet, not hurting them much, but frightening them terribly. As the beast came out again on the open bank of the river a score of soldiers, who had run over from the camp with their guns, gave him a dozen balls. Still he did not fall, but, dashing through the brush, entered the cavalry camp, and running up to a large gray horse that was tied to a tree, lifted the poor brute on his horns and threw him into the air. The horse was completely disemboweled, and dropped down dead. The buffalo next plunged his horns into a fine bay horse, the property of an officer in the Seventh Iowa Cavalry, and the poor fellow groaned with pain until the hills resounded. Exhausted by his exertions and wounds, the bull laid down carefully by the side of the horse, as if afraid of hurting himself, and in a moment rolled over dead. We skinned and dressed him, and carried the meat into camp for our suppers; but it was dearly bought beef, at the expense of the lives of two noble horses; and Col. Brown notified us he wished no further contracts closed on such expensive terms.

A RACE FOR LIFE

WHILE we lay encamped at the depot of supplies, on the Republican, Colonel Brown called for volunteer scouts, stating he would give a purse of five hundred dollars to anyone who would discover a village of Indians and lead the command to the spot. This glittering prize dazzled the eyes of many a soldier, but few had the courage to undertake so hazardous an enterprise. Sergeant Hiles, of the First Nebraska, and Sergeant Rolla, of the Seventh Iowa, came forward and said they would go upon the expedition provided they could go alone. Both were shrewd, sharp men, and Colonel Brown readily gave his consent, well knowing that in scouting, where the object is not to fight, but to gain information and keep concealed, the fewer men in the party the better their chances of escape.

On the day after Hiles and Rolla had left camp, Nelson, who had come down and joined the army as a guide, proposed to me that we should go out and hunt an adventure. My old love of Indian life was upon me, and I joyfully accepted his proposition. I applied to Colonel Brown for permission to set out at once, but he declined to grant my request, on the ground that it was not necessary or proper for an officer to engage in such an enterprise. I, however, coaxed the colonel a little, and he finally told me I might go.

Packing several days supplies on a mule, as soon as it was dark Nelson and I started, he leading the mule, and I driving him from behind. We traveled over to the Little Beaver, then up the stream for some distance, when we crossed over and camped on Little Beaver. Here we expected to find Indian signs, but were disappointed. We rested for a short time, and then traveled down the Beaver until opposite Short Nose Creek, when we crossed the divide and camped on that stream. Two days later we pushed on to Cedar Creek, and then crossed over to Prairie Dog Creek. We had traveled only at night, hiding away all day in the brush that lined the creeks, and keeping a sharp lookout for Indians. So far we had seen no Indian signs, and began to despair of finding any, when one morning, just as I was lighting the fire to cook our breakfast, I heard several shots fired, apparently four or five miles up the creek. Nelson run out on the bluff, and, applying his ear to the ground, said he could distinctly hear the reports of many rifles. We could not imagine what this meant, and withdrew into the bluffs to "make it out," as the old trappers say.

Nelson was the first speaker, and he gave it as his opinion that Colonel Brown, who had told us before leaving camp he would soon start for the Solomon, had set out earlier than he expected, and was now crossing above us. I set my compass, and, finding we were nearly on the line where Brown would cross, readily fell in with Nelson's reasoning. So sure was that the guns we had heard were Colonel Brown's soldiers out hunting, that I proposed we should saddle up and go to them This move came near proving fatal to us, as will presently appear. We rode boldly up the stream, in broad daylight, some five miles, when, not finding any trail, I began to express my surprise at the long distance we had heard the reports of the guns; but Nelson told me it was no uncommon thing, when snow was on the ground, to hear a rifle shot ten to twenty miles along a creek bottom, and, incredible as this may seem, I found out afterward it was nevertheless true.

We rode on about five miles further, when suddenly Nelson halted, and, pointing to an object a long distance ahead, said he believed it was a horseman. We lost no time in getting into the bluffs, where we could observe what went on without being seen, and soon saw an animal coming rapidly down the creek bottom. As it drew near, we discovered it to be a horse, evidently much frightened, and flying from pursuers. The horse galloped past, but stopped half-'a mile below us and quietly went to grazing, every now and then raising his head and looking up the creek, as if he expected to see some enemy following him. We lay for several hours momentarily expecting to see a body of Indians coming down the creek, but none came, and at noon Nelson said I should watch, and he would crawl down the creek and see if he could discover anything from the horse. I saw Nelson approach quite near the animal, and heard him calling it, when, to my surprise, it came up to him and followed him into the bluffs. The horse was the one Sergeant Hiles had ridden from the camp a few days previous, and was well-known to Nelson and me as a superb animal, named "Selim."

It did not take us long to come to the conclusion that Hiles and Rolla had been attacked, and that the firing we had heard in the morning was done by Indians. From the fact that Hiles's horse had no saddle on when found, we concluded he had been in the hands of the Indians, and probably broken away from them, and we doubted not that at least Hiles was dead.

Fearing the savages would come down upon us next, we lost no time in getting down the creek. We soon passed where we had encamped the night before, and, finding the fire still burning, put it out, and, covering up the ashes, pushed on for several miles and camped among the bluffs. Nelson carried up several logs from the creek, with which to make a barricade in case of attack, and, Nelson taking the first watch, I laid down to sleep, without fire or dipper, except a piece of raw pork.

At nine o'clock I arose to watch, and soon after midnight, the moon coming up bright and clear, I awoke Nelson, and suggested to him we would saddle up and cross over to Cedar Creek, for I had a strong presentiment that some misfortune would befall, us if we remained longer where we were. It is not a little singular, but true, that man has a wonderful instinct, and can nearly always divine coming trouble or danger. This instinct in the frontiersman, of course, is wonderfully developed by the perilous life he leads; but, call it presentiment or what you will, this instinct exists' in every beast of the field, as well as in the human breast, and he who follows it can have no safer guide. Several times have I saved my life by obeying the dictates of that silent monitor within, which told me to go, and yet gave no reason for my going.

We had not ridden far when we came upon a heavy Indian trail, and found it not more than four or five hours old. The tracks showed some fifty ponies and all going in the direction of the Republican. We were now convinced that Rolla had escaped and the Indians were pursuing him. Following on the trail for some distance, until we came to a hare spot on the bluff where our horses would leave no tracks in the snow, we turned to the left, and, whipping up the ponies, struck out for a forced march. We knew the Indians might return at any moment, and if they should find our trail they would follow us like blood-hounds.

All night long we pushed on, halting only at sunrise to eat a bite and give our poor ponies a few mouthfuls of grass. Again we were off, and throughout the day whipped and spurred along our animals as rapidly as possible. At night we halted for two hours to rest, and then mounted the saddle once more. On the fifth day we met a company of cavalry that had been sent out by Col. Brown to look for us, and with them we returned to camp.

We learned from the cavalrymen that Sergeant Hiles had been attacked by Indians, and Sergeant Rolla had been killed. Hiles, though he had lost his horse, had managed to work his way back to camp on foot, where he had arrived the morning they left camp, nearly starved. We had gone much out of our way to escape the Indians who had followed Hiles; but since we had succeeded in avoiding them and saving our scalps, we did not care a fig for our long and tiresome journey.

Sergeant Hiles related to me his adventures after leaving camp, and I will here repeat them as a sequel to my own. He said: "Rolla and I traveled several days, and finally pulled up on Prairie Dog Creek. We had seen no Indians, and were becoming careless, believing there were none in the country. One morning just about day-break I built a fire, and while Rolla and I were warming ourselves we were fired upon by some forty Indians. Rolla fell, pierced through the heart, and died instantly. How I escaped I know not, for the balls whistled all around me, knocking up the fire, and even piercing my clothing, yet I was not so much as scratched.

"I ran to my horse, which was saddled and tied nearby, and flinging myself on his back, dashed across the prairies The Indians followed, whooping and yelling like devils, and although their ponies ran well, they could not overtake my swift-footed Selim. I had got well ahead of them, and was congratulating myself on my escape from a terrible death, when suddenly Selim fell headlong into a ravine that was filled with drifted snow. It was in vain I tried to extricate him; the more he struggled the deeper he sank. Knowing the Indians would be up in a few minutes, I cut the saddle-girths with my knife that the horse might be freer in his movements, and then, bidding him lie still, I took my pistols and burrowed into the snow beside him. After I had dug down a little way, I struck off in the drift, and worked my way along it toward the valley. I had not tunneled far before I heard the Indians coming, and, pushing up my head, I cut a small hole in the crust of the snow, so I could peep out. As the-savages came up they began to yell, and Selim, making-a great bound, leaped upon the solid earth at the edge of the ravine, and dragging himself out of the drift, galloped furiously across the prairies. Oh! how I wished then I was on his back, for I knew the noble fellow would soon bear me out of reach of all danger.

"The Indians divided, part of them going up the ravine and crossing over to pursue Selim, while the rest dismounted to look for his rider. They carefully examined the ground all around to find my trail, but not finding any they returned and searched up and down the ravine for me. Two or three times they punched in the snow near me, and once an Indian passed within a few feet of my hole. Great drops of perspiration stood on my forehead, and every moment I expected to be discovered, dragged out, and scalped, but I remained perfectly still, grasping my pistols, and determined to sell my life as dearly as possible, and make it cost the red-skins at least three of their number.

"After awhile the Indians got tired searching for me, and drew off to consult. I saw the party that had gone in pursuit of Selim rejoin their companions, and I was not a little gratified to observe they did not bring back my gallant steed with them, from which I knew he had made his escape.

"The Indians mounted and rode down the ravine, examining every inch of ground for my trail. As I saw them move off hope once more revived in my breast; but in an hour they came back and again searched the drift. At last, however, they went off without finding me, and I lay down to rest, so exhausted was I, from watching and excitement, that I could not stand. I knew I did not dare to sleep, for it was very cold, and a stupor would come upon me. All that day and night and the next day I lay in the drift, for I knew the Indians were watching it.

"On the second night, as soon as it was dark, I crawled out, and worked my way to the foot of the ravine. At first I was so stiff and numb I could hardly move hand or foot, but as I crawled along the blood began to warm up, and soon I was able to walk. I crept cautiously along the bluffs until I had cleared the ravine, and then, striking out on the open prairie, steered to the northward. Fortunately, the first day out I shot an antelope and got some raw meat, which kept me from starving. In two days and a half I reached the camp, nearly dead from fatigue and hunger, and was thoroughly glad to be at home in my tent once more with a whole scalp on my head."

We had not found an Indian village, and none of us got the $500, but we had all had a glorious adventure, and that to a t frontiersman is better than money.

THE LOST TRAIL

WHILE we lay in camp on Medicine Creek, Colonel Brown sent for me, and ordered me to look up and map the country. I was detached as a topographical engineer, and this order, relieved me from all company duty, and enabled me to go wherever I pleased, which was not a little gratifying to one so fond of rambling about.

Packing my traps on my pony one day, I set out down the Medicine ahead of the command, intending to hunt wild turkeys until near night, and then rejoin the command before it went into camp. The creek bottom was alive with turkeys, the cold weather having driven them to take shelter among the bushes that lined the creek. I had not gone far when a dense fog arose, shutting out all objects, even at the distance of a few feet. It was a bad day for hunting, but presently as I rode along! heard a turkey gobble close by, and, dismounting, I crept through the bushes and peered into the fog as well as I could. I saw several dark objects, and drawing up my double-barreled shot-gun, fired at them. Hardly had the noise of the explosion died away, when I heard a great flopping in the bushes, and on going up to it found a large turkey making his last kicks. I picked him up and was about to turn away, when I saw another fine old gobbler desperately wounded, but trying to crawl off. I ran after him, but he hopped along so fast I was obliged to give him the contents of my other barrel to keep him from getting away into the thick brush.

I had now two fine turkeys, and, as the day was bad, determined to go no farther, but ascend the bluffs and-wait for the command. I went out on the prairie, and made a diligent search for the old trail, but, as it was covered some seven inches deep with snow, I could not find it. Knowing the command would pass near the creek, I went back to hunt, thinking I would go up after it had passed, strike the trail, and follow it into camp.

I had not gone far down the creek when I ran into a fine elk, and knocked him over with my Henry rifle. I cut off the choice pieces, and, packing them on my pony, once more set out to find the trail. I knew the command had not passed, and ascended the highest point on the bluff, straining my eyes to see if I could not discover it moving. I waited several hours, but not finding it, I concluded it had not marched by the old trail, but struck straight across the country. I now moved up the creek, determined to keep along its bank until I came to the old camp, and then follow the trail. I had not gene far when I came upon two Indians who belonged to my company, and who were also looking for the command.

Night was coming on, the wind rising, and the air growing bitter cold, so I said to the Indians we would go down the creek where there was plenty of dry wood, and make a night camp. They readily assented, and, we set out, arriving at a fine grove just before dark.

While one of the Indians gathered wood, the other one and I cleared away the snow to make, a place for our camp. The snow in the bottom was nearly three feet deep, and when we had bared the ground a high wall was piled up all around us. The wood was soon brought, and a bright fire blazing. After warming ourselves we opened a passage through the snow for a short distance, and, clearing another spot, led our horses into this most perishable of stables. Our next care was to get them some cottonwood limbs to eat, and then we gathered small dry limbs and made a bedstead of them on which to spread our blankets. Piling on more wood until the fire roared and cracked, we sat down in the heat of the blaze, feeling quite comfortable, except, that we were desperately hungry. Some coals were raked out, the neck of the elk cut off and spitted on a stick to roast. When it was done we divided it, and, sprinkling it with a little pepper and salt from our haversacks, had .as savory and wholesome a repast as any epicure might desire. After supper, hearing the coyotes howling in the woods below, I had the Indians bring in my saddle, to which was strapped the elk meat, and, cutting the limb off a tree close by the fire, we lifted the saddle astride of the stump so high up that the wolves could not reach it. All being now in readiness for the night, we filled our pipes and sat down to smoke and talk.

The Indians often feed their horses on cottonwood limbs. Officers on the plains give their horses cottonwood to eat when they can get no feed or grass, and say the bark of the cottonwood is almost as nutritious as hay.

A horse will chew up limbs as thick as a man's thumb, and in winter time eat the bark off every cottonwood tree he can reach.—Note in original

At nine o'clock the Indians replenished the fire, and, feeling sleepy, I wrapped myself in my blankets and lay down to rest. I soon fell asleep, and slept well until near midnight, when I was awakened by the snapping and snarling of the wolves near the fire. The wood had burned down to a bed of coals, and gave but a faint light, but I could see a dozen pair of red eyes glaring at me over the edge of the snow-bank. The Indians were sound asleep, and, knowing they were very tired, I did not awake them, but got my gun, and, wrapping myself in my blankets, sat up by the fire to watch the varmints and warm my feet. Presently I heard a long wild howl down in the woods, and knew by the "whirr-ree, whirr-ree" in it that it proceeded from the throat of the dreaded buffalo wolf, or Kosh-e-nee, of the prairies. There was another howl, then another, and another, and, finally, a loud chorus of a dozen. Instantly silence fell among the coyotes, and they began to scatter. For a time all was quiet, and I had begun to doze, when suddenly the coals flew all over me, and I opened my eyes just in time to see a great gray wolf spring out of the fire and bound up the snow-bank. I leaped to my feet and peered into the darkness, where I could see scores of dark shadows moving about, and a black cluster gathered under my saddle. I called the Indians, who quietly and nimbly jumped to their feet, and came forward armed with their revolvers. I told them what had happened, and that we were surrounded by a large pack of gray wolves. We had no fear for ourselves, but felt uneasy lest they might attack our horses, who were pawing and snorting with alarm. I spoke to them kindly, and they immediately became quiet. At the suggestion of the Indians I brought forward my revolvers, and we all sat down to watch the varmints, and see what they would do.

In a few minutes, a pair of fiery, red eyes, looked down at us from the snow-bank; then, another and another pair, until there were a dozen. We sat perfectly still, and presently one great gray wolf gathered himself, and made a leap for the elk-meat on the saddle. He nearly touched it with his nose, but failed to secure the coveted prize, and fell headlong into the fire. We fired two shots into him, and he lay still until one of the Indians pulled him out to keep his hair from burning and making a disagreeable smell. In about five minutes, another wolf leaped at the elk-meat and fell at our feet. We dispatched him as we had done the first one,, and then threw him across the body of his dead brother. So we kept on firing until we had killed eighty wolves, when, tired of killing the brutes with pistols, I brought out my double-barreled shot gun, and loading each barrel with nine buck-shot, waited until they were gathered thick under the tree on which hung my meat, and then let them have it. Every discharge caused some to tumble down, and sent the rest scampering and howling to the rear. Presently they became more wary, and I had to fire at them at long range.

The Indians now went out and gathered some dry limbs, and we kindled up a bright fire. Next we threw the carcasses of the nine dead wolves, that were in our camp, over the snow-bank, and knowing that the beasts would not come near our bright fire, two of us lay down to sleep, while the third remained up to watch and keep the fire burning.

The coyotes now returned, and with unearthly yells, attacked their dead-betters, snapping, snarling, and quarreling over their carcasses as they tore the flesh and crunched the bones of the dead wolves.

We rose at daylight, and, through the dim light, could see the coyotes trotting off to the swamp, while near the camp lay heads, legs, and piles of cleanly licked bones, all that was left of the gray wolves we had killed.

After breakfast, we set out to find the command, striking across the country, expecting to come upon the trail. We traveled all day, however, and saw no trail. At night we camped out again, and were scarcely in camp, when we again heard the wolves howling all around us. They had followed us all day, no doubt expecting another repast, such as had been served to them the night before. We, however, kept a bright fire burning, and no gray wolves came about; so the coyotes were disappointed, and vented their disappointment all night long in the most dismal howls I ever heard. At times, it seemed as though there were five hundred of them, and joining their voices in chorus, they would send up a volume of sound that resembled the roar of a tempest, or the discordant singing of a vast multitude of people.

While we cooked breakfast, a strong picket of wolves, watched all around the camp, feasting their greedy eyes from a distance on my elk-meat. When we started from camp, a hundred or more of them followed us, often coming quite close to the pack-pony, and biting and quarreling about the elk that was never to be their meat. When we halted, they would halt, and sitting down, loll out their red tongues and lick the snow. At length, I took my shot-gun, and loading the barrels, fired into the thickest of the pack. Two or three were wounded, and no sooner did their companions discover that they were bleeding and disabled, than they fell upon them, tore them to pieces, and devoured every morsel of their flesh. I had seen men who would .do the same thing with their fellows, but until I witnessed the contrary with my own eyes, I had supposed this practice was confined to the superior brute creation.

The third day out, finding no trace of the command, we concluded to go back to the Medicine and seek the old camp, from which place we could take the trail and follow up until we came upon it. We reached the Medicine at sun-down, and there, to our satisfaction, found the troops still in camp, where we had left them, they not having marched in consequence of the cold and foggy weather.

I was soon in my own tent and sound asleep, being thoroughly worn out with the exposure and fatigue of my long journey.

A NICE OCCUPATION FOR A U.S. OFFICER

IT WAS sent down from Camp Cottonwood (now Fort McPherson), with thirty men, to Gilman's Ranch, fifteen miles east of Cottonwood on the Platte, where I was to remain, guard the ranch, and furnish guards to Ben Holliday's overland stage coaches. In those days, Gilman's was an important place, and in earlier times, had been a great trading point for the Sioux. Two or three trails led from the Republican to this place, and every winter the Sioux had come in with their ponies loaded down with buffalo, beaver, elk, and deer skins, which they exchanged with the traders at Gilman's. War had, however, put a stop to these peaceful pursuits; still the Sioux could not give up the habit of traveling these favorite trails. The ponies often come in from the Republican, not now laden with furs and robes, but each bearing a load of beastiality called a Sioux warrior. The overland coaches offered a great temptation to the cupidity and vices of the Sioux, and they were not slow to avail themselves of any opportunity to attack them. The coaches carrier! the mails and much treasure, and if the savages could now and then succeed in capturing one, they got money, jewels, scalps, horses, and not unfrequently white women, as a reward for their enterprise.

Troops were stationed in small squads at every station, about ten miles apart, and they rode from station to station on the top of all coaches, holding their guns ever ready for action. It was not pleasant, this sitting perched up on top of a coach, riding through dark ravines and tall grass, in which savages were ever lurking. Generally, the first fire from the Indians killed one or two horses, and tumbled a soldier or two off the top of the coach. This setting one's self up as a sort of target was a disagreeable and dangerous duty, but the soldiers performed it without murmuring. My squad had to ride up to Cottonwood, and down to the station below, where they waited for the next coach going the other way and returned by it to their post at Gilman's. All the other stations were guarded in like manner; so it happened that every coach carried some soldiers.

One evening I found my pony missing, and thinking he had strayed off but a short distance, I buckled on my revolvers and went out to look for him. I had not intended to go far, but not finding-him, I walked on, and on, until I found myself some four miles from the ranch. Alarmed at my indiscretion, for I knew the country was full of Indians, I hastily set out to return, and as it was now growing dark, I determined to go up a ravine that led to the post by a nearer route than the trail. I had got nearly to the end of the ravine, where the stage-road crossed it, and was about to turn out into the road when, on looking up the bank, I saw on the crest of the slope, some dark objects. Ai first, I thought they were ponies, for they were moving on all fours, and directly toward the road. I ran up the bank, and had not gone more than ten yards, when I heard voices, and looking round, saw within a dozen steps of me, five or six Indians lying on the grass, and talking in low tones. They had noticed me, but evidently thought I was one of their own number. Divining the situation in a moment, I walked carelessly on until near the crest of the hill, where I suddenly came upon a dozen more Indians, crawling along on their hands and knees. One of them gruffly ordered me down, and I am sure I lost no time in dropping into the grass. Crawling carefully along, for I knew it would not do to stop, I still managed to keep a good way behind and off to one side. We at last reached the road, and the Indians, gun in hand, took up their position in the long grass close by the road-side. I knew the up-coach would be due at the station in half an hour, and I. now found myself in the unpleasant position of waylaying one of the very coaches I had been sent to guard. Perhaps, one of my own soldiers coming up on the coach would kill me, and then what would people say? how would my presence with the Indians be explained? and how would it sound to have the newspapers publish, far and near, that an officer of the United States army had deserted his post, joined the Indians, and attached a stage-coach? However, there was no help for it, and I lay still waiting for developments. It was now time for the coach, and we watched the road with straining eyes. Two or three times I thought I heard the rumbling of the wheels, and a tremor seized me, but it was only the wind rustling the tall grass. An hour went by, and still no coach, when the Indians, becoming uneasy—one who seemed to be the leader of the expedition, rose up, and motioning the others to follow him—started off down the hill toward the ravine. I made a motion 20 as if getting up, and seeing the Indians backs turned, dropped flat on my face and lay perfectly still. Slowly their footsteps faded away, and raising my head, I saw them mount their ponies and disappear, over the neighboring hill, as if going down the road to meet the coach.

As soon as they were out of sight, I sprang up and ran as fast as I could to the ranch when, relating what had happened, I started with some soldiers and citizens down the road to meet the stage. We had not gone far when we heard it coming up,-and on reaching it, found it had been attacked by Indians a few miles below, one passenger killed and two severely wounded. The coach had but three horses, one having been killed in the fight. The Indians had dashed at the coach mounted, hoping to kill the horses, and thus cut off all means of retreat or flight, but they had only succeeded in killing one horse, when the passengers and soldiers had driven them off, compelling them to carry two of their number with them, dead or desperately wounded.

I was more careful after that, when I went out hunting ponies, and never tried again to waylay a coach with Indians.

AN UNPLEASANT REQUEST

AMONG the soldiers stationed at Gilman's Ranch, were a number of Omaha and Winnebago Indians, who belonged to my company, in the First Nebraska Cavalry. I had done all I could to teach them the ways of civilization, but despite my instructions, and their utmost endeavors to give over their wild and barbarous practices, every now and then old habits would become too strong upon them to be borne, and they would indulge in the savage customs of their youth. At such times they would throw aside their uniforms, and, wrapping a blanket about them, sing and dance for hours.

One evening they were in a particularly jolly mood, and having obtained permission to have a dance, went out in front of the building, and for want of a better scalp-pole, assembled around one pf the telegraph poles. One fellow pounded lustily on a piece of leather nailed over the mouth of a keg, while the others hopped around in a circle, first upon cue leg, then the other, shaking oyster-cans over their heads, that had been filled with pebbles, and keeping time to the rude music, with a sort of guttural song. Now it would be low and slow, and the dancers barely move, then, increasing in volume and rapidity, it would become wild and vociferous, the dancers walking very fast, much as the negroes do in their "walk-arounds." We had had all manner of dances and songs, and enough drumming and howling to have made anyone .tired, still the Indians seemed only warming up to their work. The savage frenzy was upon them, and I let them alone until near midnight. Their own songs and dances becoming tiresome, I asked them to give me some Sioux songs, for I had been thinking all the evening of the village up the Missouri and my squaws. The Indians immediately struck up a Sioux war song, accompanying it with the war dance.

All the Indian songs and dances are terminated with a jump, and a sort of wild yell or whoop. When they had danced the Sioux war song, and ended it with the usual whoop, what was our surprise to hear the cry answered back at no great distance, out on the prairie. At first I thought it was the echo, but Springer, a half-breed Indian, assured me what I had heard was the cry of other Indians. To satisfy

217

myself, I bade the Indians repeat the song and dance, and this time, sure enough, when it was ended the whoop was answered quite near the ranch. I went inside, lest my uniform could be seen, and Celling Springer to continue the dance, I went to a back window and looked out, in the direction from which the sound appeared to come.

The moon was just rising, and I could distinctly see three Indian warriors sitting on their ponies, within a few hundred paces of the house. They seemed to be intently watching what was going on, and were by no means certain as to the character of the performers or performance. At a glance, I made them out to be our deadly enemies, the Ogallala Sioux, and determined to catch them. I quickly called Springer, and bid him kindle a small fire, and tell the Indians to strike up the death song and scalp dance of the Sioux. This, as I expected, at once reassured the strange warriors, and, riding up quite close, they asked Springer, who was not dancing, and who had purposely put himself in their way,

"What are you dancing for?"

"Dancing the scalps of four white soldiers we have killed," replied Springer.

"How did you kill them," inquired the foremost Indian warrior.

"You see," said Springer, who, being part Sioux, spoke the language perfectly, "we were coming down from the Yeobarrah, and going over to the Republican to see Spotted Tail and our friends the Ogallalas, when some soldiers fired on us here, and seeing there were but four of them, we attacked and killed them all. They are now lying dead inside," added Springer; "come, get down and help dance their scalps."

Two of the warriors immediately dismounted, giving their ponies to the third one to hold, who remained mounted. Springer seemed to take no notice of this, but leading the warriors up to the dance, joined in with them, the other Indians making room in the circle for the new-comers.

When the dance was ended, Springer said, "Come, let us bring out the scalps," and turning to the two Indians, inquired, "Will you look at the bodies?" About half the Indians had already gone into the ranch, under pretense of getting the scalps, and the two Sioux walked in with Springer, apparently without suspicion that anything was wrong.

As soon as they had crossed the threshold the door was closed behind them, and two burly Omahas placed their backs against it. If was entirely dark in the ranch, and Springer proceeded to strike a light. When the blaze of the dry grass flared up it revealed everything in the room, and there stood the two Sioux, surrounded by Omahas, and a dozen revolvers leveled at their heads.

Never shall I forget the yell of rage and terror they set up, when they found they were entrapped. The Sioux warrior outside, who was holding the ponies, heard it, and plunging his heels into the sides of his pony, made off as fast as he could. Notwithstanding my men fired a dozen shots at him, he got off safely, and carried away with him all three of the ponies.

The two Sioux in the ranch were bound hand and foot, and laid in one corner of the room; then my Indians returned to the telegraph pole to finish their dance. Feeling tired, I lay down and feel asleep.

Near morning I was awakened by most unearthly yells, and looking out, saw my Indians leaping, dancing, and yelling around the telegraph pole, where they now had a large fire burning. Presently Springer came in and said the Indians wanted the prisoners. I told him they could not have them, and that in the morning I would send them to Col. Brown at McPherson, as was my duty. Springer, who was a noncommissioned officer, communicated this message to the Indians, when the yelling and howling redoubled. In a short time Springer came in again, and said he could do nothing with the Indians, and that they were determined to have the prisoners, at the same time advising me to give them up. I again refused, when the Indians rushed into the ranch, and, seizing the prisoners, dragged them out. Seeing they were frenzied I made no resistance, but followed them closely, keeping concealed, however.

They took the Sioux to an island on the Platte, below the ranch, and there, tying them to a tree, gathered a pile of wood and set it on fire. Then they thrust faggots against the naked bodies of the prisoners, stuck their knives into their legs, arms, and finally into their bowels. They next cut off their ears and noses, and then their hands, after which they scalped and disemboweled them. The Sioux uttered not a complaint, but endured all their sufferings with that stoicism for which the Indian is so justly celebrated, and which belongs to no other race in the world.

Sick at heart, I crept back to the ranch and went to bed, leaving the Indians engaged in a furious scalp dance, and whirling the bloody scalps of the Sioux over their heads, with long poles to which they had them fastened.

Next morning, when I awoke, I found .the Indians wrapped in their blankets, and lying asleep all around me. The excitement of the night had passed off, and brought its corresponding depression. They were very docile and stupid, and it was with some difficulty I could arouse them for the duties of the day. I asked several of them what had become of the Sioux prisoners, but could get no other answer than, "Guess him must have got away."

I was sorely tempted to report the affair to the commanding officer at Fort McPherson, and have the Indians punished, but believing it would do more good in the end to be silent, I said nothing about it. After all, the Omahas and Winnebagoes had treated the Sioux just as the Sioux would have treated them, had they been captured, and so, it being a matter altogether among savages, I let it rest where it belonged.

MY INDIAN SOLDIERS

IT WAS for a time, in 1865, on duty at Fort Cottonwood, Nebraska, as adjutant of my regiment, the First Nebraska Vol. Cavalry, when the scarcity of officers at the post made it necessary for the commanding officer to detail me, with thirty Indian soldiers, to proceed to, and garrison Jack Morrow's ranch, twelve miles west of the fort, on the south side of the Platte River. The Sioux were very hostile then, and it was an ordinary occurrence for ranches to be burned and the owners killed.

Morrow's ranch, unlike the little, low, adobe ranches everywhere seen, was a large three-story building, with outbuildings adjacent, and a fine large stable for stock, the whole being well surrounded by a commodious stockade of cedar palisades, set deep in the ground, and projecting to the height of about ten or twelve feet above the surface.

Upon arriving at the ranch, late at night, my usually noisy Indians were quietly sleeping in the huge ox-wagons, which had been provided for transportation. I found the front of the ranch lit up by fires built between the stockade and the buildings on a narrow strip of ground, serving for a front yard. I had been informed by the commanding officer at Cottonwood, that Mr. Morrow was not living at his ranch, but was away, East, and the object in sending me there was to prevent the Indians from burning so valuable a property. I was not prepared to find a party encamped at the ranch, and not knowing but that they might be Indians, waiting in so favorable a spot to waylay travelers or emigrants passing the road in front of the stockade, I told my drivers to halt their teams, and, quietly awakening my Indians, I bade them be in readiness to rush up if I should give them a signal by yelling, but to remain in the wagons until I called them, and to make no noise. I then quietly rode forward to reconnoiter, and as the stockade timbers were set very close together, I had to crawl up to the loop-holes cut in the timbers to see what was going on inside. Standing on the ground, and holding my pony's nose with my hand to keep him quiet, I stood on my tip-toes, and could see through one of the loop-holes, a curious sight, but one natural enough on the frontier.

Grouped around three small fires, built close to the front of the ranch, sat some ten or twelve browned and weather-beaten men, whose hair hung to their shoulders, and each one of whom wore a slouched hat, a pair of revolvers, and a good stout knife, the inseparable companions of a western prairie man. All were intent on eating supper of fried bacon, slapjacks, and coffee.

They had no guard, doubtless feeling secure in their number and means of defense, against any Indian attack that might be made. "Hello!" I shouted, "have you got supper enough for one more?" "Yes if you are white or red; but if black, no," was answered back, with an invitation "to show" myself. I led the pony across the narrow trench which ran around the stockade, and, mounting him, rode into the yard. As I approached the party I overheard remarks, such as, "An army cuss;" "One of those little stuck-up officers. But not appearing to have heard them, I got down, and asked what party they were. "Wood-haulers," they replied; "taking building logs down the road;" followed by "Who are you, and where are you going this late at night?" I told them who I was, and that I had now finished my journey, as I intended to stop there. I was immediately informed in a curt manner that they guessed it was rather "mixed" about staying there, if I had any stock along, for the stables were full, and the ranch, too; and they had no room for any additional people or stock. I told them that I had two teams standing outside and that it was my intention to put the mules and my pony in the stable; and if there was no room there, I should make room by turning out some of their animals. To this I was plainly told that I could .neither turn a mule out or put an animal in, nor could I remain at the ranch, which they had occupied for their own quarters, Jack Morrow having left and gone East, probably never to return. They said they were a little stronger in numbers than myself and my two drivers, and I must move on or they would make me. I told them that I was a United States officer, acting under orders, and that it would be an easy matter for me to ride back to Cottonwood and get men enough to enforce my orders .unless they submitted. Several of the rough-looking fellows said that they each carried good revolvers, and that it was an easy matter to stop me if I attempted to return to Cottonwood, and swore they would do so. I remained quiet for a moment, and the leader of the party, looking at me, asked: "What are you going to do about it?" "I am going to open the stables and put my animals in shelter," I replied at the same time mounting my pony and riding out to the stables, a short distance in front of which stood my teams. Several of the frontiersmen got up, and, without saying a word, walked to the stables, and went up close to the doors. I ordered the teamsters to drive to the stables, unharness from the heavy ox-wagons, place their teams inside, and if they could not find vacant stalls enough, to untie and turn loose mules to empty the required number for my teams. The teamsters obeyed by driving up, and when they had dismounted and were about to unhitch from the wagons, one of the wood-haulers at the stable door said: "You can save yourself the trouble, mister, of unhitching them mules, for you ain't agoing to put them in this stable; and the first man that attempts it, I'll fix."

"Suppose I wish to open that door and put up my teams," said I, "without any trouble; wouldn't it be better for all of us?" "You go to h—l!" he replied; and added, "you won't get in this stable; that's settled." "I'll see about that!" and yelling "Turn out! Turn out" in the Indian language, my soldiers jumped from the canvas-covered wagons, yelling like-demons, and brandishing their carbines and revolvers in a threatening manner. Never were men so taken back as-the wood-haulers. They were sure we were Sioux, and started to run, but I called them back. Not a word was then spoken while my Indians led the mules, that were now unhitched, into the stables.

Leaving the teamsters to feed and water their animals, I turned my pony over to an Omaha, to unsaddle, and marched mv soldiers up to the house, of which I took possession. The roughs changed their tune, and tried to laugh the matter off, saying they knew all the time the wagons were full of soldiers, and they only wanted to see if I had "nerve." I told them they could leave their teams in the stables, as my teamsters told me there was room enough yet remaining for all the mules, but that in the morning they must leave. At early light they were off, not, however, before I had found out the names of the leaders of the gang. The doors of the house had been taken off the hinges, and the framed pine used to sleep and chop meat on, all being marked with gashes chopped in them with axes. The windows were also broken, the glass and sashes gone, and the building as much damaged as if Indians had been there a month. I did all I could to save the property scattered over the grounds, and remained at the ranch some weeks, until an order came for me to go to Omaha as a witness before the United States Court.

A RACE FOR LIFE

WHILE the troops lay at Camp Cottonwood, now Fort McPherson, the scurvy broke out among the men and caused terrible suffering. There were no anti-scorbutics nearer than Leavenworth, Kansas, which could be had for issue to troops, and before these could be received, the disease increased to an alarming extent. At last, however, the remedies arrived, and the men began rapidly to convalesce. The doctor advised them to eat wild fruit and berries, and to take plenty of exercise in the open air. There was a plum grove about four miles from the camp, and as this wild fruit was very wholesome, the sick men went out nearly every day to gather it.

One morning, Captain Mitchell, of the Seventh Iowa Cavalry, procured an ambulance, and, taking with him a driver named Anderson, an orderly named Cramer, and seven hospital patients, started for the plum grove. They arrived at the first grove about ten o'clock, and, finding that most of the plums had been gathered, drove on to another grove some three miles farther up the cañon. They were now about seven miles from camp, too far to be safe, hut, as no Indians had been seen lately in the country, they did not feel uneasy. At the upper grove they found two soldiers of the First Nebraska Cavalry, named Bentz and Wise, who had been sent out by the quartermaster to look for stray mules, and they had stopped to gather some plums. As both these men were well-armed, Captain Mitchell attached them to his party, and felt perfectly secure.

Bentz and Wise went up the cañon a little way, and while eating fruit were suddenly fired on from the bushes by almost a dozen Indians. At the first volley, Bentz had his belt cut away by a ball, and lost his revolver. The soldiers turned to fly, but, as they galloped off, another ball entered Bentz's side, desperately wounding him. They now rode down the cañon, hoping to rejoin Captain Mitchell's party, but soon saw a body of Indians riding down the bluff ahead of them, evidently with the design of cutting them off. Wise told Bentz to ride hard, at the same time handing him one of his revolvers, to defend himself in case of emergency. Bentz was very feeble and dizzy, so much so, indeed, that he could barely sit in the saddle.

Wise was mounted on a superb horse belonging to Lieutenant Cutler, which he had taken out to exercise, and, seeing that the Indians would head them off, and that Bentz, who was riding an old mule, could not keep up, he gave the powerful brute rein, and shot down the cañon like an arrow. He passed the intervening Indians in safety, just as three of them dashed out of a pocket in the bluff and cut off poor Bentz.

Wise saw Bentz knocked from his mule, and, knowing it was useless to try to save him, left him to his fate, and thought only of saving his own life. He rode hard for Captain Mitchell, who was not far distant, but before he could reach him another party of Sioux headed him off, and he turned and rode up the bluffs to the flat lands. The Indians pursued him, and made every effort to kill or capture him, but his fine horse bore him out of every danger. Three times he was cut off from the camp, but, by taking a wide circuit, he managed to ride around the Indians, and at last succeeded in reaching the high road above the camp. As many settlers lived on this road, the Indians did not venture to follow him along it, and he was soon safely housed in the log-cabin of a frontiersman, and relating his adventures.

Meanwhile Captain Mitchell, having seen the fate of Bentz and escape of Wise, made haste to assemble his party, and, lifting those who were too weak to climb into the wagon, they set off for the camp. Mitchell and Anderson were the only two of the party who had arms, but they assured the sick men they would defend them to the last. Anderson took the lines and drove, while Mitchell seated himself in the rear end of the ambulance, with a Henry rifle to keep off the Indians.

They had not gone far before they came upon a large force of warriors drawn up across the cañon, to cut off their retreat. The bluffs were very steep and high on both sides of them, and escape seemed impossible, nevertheless Mitchell ordered Anderson to run his team at the right hand bluff and try and ascend it. The spirited animals dashed up the steep bank and drew the wagon nearly half way up, when one of the wheelers balked and nearly overturned the wagon. .A loud yell from the savages, at this moment, so frightened the horses that they sprang forward, and before they could appreciate it they were over the bluff on the level prairie, and flying toward the camp at the rate of ten miles an hour.

They now began to hope, but had only gone as far as the first plum grove when they saw the Indians circling around them, and once more getting between them and the post. Still they hoped that some soldiers might be in the first grove gathering p ums, or that Wise had reached the post and given the alarm, so that help would soon come to them. Captain Mitchell fired his rifle once or twice, to attract the attention of any persons who might be in the plum grove, but there was no response, and Anderson drove rapidly on.

The Indians now began to close in upon the ambulance from all sides. They would ride swiftly by a few yards distant, and, swinging themselves behind the neck and shoulders of their ponies, fire arrows or balls into the wagon. Two of the sick men had already been wounded, and Captain Mitchell, finding it impossible to defend them while the ambulance was in motion, the shaking continually destroying his aim, ordered Anderson to drive to the top of a hill nearby, and they would fight it out with the red-skins. Cramer now took the lines, when, either through fear or because he did not believe in the policy of stopping, he kept straight on. Captain Mitchell twice ordered Cramer to pull up, but, as he paid no attention, he told Anderson .to take the lines from him. In attempting to obey the captain's order, Anderson lost his footing and fell out of the wagon. The captain now sprang forward, put his foot on the brake to lock the wheels, when a sudden lurch of the wagon caused him to lose his balance, and he fell headlong on the prairie. Fortunately, he alighted near a deep gully, where the water had cut out the bank, and, rolling himself into it, he looked out and saw Anderson crawling into a bunch of bushes nearby. When these accidents happened, the ambulance had just crossed the crest of a little hill, and, as the Indians had not come over it yet, they did not see either of the men fall from the wagon. The captain had only two revolvers, but Anderson's gun, a Spencer rifle, had been thrown out with him, and he picked it up and took it into the bushes.

In a few moments the Indians came up, riding very fast, and the main body crossed the ravine near where Captain Mitchell lay. Some of them jumped their horses directly over the spot where he was concealed, but in a few moments they were gone, and soon had disappeared behind the neighboring divide, leaving the captain and Anderson to their own reflections. What to do was the next question. That the Indians would overtake the ambulance, kill all its occupants, and return, the captain had not a doubt. He determined to go down the ravine, and, calling to Anderson to follow, started off. He had already crawled some distance when, hearing the clatter of horses' hoofs, he peeped over the edge of his cover, and saw about seventy-five Indians riding directly up to where he was concealed. Giving himself up for lost he laid down, drawing his revolvers and preparing them for action, for he was determined not to let the savages have his scalp without making a desperate resistance. The warriors came up, and, dismounting within thirty yards of him, began a lively conversation. The chief walked up close to the brink of the ravine, and almost within arm's length of the captain, and stood gazing on the ground. Mitchell now saw the chief was blind of an eye and wore a spotted head-dress; and he knew by these marks he was none other than the celebrated Sioux warrior, Spotted Tail.

The much-respected Spotted Tail (ca. 1823–1881) was a Brulé Lakota tribal chief. He early on recognized the futility of fighting with whites and made several trips to Washington, D.C. in the 1870s to advocate for his people.—Ed. 2015

On making this discovery the captain leveled both his revolvers at the chief's breast, and was fully determined to fire. He believed that the loss of five captains would be a small matter, if by their death they could secure the destruction of the great leader of the Sioux. Just as he was about to pull the triggers a loud shout from the warriors caused Spotted Tail to start forward and run rapidly up the hill. The ponies were led down the ravine and the warriors scattered in all directions, seeking cover. One of them ensconced himself in the ravine not more than thirty feet from Mitchell. Raising his head so he could see out, the captain endeavored to ascertain what caused all the excitement among the Indians. At first he had thought he was discovered, then that re-enforcements from the fort had arrived, and a battle was about to begin; but now he saw Anderson was discovered. When the captain had started down the ravine Anderson had followed him, and just emerged from the bushes when the Indians suddenly came up. He had dropped on the ground, and endeavored to roll himself back among the sage brush, when an Indian saw him and gave the alarm. The warriors, not knowing how many white men might be in the brush, with their usual caution, had immediately sought cover.

A hot fire was opened on Anderson's position, and at first he did not respond at all. A warrior, more bold or indiscreet than the rest, ventured to go closer to the bushes, when a small puff of white smoke was seen' to rise, a loud report rang out on the air, and the warrior fell, pierced through the heart. A yell of rage resounded over the hills, and three more Indians ran toward Anderson's cover. Three reports followed each other in rapid succession, and the three Indians bit the dust. There was now a general charge on Anderson, but he fired so fast and true that the Indians fell back, carrying with them two more of their number.

The captain now felt it his duty to help Anderson, and was about to open fire with his revolvers, when Anderson, who, no doubt, expected as much, yelled three or four times, saying, in a soil of cry, "My arm is broken; keep quiet; can't work the Spencer anymore." The brave fellow no doubt intended this as a warning to the captain not to discover himself by firing, and he reluctantly accepted the admonition and kept quiet.

A rush by some thirty warriors was now made on Anderson, and, notwithstanding his disabled condition, he managed to kill three more Indians before he was taken. He was overpowered, however, dragged out of the bushes, and scalped in full sight of the captain. He fought to the last, and compelled them to kill him to save their own lives. Nothing could exceed the rage of the Indians, and especially old Spotted Tail, as he saw the body of warrior after warrior carried down the hill, until nine dead Indians were laid beside Anderson. In his grief for the loss of his braves, the old chief kicked the corpse of poor Anderson, and the other Indians, coming up, stuck knives into it. Then they rolled it over, cut nine gashes in his back, one for each warrior he had killed, and stabbed it nine times. Next, they drove a stake in the eye, drew it out, and filling the hole with powder, blew his skull to pieces.

In a few minutes after the death of Anderson, a mounted party was seen coming over the hills, and about thirty warriors rode up to Spotted Tail, and reported that they had captured the ambulance and killed all who were in it. They exhibited to Spotted Tail the scalps of all Captain Mitchell's late companions, except that of Cramer. The ambulance horses were brought back, each carrying a greasy mass of brutality, known down east as a "noble red man."

In a few moments the warriors had their dead comrades securely strapped to ponies, and, mounting their own, set out toward the Republican. As soon as they were out of sight, and it became dark, Captain Mitchell started for the camp, where he arrived about 10 o'clock, and told the story of the "Cottonwood Massacre," as I have here related it.

Early the next morning I was sent out with a strong force to pursue and, if possible, overtake and punish the Indians. For two days I followed them hard, and, on the evening of the second day, came upon a small party as they were crossing a stream, but, in attempting to charge them, they scattered over the prairie and were soon lost in the darkness. The trail now divided in every direction, and it would have been impossible to follow it unless each soldier had pursued some half a dozen warriors, when it is not likely he would have returned. So we turned back, and marched for Cottonwood. The bodies of the dead had been brought in and buried, and everything had been found just as Captain Mitchell had stated.

Private Wise was severely censured for not immediately going to the camp and giving the alarm, but he said he had no idea the wagon and its sick men had ever left the cañon, for there were at least one hundred and fifty warriors around it when he came away, so he thought he might as well rest until morning before bearing such dismal news as he had to communicate to his fellow-soldiers.

HOW TO FIGHT SIOUX INDIANS

DURING the time when we were guarding Ben Holliday's stage coaches, and when attacks on them were of frequent occurrence, I had an adventure which I think is worth relating.

I was at one of the lower ranches, and the Indiana were very troublesome. Our guards were nearly all sick or wounded, and the coaches had to go out insufficiently protected.

One evening the coach was late, and, as to be behind time was a sure sign that something was wrong, we all felt very uneasy. The drivers made it a rule to get from one station to another on time, and if they did not arrive parties were immediately started out to the next ranch, ten miles below, to see what the matter was, the stations being all eight, ten, and twelve miles apart.

On the particular evening in question, I had got tired waiting, and gone over to the stable-keeper to see if we had not better take the change horses, go down the road, and try if we could not find the coach. It was due at the station at 8:30 P. M, and it was now ten, so I was confident it had been attacked or had broken down. While we were talking, the sentinel on the outpost, whose business it was to look out for the stage and give notice of its approach, signaled the coach was coming. We all ran down the road to meet it, and soon saw it coming slowly along with three horses instead of four, and the driver driving very slowly, as if he were going to a funeral or hauling wounded.

When we came up to the coach we learned that he was indeed both conveying a corpse and wounded. On the arrival of the party at the ranch, Captain Hancock, who was a passenger, related to me all that had happened, and I repeat the story as it fell from his lips.

"We were," said the captain, "driving along smartly in the bottom, about four miles below, when, just as we crossed a little ravine, some twenty Indians jumped up out of the long grass and fired on us. The first volley killed Mr. Cinnamon, a telegraph operator, who was a passenger, and was on his way from Plum Creek to some point up the river. He was riding on the box with the driver at the time when he received the fatal shot, and the driver caught his body just as it was falling forward off the coach on the rear horses. He put Cinnamon's corpse in the front boot among the mail bags, where it now is.

"The first fire had also killed our nigh wheeler, and, as the coach was going pretty fast at the time, the horse was dragged a considerable distance, and his hind leg becoming fast between the spokes of the fore-wheel, his body was drawn up against the bed of the coach, and all further progress completely blocked.

"The driver took it very coolly, first swearing fearfully at the Indians, toward whom he cracked his whip repeatedly, as if flaying their naked backs, and then, having vented his spleen, he quietly descended from his box and stripped the harness off the dead horse.

"Meanwhile the Indians had been circling around us, firing into the coach every few minutes, and I had got under the wagon with my clerks, the better to be protected and to fire at the Indians, who could be seen best from the ground, as they moved against the horizon.

"The driver tried in vain to extricate the leg of the dead horse from the wheel, but it was firmly wedged in, and after uniting my strength to his I found it necessary to take my knife and amputate the leg at the knee-joint. The body was at length removed, and, mounting the box, the driver bid us get in, and we were off once more. One of the clerks had been severely wounded, and, as his wound was quite painful, we had to drive very slowly; so we were late getting in.".

While the captain was talking the driver came to the door to say the coach was waiting, for on the plains stages stop not for accidents or dead men. I bade my friend good-night, hoping he would not again be interrupted on his journey by the red skins, and, the driver cracking his whip, the four fresh bays bounded forward at a gallop, and soon carried the coach out of sight of the valley.

Next day we buried poor Cinnamon, and sent the wounded man to McPherson, where he could have medical attendance, and we were pleased to learn he speedily recovered.

I rode down to where the coach had been attacked, and saw the dead horse and the ravine from which the Indians had sprung. The fight had evidently been a sharp one and I could see by the trail that the savages had followed the coach nearly to the ranch, and then struck across toward the Republican, never stopping, in all probability, until they reached it, ninety miles distant.

GENERAL SULLY S EXPEDITION AGAINST THE SIOUX

THE bloody engagements between the expeditionary forces, under General Sully, and the Sioux tribes of the Upper Missouri, have, perhaps, never been equaled in the history of Indian warfare on this continent. The incidents of that expedition, I believe, have never been published, and, as I was present and engaged in it, I will here relate some of them—General Sully's official report, as is always the case in such documents, being necessarily brief, and omitting those minor details which are of most interest to the general reader.

The troops consisted of the Second Nebraska Cavalry, Col. Furnas commanding; a battalion of the Sixth Iowa Cavalry, Major House commanding; two companies of the Seventh Iowa Cavalry, and two companies of infantry with the train, for guarding the supplies.

The forces moved up the Missouri, and established at Fort Sully a supply depot. This place is nearly opposite old Fort Pierre.

Early in August, 1863, we marched for the Indian country, with instructions to punish the savages, who had been committing horrible outrages on the whites in Minnesota. The weather was intensely hot, and we toiled slowly along, marching early in the day and lying by during the afternoons. We had reached Cannon Ball River, and were moving on to Painted Wood River, when our scouts found an old Indian, by the name of "Keg," and brought him in. This old fellow had been left by his inhuman companions to die by the side of a stream. He related that he had frozen his feet during the past severe winter, and the hot weather having inflamed his sores so he could not travel, his tribe had stolen all his ponies and blankets, and cast him out to die of starvation. Gen. Sully had his wounds dressed, gave him clothing and food; and this kind treatment so deeply touched him, that he felt bound to answer all the general's inquiries concerning his ungrateful tribe.

He said they had gone to the lakes, some hundred miles distant, to hunt buffalo, and would be there a long time, as they wished to take enough meat to last them during the fall and winter. On this intelligence, the general moved forward, taking with him old "Keg" as a guide.

Every day the sun poured down his intense rays from nine o'clock in the morning until four o'clock in the afternoon, and so great was the heat that we could only march very early in the morning and late in the evening; nevertheless, we made good days' journeys. The nights were so cold we had to wear thick woolen clothing and sleep under blankets. This condition of the weather kept us constantly peeling off to keep from roasting, or shivering in great overcoats.

Scouts were out daily looking for Indian camps, and fresh trails and skeletons of recently-killed buffalo warned us that the Indians were not far off. One evening we came to a lot of fresh carcasses that had evidently been slaughtered but a few hours before, and General Sully, halting, sent out Major House to scout.

We were now moving among a tier of beautiful little lakes, some ten miles apart; and these were the ones alluded to by old "Keg" as the hunting-grounds of his tribe. The general had instructed the scouts to move with great caution, and not alarm or engage the Indians, but simply report what they saw.

On the day in question, after Major House had gone out, I lay down in my tent to sleep, and, as was the custom, the whole camp, except the guards, was asleep, for we had been marching nearly all night. About three o'clock I was awakened by a great uproar, and, rushing out of my tent, saw troops streaming over the prairie to the westward. It took but a moment to learn the cause of all this excitement, and it was to the effect of that Major House had found the Indians posted in force on a ridge not far off, and a great battle was about to begin. Not waiting to dress, I buckled on my revolvers, and, mounting my pony placed myself at the head of a squad of my men, and galloped hard for the battle-field, eleven miles distant. It was a long ride on that hot day, but we reached it at last just as the sun was going down over the western hills. We found the Indians drawn up on a jutting ridge, with their women, children, and ponies corralled behind them in a hollow. General Sully was already on the ground, and directing the movements of the troops as they came up. The savages were soon' completely surrounded, and we impatiently waited for the action to begin. The Indians kept falling back on a spur that put into a deep ravine, and were, in a short time, closely crowded together on the extreme point. They had evidently only halted to fight Major House's force, and were appalled on seeing our great numbers.

The troops were dismounted, and, No. 4 holding the horses, Nos. 1, 2, 3, of each set of fours in the cavalry advanced to fight on foot. We had approached quite near the savages and halted, when an orderly was seen to gallop up to Major House and deliver an order from General Sully [The order referred to was from General Sully, to hold the Indians in check and not attack until he had concluded the council he was then holding with some of their chiefs]. We saw House's men slinging-their carbines, and in a moment we knew it was an order not to attack. A murmur of disappointment ran along the lines; and, at that moment, Captain Bayne, of the Second Nebraska Cavalry, stepped out in front of the men, and said:

"Boys, we have come a long way to fight the Indians, and now that we have got them, I am in favor of whaling them. Shall we advance?" "Yes! yes!" ran along the lines, and Bayne cried out: "Each man pick his Indian." There was no order to fire, but every soldier leveled his carbine. An Indian was now seen advancing, wrapped in a garrison flag, and crying, "How! how!" moving his hand up and down, as if shaking hands. As yet not a gun had been fired, and the Indians stood wrapped in their blankets, their arms concealed, and only the top of a bow in sight here and there. They were very cool, and stood perfectly still. The Indian in the flag continued to advance, and when he was close to our line, a little Dutchman on the left fired and killed him, he gathering tire flag about him as he fell, and making of it a winding sheet. There were two or three more shots along the line, then a scattering volley; and the Indians on the hill throwing off their blankets, nearly everyone was seen to have a gun. The action soon became general along our line, and Major House's battalion wished to join in the battle, but their officers, stepping in front of them, declared they would cut down the first man who fired a shot. About one hundred and twenty-five Indians had gone up on the hill where General Sully was, and were holding a council with him when the battle began. They immediately began to withdraw, but General Sully ordering his body-guard, two companies of cav airy, to surround them, they were all taken prisoners.

The Indians were now fighting desperately, most' of them having mounted their ponies, charging and yelling furiously. It was growing dark, and, as the darkness increased, the savages became more bold, dashing among our men and tomahawking them as they forced their ponies through the lines. The soldiers, with clubbed guns, resisted them, and many a pony, Indian, and white man went down together in death in that bitter hand-to-hand struggle. House's men had become engaged, and the battle surged and roared over the hills, the flashes of the guns lighting up the darkness of the fearful scenery. Despite our exertions, many of the Indians escaped, and the remainder held firmly to the hill. We lost a little ground after dark, and the battle lulled. All night we lay on the ground near where we had fought, and within hearing of the cries of our wounded, many of whom had been left behind in the hands of the Indians. Little did we know of the fearful tragedy that was enacting on the hill above us under cover of night; for if we had, we would have advanced and ended it, though it had cost the lives of one-half the men in the command.

As soon as it was dark the squaws had descended from the hill, and attacking our helpless wounded with long-handled tomahawks, beat their brains out, after which they took a butcher-knife and cut out their tongues.

Lieut. Levitt was wounded early in the action, and his horse at the same time being shot, and falling on his leg, held him fast, so that when the men fell back he was, unfortunately, left behind. He said next day, he saw the squaws come down the hill and attack our wounded and dying men, nearly all of whom bravely defended their lives, wounding many of the squaws. He lay close to his dead horse, partly hidden by his „ saddle, and he hoped they would not discover him. Presently, however, he saw a squaw approaching, evidently with the design of rifling the saddle-bags. While she was engaged in this occupation she saw the lieutenant, and, springing quickly back, struck at him with her tomahawk. He made a thrust at her with his saber, but could not reach her. After trying for some time to kill him with her long-handled weapon, she screeched, and brought half a dozen other squaws to her assistance. They all now attacked him, making feints and motions, and then suddenly striking him. Using his saber as well as he could in his cramped and disabled condition, he, for a long time, kept them at bay. He held his left hand over his head, and with his right thrust out with the sword. The fingers of his left hand were nearly all broken, and the flesh on his arm so gashed and bruised, that it was laid bare to the bone all the way from the wrist to the shoulder, and the tendons severed at the elbow. At length, making a desperate thrust, he severely wounded a squaw, and she set up a fearful howling; the rest carried her off, and did' not again return to molest him. So weak was he, from fatigue and loss of blood, that he fainted as Boon as the squaws left him. Next day we found the poor fellow in a terrible condition, and brought him to camp, where everything was done for him that kindness could suggest, but he died after a day of great suffering.

To return once more to the battle-field. After the fighting: for the day had ceased the Indians crept away, and before morning nearly all had escaped. We followed them up, and found nearly every buffalo wallow, filled with their dead and wounded. They would carry them along until they came to a wallow, and then, depositing them, leave them to their fate. We counted in all two hundred and twenty-five dead Indians, and we had one hundred and twenty-five prisoners. There were also seven hundred head of-Indian stock killed, wounded, or captured. Our own loss amounted, in killed and wounded, to fifty-eight men, eighteen belonging to the Second Nebraska Cavalry, and forty to the Sixth Iowa Cavalry.

DESPERATE SITUATION—NOBLE SACRIFICE

SEVERAL of us were standing by the bed-side of poor Lieut. Levitt, who had just finished his story of suffering and honor on the battle-field, and now lay dying. It was sad in the extreme, for we all loved him dearly, and not a man of us, as we watched his heavy and painful breathing, could refrain from hating the authors of so much misery. As for myself, I made a resolve I would not rest until I had at least two scalps at my girdle for Levitt's death, and I fear there were many similar resolves made by the hardy and hardened men who surrounded that death-bed.

Scarcely had we reached our tents, when "bang!" "bang!" went the guns of the pickets on the hill, and the cry of "Indians! Indians!" resounded through the camp. There was rushing to and fro, and mounting in hot haste; but, in less time than it takes to record it, a hundred horsemen were flying to the support of the pickets. I did not go out, thinking it a feint; it proved, however, to be a real attack of the red rascals, who had returned, hoping to surprise us, and, by a dash, succeed in liberating the 125 of their people we held prisoners. The assault was a feeble one, and soon repelled, not an Indian escaping from our camp to reward the savages for their enterprise.

As soon as the Indian attack was over, General Sully ordered the Indian camp and supplies to be destroyed. It was a very large camp, well stocked with provisions and robes, and the burning of it was no small, job. Teepees were pulled down and heaped up on the lodge-poles, and on top of these were thrown bales of robes, parflechees of meat, and pieces of wood. The whole was then fired, and stirred up until it burned down. Thousands of articles were consumed, and the soldiers, in the light of this burning town, looked like real fire fiends as they ran about in their red shirts thrusting their torches in every combustible pile.

While the town was burning a most lamentable sight was witnessed. The Indian dogs that had been left in the village with the property, as was customary, trotted about, howling most dismally. They had little shafts strapped to their sides, and on these were tied cooking utensils, and, not unfrequently, Indian babies. During the battle many of the dogs had become frightened, and hid away in the rocks and ravines, and the Indian mothers, making their escape in the night, had to go away without their babies. The dogs, true to their charges, would not allow the soldiers to approach their loads, but fled over the hills when anyone went toward them. In a little while they would return, and, sitting on a hill-top, gaze at the burning town and cry piteously. The little babies, that the dogs were dragging about on their travois, never cried, but lay perfectly still, though the dogs galloped over ditches and gullies, shaking and jolting them at a terrible rate. The soldiers, not being able to catch the dogs, shot them, and it sometimes happened the dog would move, or the aim not be good, when the baby, instead of the dog, would receive the ball. It was, perhaps, well it was so killed, for if left out on the prairie it would have starved to death; if brought in, we had no way to keep it or take care of it, but if dead it was at rest. Poor little creatures, however much we pitied them we could not help them.

When the camp was burned, General Sully determined to follow up the Indians and administer still further punishment, as they exhibited no signs of coming to terms. It was deeply to be regretted they had not been attacked in the first fight, but the only way now was to fight it out and conquer if possible. The general detached Lieut. Bayne with sixty men, to scout and find the Indians. Taking the old trail, Bayne pushed on, and the first day out came upon two Indians who were making their way on foot to the bluffs. One of them seemed to be wounded, and was leaning on the shoulder of his companion, who pretended to be helping him along. When first noticed they were moving slowly, but, on Lieut. Bayne calling out to his men, "There are two; of the rascals, let us go for them, gallop, march," the Indians began to run. The guide, who was an old and experienced frontiersman, no sooner saw the Indians set off than he rode up to Bayne, and called out:

"Look out, lieutenant, they are a decoy; see how that lame Indian mends his pace."

"Silence, sir," retorted Bayne, angrily, to this well-meant admonition; "I, not you, command here."

The guide, without uttering a word, reined up his horse and allowed the column to pass him, and then turning toward the camp, plunged the rowels into his steed's flanks, and in a moment had disappeared behind a protecting bluff.

Bayne kept straight on following the two Indians up a narrow cañon, and gaining on them every moment. He was now within pistol shot of them, and they were running for dear life, when suddenly they disappeared, and instantly the hills swarmed with Indians.

"They are in our rear," shouted several soldiers, and, halting the command, Lieut. Bayne looked down the cañon and saw three or four hundred savages coming out of the bluff, and completely closing the passage along which he had just marched.

"Look! look!" shouted the sergeant, and directing his eyes up the valley, the lieutenant discovered two solid lines of savages advancing upon him, stretched out from bluff to bluff.

"We are lost!" cried Bayne, and, for the moment, seemed completely prostrated by the sad predicament into which he had got himself and his devoted troopers. "Fours, right about, wheel," shouted the sergeant, and the men mechanically obeyed the order. "Now," cried the brave sergeant, "ones and fours, cut right and left, and twos and threes, go ahead; steady column! forward! gallop, march!"

Away went the troopers, and dashing at the solid lines of Indians, rode or cut them down. Fast and furious fell the saber strokes, and the savages, appalled at the sudden and terrific onset, parted in twain, and allowed the column to pass through to the open plain. Many horses were wounded, but strange to relate, not a man was killed. Lieutenant Bayne fought desperately at one time with his single saber, holding the Indians in cheek, until some troopers, who had got behind, came up and passed through the gap.

Once out on the plain the column headed for camp and rode swiftly forward. Suddenly the brave sergeant's horse was seen to stagger and reel under his weight, and then fall to his knees. He reined him up and allowed the column to pass, then calling to some troopers, who were behind, to stop and take him up behind on one of their horses, he dismounted, but the demoralized soldiers, paid no attention to his request, and the column swept on. Once more mounting his steed, the sergeant pushed him to his utmost speed, hoping to overtake the column, but seeing he was each moment losing distance, and the noble horse becoming more and more feeble, the sergeant turned him off the trail and rode him across the prairie. This he did for the purpose of drawing as many of the Indians as possible after him and thus, by sacrificing his life, increase the chances of escape for his comrades. We saw the gallant fellow dashing over the prairie followed by a horde of hooting savages. Suddenly the horse stopped, sank to the ground, and rolled over dead. The sergeant lay down behind his horse, and taking deliberate aim at the foremost Indian in the chase, killed him at the first fire from his Enfield rifle. Quickly loading, he fired again, and another Indian fell. He now drew his revolvers, and sheltering his body from the arrows and bullets of his savage assailants, fired away at them. It was not until he had killed eight Indians, and fell weak and bleeding from wounds, that they could get him from behind his horse; then they dragged him out and scalped him, but seeming to respect his bravery, refrained from mutilating his body.

The guide, after leaving Lieutenant Bayne, had waited only to see the attack begin, and then rode straight to camp, where he informed General Sully of all that had happened. General S. lost no time in sending re-enforcements to Lieutenant Bayne who was met a short distance from camp, quietly returning, the Indians having given up the pursuit after killing the brave sergeant. The whole party returned to camp, and Lieutenant Bayne was immediately ordered to make out a full report of the affair. He did the sergeant justice, and when General Sully read the report, he sent out a strong force, brought in the body of the sergeant, and buried it with all the honors of war.

The sergeant here referred to, was Sergeant Bain, of the Second Nebraska Cavalry. A short time before Lieutenant Bayne's scout took place, Sergeant Bain had been reduced to the ranks for having scalped twenty-seven Indians. The circumstances were these:

Sergeant Bain, while out following the Indians after the battle fought by General Sully, near Goose Lake, on the third of September, 1863, came upon a buffalo-wallow, filled with sick and wounded Indians, some of whom were in a dying condition, and others barely able to sit up. With a ferocity unparalleled, he sprang into the wallow, tomahawked twenty-seven of the Indians with their own tomahawks, and scalped them with their own scalping-knives. He did this, he said, in revenge for the squaws cutting the tongues out of the mouths of our wounded the night before, and in order, as he observed, that the Indians might know how it went to have their own barbarity applied to themselves. He was, undoubtedly, influenced by honest, but, nevertheless, mistaken motives; but, for his cruelty, he was broken by General Sully, and reduced to the ranks as a private.

After Bayne's scout, in consideration of the signal services he had rendered the command on that occasion, the order was revoked reducing him as sergeant; he was reappointed a sergeant, and then his poor body was laid to rest, and there was not an officer or soldier in the command, but felt a regret for his untimely and sad death.—Editor.

SCOUTING ON THE REPUBLICAN

IT was while I was with Colonel Brown that I had an adventure which came near being my last, and, as I have omitted to relate it in its proper place; I will here insert it.

We were camped on a tributary of the Republican, and I had been sent out with a small party to scout. Our numbers were too few to travel by daylight, and, besides, it was not our business to be seen, but to see. We had-been traveling through a buffalo range, and one evening, unable to resist the temptation to hunt, I sallied out down the little creek on which we had been hiding, hoping to stalk a buffalo calf. I had not gone far when I saw a fine fellow grazing near the water's edge, and, firing, broke his shoulder. He made off for the herd, which was feeding nearby, and thinking I could soon overtake and finish him, I mounted my pony and made after him. Notwithstanding his three legs, he ran along so smartly that, before I could overhaul him, he had joined his dam and mingled in the herd. The buffaloes started across the prairie, and, chagrined and excited, I followed, determined to get some buffalo meat before I returned to camp. I knew I was getting too far from the camp for safety, but still on we went, uphill and down, my little pony each moment gaining on the herd. I had got quite close, and was about to shoot, when I saw another herd coming in the opposite direction at a full run. Knowing buffalo did not move so rapidly unless frightened, I stopped and' looked hard at them, but seeing nothing, I concluded they had been started by prairie wolves, and, plunging the rowels into my pony, continued the pursuit after my own herd. They soon swung round to the left, and joined the herd I had seen flying across the flat. I was on the right of the herd, which was now very large, and had just singled out a fine young bull, and was about to fire, when, seeing the head of the drove suddenly lurch to the left and change the direction of the whole body, I looked, and, to my horror, saw two Sioux Indians hunting on the right of the herd. Quickly reining my pony up, I dodged into a ravine in rear of the buffalo, and, riding around the bluff, waited with fear and trembling the events of the next few minutes. I scarcely dared hope I had not been seen, and yet, singular as it may appear, such was the case. Riding up on the bluff when I found no one was after me, I saw the buffalo in full flight, and a dozen Indians firing arrows into the now thoroughly frightened beasts. I at once took the back track, and as my route to camp carried me along the trail the second herd had run, I fortunately found the carcasses of two fine buffaloes sticking full of Sioux arrows. I cut out some choice steaks, and then, haggling the meat so as to make the Indians think a wolf had been at their game, I rode back to our hiding-place, taking good care to keep in the ravines until I reached the creek.

Hastily broiling some of the buffalo on the coals, we saddled up and left the place, well knowing that the Sioux would return to skin and dress their game, and fearing they might discover it was a two-legged wolf that had been cutting up their beef for them.

Had I fired a single shot at the herd, it would probably have proved my last buffalo hunt, as subsequent events showed I was near an Indian village, and in' the midst of a large Sioux hunting party.

Under cover of night we crept away, and by building only small fires, eating sparingly, and riding hard, we succeeded in making our escape, and returning in safety to the military camp.

APPOINTED A SECOND LIEUTENANT

IT was on the 10th of July, 1867, that I was informed I had been appointed Second Lieutenant in the regular army, the appointment to date from the 9th day of June. This commission was given me for services rendered during the war, and was not a little gratifying to me, as a position in the army would enable me to continue, in a more regular form, the wild life on the frontier, of which I had become so fond.

As the law then required all officers to be examined before being assigned to duty, I immediately set out for Washington, to report to General David Hunter, who was President of the Board of Examiners. In due time I passed the ordeal, and was assigned to the Second United States Cavalry, then serving in the Department of the Platte. On my return home to the West, I stopped for a short time at New Philadelphia, Ohio, to visit some relatives and friends, and spent several delightful days with them. All the way through the East, I could not help noticing how crowded together the people lived, and I cannot to this day understand how it is possible for men to be contented where there are no prairies or wild game.

On the 8th of September I started to join my company, which was stationed in the Powder River country of .the Rocky Mountains. Our route lay up the Platte River to Julesburg, and thence to old Fort Laramie, where I was placed on temporary duty, with .Company F of the Second Cavalry. We marched to Fort Fetterman, and then to Reno, where I met the command of General Sweitzer, and reported to that officer.

My first military duty was to pursue three deserters, but, after searching several trains, and following them thirty-three miles, I lost all trace of them, and returned, having made a dead failure, for which I received the comforting assurance of the commanding officer that I "would do better next time."

General Sweitzer sent me to Fort Phil. Kearney, and immediately on my arrival there, I was ordered out, with forty soldiers, to guard some workmen who were cutting hay near the post. The country abounding in game, I amused myself by hunting, and the first day out killed four elk, one black-tail deer, and an antelope. The next day I killed three wolves, one of which was a large gray fellow, and the day after that shot a black-tail deer and a fine young antelope. Going into the garrison to draw rations for my men, I carried in my game with me, having several hundred pounds of meat, which I gave to the officers. From the 10th to the 27th of October, during which time I was stationed near the hay-fields I killed the following extraordinary quantity of game: two buffalo, four elk; four Rocky Mountain sheep, eight black-tail deer, seven antelope, five wolves, five prairie chickens, one mountain grouse, one jack rabbit, one small rabbit, and one fox squirrel, besides wounding nineteen animals, which I did not get. This was considered good hunting, even in that prolific country.

In the last days of the month the Indians fired the grass all around the post, and for a time we thought we should be burnt up. The slopes of the hills, as far as the eye could reach, were covered with lines of fire, and tall sheets of flame leaped up from the valley or run crackling through the timber. The parade ground of the garrison was lighted up at night so one could see to read, and for a distance of many miles every tree and shrub could be distinctly seen. The crackling of the fire sounded like the discharge of thousands of small arms, and every few moments the bursting of heated stones would resound over the valley, resembling the booming of distant cannon. In all my life I had never seen so grand and imposing a sight, and never expect to witness one like it again. For three days the flames raged over a vast extent of country, and then, having consumed all the grass and dry trees, went out, doing us no harm, owing to the streams around the fort, which completely checked the advance of the destroying element.

The first day of November a horseman approached the fort, riding at full speed, and his horse covered with foam. The officers gathered around the head-quarters, to learn what was up, and we were soon informed that the messenger had brought a note from Lieutenant McCarthy, which stated that his whole command, while escorting a train to Big Horn, had been surrounded by Indians, and, that he was then hard pressed, but would endeavor to hold out until forces could be sent to his f relief. The messenger said he had cut Id's way through the Indians, and had to ride for his life all the way to the fort, General John E. Smith, who commanded the post, ordered me to take Company D, Second United States Cavalry, and go immediately to the assistance of Lieutenant McCarthy. In an hour we were well on the road, and soon reached the beleaguered command, which had driven off the Indians before our approach, and was then moving on its journey.

As we returned to the fort, we rode over to the Phil. Kearney massacre ground, and Major Gordon pointed out to me the places where the hardest fighting had taken place. There, on the 21st of December, 1866, three thousand Sioux, Cheyenne, and Arrapahoe warriors, under the noted Sioux chief, Red Cloud, surrounded Colonel Fetterman and his command, and killed everyone.

Near present-day Sheridan, Wyoming, the ground is now a national historic site.—Ed. 2015

The ground was still covered with the debris of the fight. Skeletons of horses and mules, human bones, pieces of skulls, knapsacks, torn uniforms, and broken guns lay scattered over the ground for a mile or more. Major Gordon showed me where Fetterman made his last stand, and where eighty-six soldiers and citizens lay dead in one pile. He also pointed out to me the rock behind which Jim Wheatley, the guide, and Captain Brown had taken shelter, and in front of which fifteen Indians lay dead. This massacre was unparalleled in the history of savage warfare. The fight was desperate in the extreme, each soldier firing until his ammunition gave out, and then defending himself with rocks and the butt of his gun. One bugler boy was seen to "knock two Indians down with his bugle before he was run through by an Indian lance. The stones and rocks were still stained with blood and covered with hair where the Indians had beat out the brains of the white soldiers with their war clubs. I picked up an old flint-lock Indian gun, and it bore the brand, "London, 1777." The history of that gun would certainly be curious could it be written—how many battles and skirmishes had it been in? where had it traveled, and how many wild animals, Indians, and white men had it slain? These and many other questions suggested themselves to my mind while looking at this relic of by-gone days.

I now remained in the fort for several days, engaged in military duties, but found time to ride out occasionally and shoot a buffalo or elk, these animals often coming down in full sight of the post.

It was the 5th of November when a runner came hastily into the fort to announce that Lieutenant Shirly, who had been sent out with a detachment of men, had been attacked by two hundred Indians, and a severe battle had been fought. The lieutenant had been shot through the foot and severely wounded, one soldier killed, and seven wounded. It was late in the evening when the news of the battle reached us, and at one o'clock at night Colonel Green left the fort with two companies of cavalry, and arrived at the-scene of the battle about daylight the next morning. We found wagons overturned, and sacks of flour, sugar, rice, and bacon scattered over the ground. Boxes of crackers, packages of stationery, pipes, tobacco, books, belts, scabbards, swords, and broken guns lay every-where. A dead horse, and a mule with a saddle yet on, lay on the road, and further out on the plain were a dozen dead ponies, where the Indians had charged. All the savages had left, but the trail was only a few hours old, and leading eastward. While most of the soldiers went in pursuit of the Indians, the rest of us busied ourselves in looking after the wounded. One corporal had his thigh broken, and another his hand shattered, rendering amputation necessary in both cases A soldier was shot through the lungs, another in the knee another in the shoulder, and still another in the arm. A citizen, who had acted as postilion to a mounted howitzer, received a ball in the thigh. Lieutenant Shirly's wound was very severe and painful, the ball having passed through the instep and flattened against' the sole of the boot. Shirly said the principal object of attack by the Indians was the howitzer, they having killed or wounded every man around it in their efforts to capture it. They no doubt wished to secure the piece, so as to shell and annoy the forts with it.

We gathered up the stores as well as we could, and, taking the wounded men, returned to the fort. Soon afterward the cavalry came in, having failed to overtake the Indians.

I started out to scout with Major Gordon's company of cavalry, and the second day a violent rain and snow-storm broke upon us. The wind blew a gale, and we went into camp as soon as we could find shelter. Toward evening the wind fell, the rain ceased, and the sun came out bright and warm, dispersing the gloomy clouds. Next morning, however, it was very cold, and we took the road as soon as it was light, pushing on smartly until we reached Fish Creek, a distance of fourteen miles. During the day I shot several prairie grouse, and some birds. In the evening, after we had pitched our camp, a band of Indians appeared on the hills to the west, and, on being hailed, answered they were friendly Crows, and asked permission to come in and visit us. Major Gordon said they might come, but they soon annoyed us so the major was obliged to drive them off.

We marched to Muddy Creek the following day and encamped, where the Crow Indians again visited us, and begged everything they could, even to small pieces of straps. The chiefs: Bad Elk, Little Wolf, and Bird-in-the-Neck were with them, and these noble red men were not too proud to beg, or so honest they would not steal.

Our march now lay to Big Horn, and, on the third day, which was the evening of the 13th of November, 1867, we

SIEGE OF MCPHERSON'S TRAIN

HUNTING, scouting, and reading occupied my time till the end of the month, when I went out to kill buffalo and Rocky Mountain sheep. We soon saw three sheep standing on some shelving rocks, far up the mountain side, and leaving the corporal, who was with me, to hold the horses, I climbed for an hour among the rocks, and at the end of that time found myself within three hundred yards of a fine buck. I fired, and he fell over, when the ewes that were with him started to run away, and, although I succeeded in putting two balls into one of them, she got off. The buck had both his fore-shoulders broken; but was very anxious to fight me, striking with his horns, and kicking like a mule with his hind feet. I soon laid him out with my big butcher, and started in pursuit of the wounded ewe. Following her trail for over a mile, often getting heavy falls, she at last had ascended the rocks, where r it was impossible for me to climb, and I turned back to secure and dress my buck. His horns were enormous, and cutting off his head, I carried it to the fort, where I presented it to our accommodating quartermaster, Gen. Dandy, who wished it send it to some friends in the East.

Next morning I again started out, accompanied by Colonel Smith, Dr. Gisedorf, and some soldiers. It was snowing, and the thick undergrowth made so much noise that, although we saw several deer, we did not succeed in killing any. Leaving my companions, to see if I could not scare up something by myself, I soon came upon a fresh bear track, and followed it for six miles, when I gave out, and sat down. Fortunately, one of the soldiers had followed me with my horse, and mounting, I rode back to camp, having shot nothing during the day but a mountain grouse." This was the poorest day's hunting I had ever done in that country.

On the 29th of November the pickets on the hill overlooking the fort signaled "Indians," and a few minutes afterward reported that they were attacking the ox train, three miles distant. I immediately saddled up some horses, and, accompanied by a small party of cavalrymen, set out for the train. On our approach the Indians, ten in number, made off, and we gave chase. After following them about seven miles, we overhauled four savages, and killed them. A dozen times we got within a hundred yards of the others; but could not get any more of them.

It was wonderful to see the coolness and agility of the savages. When one would get wounded or killed, the rest would, halt, and, in a moment, lash him to his horse, when they would set off again at a full gallop. We succeeded in getting two ponies; but the Indians put the dead bodies of their comrades on other ponies, and carried them off. One Indian was tied by the neck to the bow of his saddle, and by one leg to the cantle, the other one dragging on the ground.

Early in December a messenger came to the fort, and reported that a train belonging to Mr. McPherson had been attacked and corralled, about forty miles out on the Phil Kearney road. The same night Mr. McPherson's herder came in, and confirmed the report, stating that the men with the train had been fighting since Sunday morning, and when he left one had been killed and seven wounded. I was ordered out with the cavalry company and one mountain howitzer, and directed to go, with all possible haste, to the assistance of the train.'

We had not marched more than ten miles from the fort, when, near Rock Creek, we were fired upon by a small party of Indians, who were concealed in the bluffs. Their fire did no harm; and we pushed on until near morning, when we were challenged with "Who goes there?" and upon answering, "Relief from the fort," cheer after cheer burst from the throats of the besieged men. They were wild with joy, and many sat down, and cried like children, when they knew they were really delivered from a horrible death. Over two hundred Indians had surrounded them, and only left when they learned of our approach. So closely had they watched, that it was impossible to get word to the fort, and one man was killed while attempting to steal through the Indian lines. The herder had only escaped at great risk, and by keeping in a ravine until he got among the rocks, where he crawled for over a mile on his hands and knees.

The battle-field bore marks of a desperate conflict, arrows, guns, blankets, dead oxen, and ponies lying thick over the ground. We saw white human bones, where the wolves, in the night-time, had dragged the bodies out on the prairies, and eaten every particle of flesh off of them. Even the skulls were broken in, and the brains sucked out by the ravenous beasts.

Gathering up the wounded, we set out with the besieged train for the fort; and on the first night of the march camped on Clear Creek, where we saw, in the evening, signals being made by the Indians on the mountain sides with poles and red feathers attached to the end of them. Pushing out a small party in the direction of the savages, they soon came upon a lodge the Indians had just left, and which still contained cooking utensils, pipes, tobacco, and some robes. Destroying the lodge, the party returned to camp; and we saw nothing more of the Indians. In the morning I witnessed a curious contest between an old buffalo bull and a pack of wolves. Nearly a hundred of these fierce brutes had attacked the old fellow, and were endeavoring to pull him down. They had torn open the scrotum, and terribly lacerated his hams. After watching the unequal battle for some time, we put an end to it by firing a volley into-the wolves, who scampered off. We then killed the old buffalo, and started on our march for Shell Creek. We camped there all night, and the next day reached the fort, the day being very cold and a rain falling at the time we entered the stockade.

I now busied myself in making a suit of buckskin, making my tour as officer of the day, and occasionally shooting a few sage hens and rabbits.

So time passed until the 9th of December, when I went out one morning to hunt blacktail deer; and on my return to the fort in the evening, I learned that the Indians had been there, and attempted to run off the herd. I determined to be more careful in the future, and remain in the fort, lest I should lose my scalp.

1 had employed, as cook, an Indian girl named Basache; and us she was good looking, I was constantly annoyed by young warriors of the friendly Crow tribe, who came to court her. Basache had a history, which is worth relating. She was a Crow; and one fall, when her tribe was out hunting, a startling adventure befell her, she then being a mere child. The village was pitched in a valley, beside a heavily-timbered stream; and the men were killing buffalo while the

squaws were engaged in cutting up and preserving the meat and hides. Basache had gone out into the woods to gather berries, and was climbing up a vine on an old tree, to pick some grapes, when, through an opening in the leaves above her head, she saw two great eyes glaring at her from a hole in the trunk. In a moment she knew it was a bear, and began to descend as rapidly as possible; but the bear also slid rapidly down the inside, and came out just as Basache reached the ground. She started to run, the bear following close at her heels. When she emerged from the timber several warriors, who were strolling near the village, saw her, and aimed their guns to shoot the bear, but feared to fire, lest they should hit the girl. Seeing the bear would catch her, they called out to her to lay down; and instantly she dropped as though she was dead. Bruin came up, smelt her face, and, taking his paw, rolled her over and over. She kept her eyes shut; and presently the bear sat down beside her, as if to meditate upon the matter. Bears will not touch a dead human body; but Bruin seemed to have his doubts as to whether Basache was really dead. Meanwhile, the warriors resorted to various artifices to attract the attention of the bear, and, if possible, draw him off in pursuit of themselves. At length they succeeded, and told the girl to run for the village; but no sooner did she rise to her feet than Bruin left the warriors, to pursue Basache. She ran as fast as she could; but the bear was soon again close upon her; when, seeing no chance of escape, she stopped, drew her tomahawk, and, as he came up, dexterously struck him between the eyes, sinking the sharp blade deep into his brain. The brute turned around, fell to his knees, and, roaring furiously, rolled over on his side, and died. So the Indians named the girl, who, before this occurrence, had no name. Basache, "the bear-runner."

SMOKE AND BAD BLOOD

ON the 13th of December we had a serious alarm, the friendly Crows reporting a large body of Sioux warriors approaching the post, evidently with the intention of making an attack, as they were in war paint, and had sent all their pack-horses and women to the rear. The companies were all got out, the cannon and arms cleaned, and every preparation made for battle. We remained under arms all night, but morning came and we were still unattacked. About eight o'clock it was announced that our outpost, at Piney Creek, near the fort, where the wood-cutters were, had been attacked, five Indians killed, and six wood-choppers wounded, four of whom had since died. The Indians had captured all the oxen and wagons, and driven them off. A half-breed, who came into the fort, said a number of Crow Indians were in the fight with the Sioux, and, on going out, we picked up several Crow arrows, which had been fired at the wood-cutters. This was not, however, considered conclusive evidence against the Crows, as we knew the wily Sioux had, in all probability, fired the arrows, in order to get the Crows into trouble, they having, of late, made several efforts to induce the Crows to join them in their war against the whites.

We marched out to the relief of the wood-cutters, and, although the hills were full of Indians, we could not induce any of them to come down and give us battle. We found most of the cattle, and brought in the wood-men, five of whom were dead.

Sioux, Cheyennes, and Arrapahoes in great numbers continued around the fort, causing us much uneasiness—as we knew from their sullen deportment, they were bent on mischief. One night, just as we were going to bed, several shots were fired by the sentinels, and we all sprang from our beds, anticipating every moment an Indian attack. The alarm proved, however, to be caused by a fire, which had broken out in the barracks, near the corral. The wind was blowing stiffly at the time, and, for awhile, the whole garrison was in danger of being burned, but the prompt exertions of the soldiers extinguished the flames, and restored safety. To add to our troubles, while the fire was burning, the Indians came around, and we were by no means certain that it was not a ruse to get us off our guard and then attack us. The gates were closely watched, however, and the savages finally retired without making any hostile demonstrations.

In the last days of December I was ordered down to Fort Reno with the mails, and set out, taking with me thirty men and two wagons. In three days I reached my destination in safety, having had a pleasant journey, and without seeing any Indians. After waiting three days for the return mails, I started for Kearney, and reached that place on the 31st of December, thus closing the year with a most dangerous, but successful trip.

Next day I ate a New Year's dinner with Lieut. Warrens and his accomplished lady, and spent some delightful hours.

On the second of January, the Indians again appeared around the fort, and Dr. H. W. Matthews, one of the Peace Commissioners on the part of the United States Government, called them to meet him in council. A number of chiefs and principal warriors came in, and, after they were all assembled, Dr. Matthews rose, and said:

"Chiefs and warriors: There was a time when the Indian and white man were friends. The Great Spirit and the white father at Washington desires they should still be friends. Your father has sent me to tell you this, and to try and induce you to listen to his words. He is anxious to please you, and wishes you to live at peace with his children. Yesterday was a great medicine day among the whites. Resolutions and good intentions made on that day are sacred, and will be kept throughout the year. We resolved to be at peace with you, and have sent for you, that we might talk together and understand one another. I hope that the peace we now make will be a lasting one, and kept, not only throughout the year, but forever. I would like to make a treaty now, but the great father will not permit me to do so, as I am but a subordinate chief. He has authorized me, however, to say to you, that if you will cease from war on his people during the winter, early in the spring he will send his commissioners, who are great chiefs, to sign your treaty at Laramie. This offer he makes you as a last offer, and if you reject it, the white father will be very angry. He loves you, but is not afraid to punish you I hope you will consider well what I have said, and decic wisely on peace."

When this speech had been translated into Sioux, Cheyenne, and Arrapahoe, so that all the Indians understood it, the doctor sat down, and a Sioux warrior, named "Stabber," addressed the council as follows:

"Whoever our father, who has just spoken, is, I believe he is a good man. We-are told that the great father (President) sent word some time ago for his soldiers to leave the country, and I want to tell you that we want them to hurry and go. Send word to the great father to take away his warriors with the snow, and he will please us. If they can go right away, let it be done, so that we can bring our old men, women, and children to live on these grounds in peace, as they did before you all came here. The Sioux, Arrapahoes, and Cheyennes never fought each other until you came and drove away the game (meaning in the whole West), and then attempted to drive us away. Now we fight each other for sufficient ground to hunt upon, though all the lands to the East were once ours. We are talking to-day on our own grounds. God Almighty made this ground, and when he made it he made it for us. Look about you, and see how he has stocked it with game. The elk, the buffalo, and deer are our meat, and he put them here for us to feed upon. Your homes are in the East, and you have beef cattle to eat. Why, then, do you come here to bother us? What have you your soldiers here for, unless it is to fight and kill us? If you will go away to your homes and leave us, we will be at peace; but if you stay, we will fight. We do not go to your homes; then why come to ours? You say we steal your cattle and horses; well, do yen not know that when you come into our lands, and kill and drive away the game, you steal from us? That is the reason we steal your stock. I am done."

When "Stabber" sat down, "Black Hawk" came forward, and said:

"Where was I made? I was raised in the West, not in the East. I was not raised in a chair, but grew upon the ground. (He then sat down on the earth, and continued:) Here is my mother, and I will stay with her and protect her. Laramie has always been our place for talking, and I did not like to come here. You are getting too far West.

257

You have killed many of our young men, and we have killed some of yours in return. I want to quit fighting to-day. I want you to take pity on us and go away."

A Cheyenne chief next addressed the council. He said:

"We have been told that these forts are to be abandoned and the new road given up, and we have come in to see about it. If this is true, tell me so. I never thought, we would come to a Council so far west; but the old men prevailed, and we are here. All last summer we heard that Gen. Harney wanted to see us at Laramie; but we would not go. Gen. Sherman also sent for us; but we would not listen while you were here. I don't know the name of my father there (pointing to Dr. Mathews), nor who at present is my great father (President) at Washington; but this I do know, my father (his parent) when he raised me, told me to shake hands with the white man, and try to live at peace with him, for he was very powerful. But my father also told me to fight my enemies, and since the white man has made himself an enemy, I fight him. How are you our enemy? You come here, and drive away our game; and he who does that steals from us our bread, and becomes the Indian's bitterest enemy, for the Indian must have food to live. I have fought you, and I have stolen from you; but I have done both to live. The only road you have a right to travel is the Platte road. We have never crossed it to fight you. I am a soldier. I have a great many young men here who are soldiers, and will do my bidding. It is our duty to protect and feed our old men, women, and children, and we must do it. If you are friendly, why don't you give us powder and bullets to shoot game with? We will not use them against you, unless you do us harm. I want ten kegs; and when the other tribes know that you have given them to me, they will know we are good friends, and will come in and treat, and we will all live at peace. I came here to hear talk; not to make talk. We are poor. Take pity on us, and deal justly by us. I have done."

The next speaker was a Crow chief, who, standing by the council table, said:

"Sioux, Cheyennes, Arrapahoes, Crows, Father: I have been listening to your words, and they sound good. I hope you are not lying to each other. The Crows have long been the friends of the whites, and we want peace for all. We want powder; and when the white father makes us presents, I want him to give us a good deal of ammunition."

An Arrapaho chief said:

I want to say this: "You are here with your soldiers; and what for? Soldiers are your fighting men. Do you then want to fight? If so, tell us. If you desire peace, send your soldiers away. I have some of your stock. I would like to see you come, and try to get it back."

This closed the speaking on the part of the Indians, and Dr. Matthews replied. He said that the Peace Commissioners would as willingly meet at Laramie as at any other place; but that it was more convenient for the Indians to come to Fort Kearney. He did not say when the posts would be abandoned, or the country and roads given up. He made no reply to the demands for powder; but simply said: "If the Indians cease fighting, and keep the peace during the winter, the Commissioners will meet them in the spring, and make a treaty which, will be satisfactory to both parties."

The council broke up, having effected no good result; and the Indians left more dissatisfied than ever. When asked why Red Cloud did not attend the council, a chief replied: "He has sent us, as the great father has sent you. When the great father comes, Red Cloud will be here." This evidently meant that the haughty chief would only treat through his agents or ministers, unless the President was present in person.

After the council I went down to the Arrapahoe camp to trade for some buffalo robes, and finally succeeded in getting a fine bridal robe; but had to pay the enormous price of $98 for it. I brought it up to the post, and showed it to the officers, some of whom had never seen so fine a robe; and all wanted to buy it. Gen. Smith wished me to get' him one, and seeing he had taken a great fancy to the one I had, I presented it to him; but had hard work to prevail upon the good old man to accept so valuable a present. Next morning I went into the Sioux camp to buy another robe; but could not induce the Indians to sell any for money, though they offered me anything they had for powder and bullets. A single charge of powder was worth $4, and four ounces of the little black grains would bring $40. The officers were not allowed to sell the Indians ammunition, however; and so I failed to make any trades.

One day Basache, my Indian cook, came to me in great glee, and announced that the Upper Missouri Crows, who had not visited the Montana Crows for some years, were coming down to live with them. She said her father was the head chief of the Upper Crows; and she must go immediately on their arrival, and join her tribe. I readily acquiesced, and gave the happy girl a present of a new dress to wear on the occasion. I asked her to stay a few days longer, and tan some skins for Gen. Smith, which she said she would be pleased to do. On the eighth day she went away; and I was sorry to part with her, for she really was a very kind-hearted and useful servant.

AN AMUSING OCCURRENCE

ABOUT the middle of January, Red Cloud came down and encamped within ten miles of the fort, sending word he was for peace, but would not come to the post, or talk with any of the officers. At the same time, Basache came back and begged me to take her again into my service. She found it much pleasanter, and far preferable, to being even a great chief's daughter. These chiefs had little else for women, she said, than plenty of hard work; so I returned her to my pots and kettles, and she was once more happy. She had .been with me but a short time, when her father sent her word to return to the, and notified me that Basache must not live any longer with the whites. I advised her to go back to her father's lodge, but this she positively declined to do.

The routine of garrison duty occupied us until the fifth day of February, when I received letters from home informing me of the marriage of my eldest sister, and the death of a lady who was an old and esteemed friend of the family. The letter of the husband of this lady, written to a brother then at our post, was, to me, one of the most touching epistles I had ever read, and it made a deep impression upon my mind.

While at Fort Phil. Kearney, I was called upon to participate in the curious ceremony of christening an Indian child. His father, Raphael Galleges, was a half-breed, and the mother a Sioux Indian. A Sioux warrior stood up on the mother's part, and I represented the father. All the women, except the mother, were excluded from the building, and then a bunch of sweet-scented grass was rolled up with some "Indian medicine," in a piece of elk skin, and set on fire. The room was soon filled with smoke, and the mother, taking the child, held him over the ire until the little fellow was completely smoked, when the father, taking him by the left hand, called him by name, "George Galleges." The mother next dropped some clear water on his face, and rubbing him thoroughly, the ceremony was ended. It was considered a good omen, that during the ceremony the child did not cry, for if he had, it would have men emblematical of a troublesome life, and that he would become an enemy of his "godfather." I was thoroughly glad, therefore, when the little fellow thus showed his good temper, or it would have given me great pain to reflect that, in after life, I should be obliged to kill my Indian namesake.

About this time there was an amusing occurrence at the garrison that will bear relating. The post had become filled with dogs, and General Smith, the commanding office determined to get rid of the nuisance. An order was accordingly issued to shoot all dogs found running at large during the daytime; and soon several curs who had no masters to tie them up were killed and thrown outside the stockade. The Indians, who were camped near, were not long in learning of the order; and every morning, presented themselves to receive the dead carcasses. One day, the officer of the day-shot a large dog near the guard-house, and, on turning around, to his horror saw his own favorite dog following him. He ordered the sentinel not to shoot him, and immediately sent him home and had him tied up; but the officer to whom the dog that had been shot belonged, watched his chance, and threw the dog belonging to the officer of the day over the stockade, when he was immediately nabbed, killed, and cooked by the Indians. This created a great row about the dog-law, but it was finally decided that it would not do to be partial, and that, if one loose dog was killed, all must share the same fate.

It was now well along in the month of March, and the sun was becoming quite warm, so that we knew the spring was approaching. Birds were numerous, and I often went out hunting near the post and met with good success, but did not dare venture far enough away to kill larger game than rabbits, sage hens, and occasionally an antelope or deer.

TWENTY AGAINST TWO

ON the 8th day of April the Sioux, mounted on fleet horses, appeared in large numbers on the bluffs north of the fort, and rode furiously around the hilltops, yelling and brandishing their weapons in a hostile manner. Many of them carried scalp poles, and were dressed in feathers and war paint. Most of the former parties had professed friendship, but these fellows would not come down to the fort, and were defiant in their actions. Some of the officers went outside of the stockade to see the Indians, but the savages would not allow them to approach the hill on which they were. General Smith then signaled them to come into the fort, but they refused. Three or four of them crossed the creek and galloped' toward the fort, but wheeled suddenly and made off. Presently we saw three infantry soldiers, who had been out hunting, running for the fort, and a long line of Indians, stretched out like skirmishers, following close in pursuit of them. The men were nearly exhausted, and the Indians could easily have overtaken them, but seemed only desirous of giving them a good fright. We opened the gates and let the poor fellows in, who, perhaps, never were so happy in their lives as when they saw the gates of the fort close between them and their enemies. The stockade was crowded with men, and the Indians sat quietly on their horses, apparently watching to see what we would do. General Smith ordered the cavalry to saddle up and stand to horse, and then, taking Boyer,* the interpreter, rode out of the fort and approached the hill where the Indians were.

*This may have been the well-known guide and interpreter, Mitch Bouyer, who was of Sioux and French heritage. He was married to a Crow woman and lived many years with the Crows, so was an enemy of the Sioux. He was with George Armstrong Custer's 7th Cavalry and warned Custer not to go into the Little Bighorn Valley on June 25, 1876. They both died there on that day along with five companies of the 7th Cavalry.—Ed. 2015

He wished to go up to the savages, but Boyer advised him not to do so, and, yielding to his advice, General Smith told him to call to the Indians to come down and talk with him, which he did, but for some time could succeed in getting no reply, when General Smith, advancing a few steps, cried out, "How!" This was immediately answered by someone on the hill with "How!" The general then directed Boyer to repeat again that he wished to talk with them, and an Indian, who seemed to be a chief, inquired, "What do you want to talk about?"

Gen. Smith (to Boyer). "Ask him who they are and what they want."

The Chief. "We are part of Red Cloud's warriors, and come to see when you are going to leave our country with your soldiers."

Gen. Smith. "Ask them where they have come from, and where they are going."

The Chief. "We have been fighting the Snakes on the Laramie road, and are going north."

The chief and three or four warriors then rode down quit near the general, and the interview continued.

Gen. Smith. "Tell them they have been expected for some time by the Peace Commissioners at Laramie, to sign the treaty al out, these lands."

The Chief. "We have been at the big talk at Laramie, and the Commissioners promised us the forts should be pulled down and the country abandoned in two months."

Gen. Smith. "Ask him if the time is up."

The Chief. "It is, and we want to know why you stay here with your soldiers."

Gen. Smith. "We have made preparations to go, and will leave as soon as we are ready, but if your warriors commit depredations or kill any more white men, we will not go at all, but stay here, kill you, and drive off your game."

The Chief. "We are not afraid, but I want you to go, and meantime give me some food for my young men to eat. Do you see that creek over there? Give me something to eat, and I will go over and encamp on its banks to-night."

Gen. Smith. "I have nothing to give you, but I want to warn you to restrain your young men from committing any depredations around here."

At this stage of the interview, the cavalry company, which General Smith had ordered to saddle up and stand to horse, but not to show themselves, was seen marching out of the gates of the fort, and as soon as the Indians caught sight of it they wheeled their ponies, and, putting the whip to them, never stopped until they were out of sight.

General Smith ordered the company back, and was much provoked at the interruption of his talk, as well as the false impression it had made on the minds of the Indians of treachery on his part. Toward evening the Indians again returned to the hill, but they could not be induced to come down or talk. One of them, who was Red Cloud's son, rode down, and, passing around the fort, minutely examined the works, but would not come in, or talk.

Near sunset the Indians were seen crossing the flat toward the creek where the chief had indicated that he would camp. The evening gun was fired as they crossed the stream, and the whole party halted and looked at the fort. After consultation, they seemed to think some sort of defiance had been given them, and a warrior, aiming at the fort with his gun, fired. The ball struck on the parade-ground, but did no harm. The Indians then went into camp, but left the next morning for Red Cloud's head-quarters, which were supposed to be nearby.

Two days later, another party of Sioux came down near the fort, and, on the day following, a large band of Arrapahoes encamped within a mile of us. There was no doubt now in our minds that the Indians meant mischief, and were gathering around the fort with the intention of attacking it as soon as their numbers should be sufficiently strong.

All remained quiet, however, until the 10th of June, when, about five o'clock in the evening, the pickets signaled a train was approaching, and I rode out with Lieutenant McCaulley, of the Twenty-seventh Infantry, to meet it. We had gone across a small knoll to the south of the pickets, and passed out of sight of them but a short distance, when suddenly we saw ten Indians riding down upon us. I called out to McCaulley that they were hostile, and we must ride for the fort as hard as we could. Turning our horses, we set off at full speed, and had got within full sight of it, and only about a mile and a half from the gates, when we observed some twenty Indians passing directly between us and the fort, evidently with the design of cutting us off. We were passing along the base of a steep hill at the time, and I told McCaulley we must climb, the hill and fight it out until help could reach us. Dismounting, we clambered up the hill, dragging our horses after us, who made the ascent with the utmost difficulty. When we had got about half way up, several Indians came to the foot of the bluffs and fired at us. We had no guns, but I could easily have killed one of them with my revolver, and was about to fire, when McCaulley called out not to shoot until they came closer.

We had now got to the top of the hill, and took up our position on the very crest. The Indians, going around to where the ascent was not so steep, were soon seen coming up, so as to surround us on three sides. Sheltering our horses behind the crest, on the side where there were no Indians, I told McCaulley to hold the animals while I drove back the enemy. Covering a big savage with my revolver, I was again about to fire, when McCaulley said, "Don't shoot until they charge," and at the same time the Indian, seeing my pistol pointed at him, turned and ran down the hill, followed by several others. I now brought it to bear on other parts of the line, and the cowardly rascals ran whenever I aimed at them.

We were in full sight of the fort, and anxiously looked for help, but as yet could see no one coming to our assistance. I now examined my revolvers, and to my horror, discovered I had but two charges in the barrels, and no ammunition with me. The situation was perilous in-the extreme, and I almost gave myself up for lost, but determined not to die without a struggle.

Suddenly McCaulley called to me to look out, and turning my head, I saw an Indian crawling on the ground within twenty feet of the horses. As McCaulley spoke, the savage fired an arrow, which barely missed the lieutenant, and buried itself deep in the shoulder of his horse. The animal reared and plunged with pain, but McCaulley hung to him, while I pointed my revolver at the Indian, who sprang to his feet and ran down the hill, leaping twenty feet at a jump.

I now had to be very active, and bring my pistol to bear in every direction, but observing I did not fire, the Indians became more bold, and approached within a few yards of us. Then, taking deliberate aim, I pulled the trigger, and an Indian dropped from his pony and rolled down the hill. The other savages fell back some eighty yards and commenced firing at us. The wounded horse was very restive, and I told McCaulley to let him go, which he did, when the animal bounded down the hill, and, to our delight, most of the savages put after him. About a dozen, however, again began to ascend the hill, and borrowing one of McCaulley's revolvers, I waited until they were within thirty feet of us, when I fired, and one fellow fell, but clung to the neck of his pony, and with the help of his comrades got away.

They were close upon us again, when a shout of joy burst from the lips of McCaulley, and turning hay eyes toward the fort, I saw the gates swing open, and the cavalry come streaming out. The Indians had seen it, too, and were preparing to charge, when I called out to McCaulley, if we could hold on a few minutes longer, we would be saved, at the same time directing him to let the remaining horse go and give me his other revolver. He did as I desired, and, running around the hill-top, I fired seven shots in rapid succession, with such good effect as to cause the Indians to take to their heels. The shouts of the approaching troopers could now be distinctly heard, and the Indians, putting whip to their ponies, soon disappeared over the hills.

During the fight, one red rascal, who had a rifle, had gone up on the ridge opposite us, and which commanded our position, and taking shelter behind a rock, had amused himself by firing at us for over an hour. One of his balls ripped open my jacket, and another cut Lieutenant McCaulley's sleeve. I also got an arrow through my collar, and one struck the vizor of my new uniform-cap, completely ruining it. We lost one horse which belonged to me, and had on when captured, a fifty-dollar saddle, and a Mexican hair-bridle, that I had paid one hundred and twenty-five dollars for, but a few days before.

The cavalry that rescued us, pursued the Indians and overtook them, when they had a sharp fight, but it is not known how many were killed, as it was took dark to see. We had had a narrow escape, and late in the evening, when we returned to the fort, and received the congratulations of our friends, I felt happier than I had done for many a day.

A YOUNG OFFICER'S LIFE

I DID not get along very smoothly in the army, the wild life I had led having in a great measure unfitted me for the duties of a soldier. Thus, one day, after finishing my nice new buckskin suit, I put it on and went out to show it to my friends, when the Adjutant of the post placed him under arrest for not wearing the United States uniform. On another occasion I was caught with a pair of moccasins on, and immediately sent to my quarters and threatened with arrest. Then I could not be at roll-calls at the precise moment I should have been there, and this enraged that peculiar old clock, Major Gordon, who was constantly, blowing me up. Other sources of annoyance, such as omissions to cross a t or dot an i in proceedings of courts-martial and boards, constantly presented themselves, so it did not take me a great while to become thoroughly disgusted with the service. Those who think an officer has an easy time of it are most woefully mistaken, for I certainly know of' no harder or more thankless labor than serving in the army of the United States. Every man who ranks you is your master, and you are, to all intents and purposes, his slave, though they call it by the polite names of senior and junior. I. did not like the dry old "Blue-book," and still less that excellent and entertaining cobweb of Hardee's, called "Tactics," while as to the unwritten "customs of service," there was no end to them, and they were, if anything, more obnoxious than the written ones.

A single example will serve to show some of the difficulties that beset the young officer on entering service, and I can assure the reader the problem given is only one of many more difficult that the youthful soldier is compelled to work out immediately on joining his regiment. A day or two after reporting at the garrison, he receives a neatly-folded three-cornered note, elaborately done in red ink, informing him that he has been detailed for "Officer of the Guard to-morrow." The ceremony of "Mounting the Guard" generally takes, place in the cool hours of the morning, in the presence of the commanding officer, the old officers, and the ladies. If a new lieutenant is to mount guard for the first time, the turnout is always unusually large and should the poor devil make a single mistake in the long rigmarole that follows, he is not only laughed at by his comrades, but severely scolded by the commanding officer. There is a form in the "Blue-book" for mounting the guard, which is about as clear as the "Rule in Shelly's Case," but much of what takes place is the "custom of service," or the whim of the commanding officer, who wishes his guard mounted in a "particular manner." These old bummers, who sail through the world under the general title of "commanding officer," are mostly dried up with age, and as cross as a Texas cow. They scrutinize every movement, and a saber held a little out of the perpendicular, or a hand half an inch too high upon the piece, will cause them to rear and charge like a bull in a china-shop. As to a downright mistake, should you be so unfortunate as to make one, they no sooner observe it than they grow purple in the face with rage, and if they didn't swear they certainly would burst.

I give the problem of guard mounting in the regular army, as I worked it out when in the service, though it is a long time since I "mounted a guard" and it is probable I may have forgotten something.

The line has been formed, and the officer of the guard takes his post in front of the center of his guard and about four paces from it. At the command, "Front!" given by the adjutant, the officer of the guard marches forward eight paces, and at' the command given by the adjutant, "Officers and non-commissioned officers! About face! Inspect your guard! March!" the officer of the guard makes an about-face, stands fast until the sergeants and corporals reach their stations, when he commands, "Order arms! Inspection arms!" and, returning his saber, marches to the center of the guard, faces to the left, and, marching to the right of the guard, inspects the arms from right to left of the front rank, then passes in rear of the rank from left to right, scrutinizing the uniforms of the front rank men. Next he goes to the rear rank, which is inspected from right to left, and the uniforms of this rank are examined, and then the sergeants and corporals are inspected. He then marches from the—rear to the right of the front rank, draws his saber, and, stepping one pace to the front, faces to the left, and commands,

"Open boxes!" If there is cavalry in the front rank, he passes it, going down the front line, and inspecting only the boxes of the infantry. The rear rank is then inspected, and, after all is done, he takes post four paces in front of the guard, and the adjutant commands, "Parade rest!" when the officer of the guard lowers the point of his saber to the ground, places the center of the right foot in rear of the left heel, and, crossing his hands on top of the hilt of his saber, stands still. The adjutant next commands, "Troop beat off!" when the musicians march to the front, turn to the left, and play down in front of the officer of the guard. When they have returned to the right again, the adjutant commands, "Attention guard! Carry arms! Close order, march!" at which the officer of the guard brings his saber to a carry, and, facing his guard, marches to the center, then turns to the left, and takes his position on the right of the guard. The adjutant, seeing his last orders complied with, commands, "Present arms!" when both the officer of the guard and the adjutant salute with the saber, and the adjutant, facing about, reports to the officer of the day: "Sir, the guard is formed." The officer of the day then instructs the adjutant how he shall march the guard, generally commanding, "March the guard-in review, sir!" when the adjutant faces about, and commands, "Carry arms!" at which the officer of the guard also comes to a carry with his saber. The adjutant then commands, "Platoons right wheel, march!" and the officer of the guard repeats the command, and then steps to the left of the first platoon, and commands, after it has wheeled, "First platoon left dress!" and, seeing it dressed, takes his position in front of the center of the leading platoon and one pace from it.

The adjutant now commands, "Forward, guide left, march!" and, as the guard marches in review past the officer of the day, the officer of the guard salutes with his saber. He also must command the guard in its march, and give all necessary orders.

When he leaves the parade ground, he will command, "Right shoulder shift arms!" and march his guard to the guard-house. The old guard has turned out and formed in line, and, on approaching the left of it, the old guard will present arms, at which the new officer of the guard will command. "Carry arms!" and march down the front of the old guard. Arrived on the right, he will halt and dress on the old guard, and command, "Present arms!" and salute the old officer of the guard. Both guards now come to an order arms, and await the approach of the old and new officer of the day, and when they come near, the new officer of the guard will command, "Old and new guard carry arms! Present arms!" at the same time saluting with the saber. The guard is then brought to a carry and an order arms, when the prisoners are turned over, the reports examined, the old guard relieved, details for the day made, and the posts relieved, all of which, without going further into details, takes about as long as what has gone before.

All this duty has to be done with a minuteness and precision wonderful to behold, and if an error is committed, the unfortunate officer is sure to catch it from the commanding officer.

HARDSHIPS OF A SOLDIER'S LIFE

AS soon as the traveler crosses the Missouri, and enters the territories, he begins to find the bluejackets, and the farther west he goes the more numerous they become. It is only just to the army to say that it has ever been the pioneer of civilization in America. Ever since Washington crossed the Alleghenies, and, with his brave Virginians, pushed to the Ohio, the work has been steadily going on. From Pittsburg, far down the Ohio to the Mississippi, and thence along the Father of Waters to New Orleans; next west to the Miami, and far up the lakes; then to the Missouri, and so on for thousands of miles until the other ocean was reached through Oregon and California. A. line of forts are pushed out into the new and uninhabited country, and presently people come in and settle near the posts. A few years elapse, and there are hundreds of citizens in all directions. Then the forts are sold or pulled down, and the troops march farther west to found new posts.

The knapsacks are packed, the cavalry are mounted, and we are ready to occupy a new line of country. "Head of column west, forward, march!" and away we go. What an outfit'. The long lines of cavalry wind over the hills, and then follows the compact column of infantry. Then come a few pieces oi artillery and the train. What a sight! Hundreds of wagons, filled with every conceivable article of food and implement of labor: steam-engines, saw-mills, picks, shovels, hoes, masses of iron, piles of lumber, tons of pork, hard bread, flour, rice, sugar, coffee, tea, and potatoes, all drawn in huge wagons. Six mules or ten oxen are seen tugging the monster wheeled machines along. The train is generally preceded by a score or two of carriages, ambulances, and light wagons, containing the families of officers, women, children, and laundresses. In rear of the train are driven the herds of cattle and sheep, and, last of all, comes a company of infantry, and, perhaps, one of cavalry.

Day after day the living, moving mass toils on toward the setting sun. Bridges are built, galleys filled, hill-sides dug down, and roads cut along precipices. We wonder how the pioneer corps can keep out of our way; but each day we go steadily forward, seeing only their work, never overtaking them. A ride to the front will show us how this is done. It is midday, and a company is going out to relieve the pioneers. The knapsacks are lightened, and off we go at a quick pace. At sundown we come upon the pioneers, and find some building a bridge, while others cut down the hill so the wagons can pass. We relieve them of their shovels, picks, and axes, and one half of the company goes into camp, and the other half goes to work. At midnight we are aroused by the beating of the drum and the half of the company that is in camp goes out to relieve the working party. At daylight we are relieved in turn; the work goes on day and night, and that is the way die pioneers keep ahead of the train.

Let us return to the column. It is near sunset, the bugles sound the halt, and the columns file off into camp. The cavalry horses are sent out to graze, the tents put up, fires lighted, and the suppers put on to cook. The white canvas gleams in the setting sun, and the camp resounds with mirth and laughter. Water is brought from the brook, and soap and towels are in great demand to remove the dust and stains of travel. Folding chairs, tables, beds, mattresses, are opened out, and carpets spread on the ground. The butchers have slaughtered a beef or two, and the fresh meat is brought in for distribution. The commissary wagons are opened, and sugar, coffee, rice, hominy, and canned fruits dealt out. In an hour we sit down to a smoking hot dinner and supper of roast beef, hot coffee, fried potatoes, fresh biscuit, and canned peaches. If the air is cool the little peaked Sibley stoves are put up, and the evening is spent in telling stories, playing at cards, and singing songs. Here is heard the thrumming of a guitar, and the sweet voice of woman; there are a lot of officers playing euchre, and yonder a group of soldiers gathered about their camp-fire telling tales of how they campaigned in Oregon, or fought the Comanches and Apaches in Texas and New Mexico twenty years ago.

The bugles sound tattoo, the rolls are called, taps blow, the lights are put out, and the busy camp sinks into stillness. Only here and there a light is left burning, where the quartermaster, in his tent, is busy over his papers, the adjutant making the orders for the morrow's march, or a noisy trio of officers continuing to an unseasonable hour their jests and songs. No soldier is allowed to have his light burning after taps, but the officers can do as they please everyone sleeps soundly, for each knows he is well guarded. It is near midnight, and, if you like, we will walk about the camp a little. Here is the officer of, the day, and we will accompany him. We go out to the edge of the camp, where a large group of men are gathered about a blazing fire. "Who comes there?" rings out upon the still night air. "Friends," is answered back. "Advance one and be recognized." This is done, and then comes the cry of "Officer of day, turn out the guard." There is a rattling of muskets, a hurrying and bustling to and fro, and the guard falls into line and is inspected—so far as to ascertain that all are present and everything right. Frequently an officer, but most generally a sergeant of experience, commands the guard, and all the sentinels are posted according to the directions of the officer of the day, who receives his instructions from the commanding officer of the camp.

The wagons are drawn up in long lines or semicircles, with the tongues inward, to which are tied the mules and oxen. Sentinels pace up and down to see that all goes right, and rouse the teamsters to tie up the mulcts that are constantly getting loose. The cry of "loose mules" will bring a dozen teamsters out of their wagons, and at least a hundred oaths before the animal is caught and secured. The cavalry wagons are placed twenty or thirty feet apart, and long ropes drawn through the hind wheels, to which are picketed the horses. Guards are every-where, and the sentinels are keenly on the alert. Each hill-top has its silent watcher. The herds are kept where there is as much grass as possible, and mounted herders constantly watch them, ready for an Indian alarm or a stampede. A cry of "Indians, Indians," produces great life and commotion among Abe herders, guards, and sentinels, but the body of the camp does not deign to move unless the firing is very heavy, and the order given to "turn out." This is the Regular Army on the march.

When the troops enter the Indian country, and the attacks become frequent, the column marches more compactly; the herds and wagons are kept well up; the women and children put among the infantry; flankers thrown out, and a howitzer sent to the front to throw shells and frighten off the savages. The boom of a cannon seems to be the voice of advancing civilization, and greatly terrifies the Indians.

At last the line of country that is to be occupied has been reached, and a fort is built. This consists of a stockade, log-houses, and shelters for the stores. Then the troops are divided, and another fort is built fifty or a hundred miles from the first, and so on until the whole line is "occupied." If there is danger, earthworks are thrown up, and one or two pieces mounted. Now begins the work in earnest; keeping open the communication between the forts; getting up supplies from the rear, and securing the way for immigration. The country is mapped, the land surveyed, the streams looked up and named, and saw-mills built. Settlers come in and open farms near the forts, and they creep up and down the valleys, and over the hills, until they stretch away for hundreds of miles. Meanwhile, there are Indian battles, surprises and massacres by scores. Hundreds lose their lives, but the settlements go on. There is a little grocery, a rum shop, a town, and by and by a city.

Every spring, as soon as the grass grows, the cavalry takes the field and scours over the country for hundreds of miles.

The infantry remains in the posts, or guards trains to and fro From April until December, the cavalry is on the go constantly, and the officers separated from their families. When the snows fall they come into the forts to winter, but are often routed out by the approach of their savage foes, and made to march hundreds of miles when the thermometer is far below zero. It is this that makes the troops so savage, and often causes them to slaughter the Indians without mercy. After a long and hard summer's campaign, the officers and men come in tired, weary, and only too glad to rejoin their families and rest, when scarcely have they removed the saddles from their horses' backs, when murders, robberies, and burnings, announce the approach of the fierce foe, and they are ordered out for a winter campaign. Full of rage and chagrin, they go forth breathing vengeance on all Indians, and after toiling a month or more, through ice and snow, with freezing hands, feet, and ears, they overtake the savages and punish them with terrible severity.

276

The soldier's life is, indeed, one of danger, exposure, and trouble. The hard-earned reputation of twenty years, often, is lost by the misfortunes of an hour. Old gray-headed officers, who have gained a score of Indian fights, are surprised once, lose their stock, and if they survive the conflict, are dismissed the service for "neglect of duty." Others, after years of toil, in a moment of rage, utter some hasty words, and are dismissed for "disrespect to their superiors," and others, again, for, in an unhappy mood, taking too much barleycorn. .

Nothing will give a man more aches, make him feel old sooner, or is a more uncertain business, than soldiering. I know that a different opinion prevails in the east, but it is founded wholly in error, and is dispelled the moment one arrives on the frontier, and sees what an important part our little army plays in the great work of civilizing and developing our country.

*A recent book by a Little Bighorn archaeologist stated, "Today the army advertises that it will take healthy young boys and make strong men out of them. The frontier army took healthy young men and made physical wrecks out of them" (Health of the Seventh Cavalry, Scott, 2015).

Even in winter time, when in quarters and resting, the soldiers are kept very busy. At day-break there is reveille, and immediately afterward, grooming of horses for one hour and a half. After stables, three-quarters of an hour for breakfast; then fatigue call and sick call. At 10 o'clock drill for one hour. Dinner call at 12 o'clock; fatigue call at I o'clock; drill at 2 o'clock; stables at half-past 3 o'clock to half-past 4; supper and retreat at 5 o'clock, and to bed at 9 o'clock, to go through the same routine to-morrow. Besides these duties, there are boards of survey, boards of inspection, schools of instruction in tactics, signals, and various other matters. Where is the business man, or the professional man, who works more steadily?

For these services, it is generally supposed the officers receive large pay, yet, the fact is, they get but a miserable pittance, as the following list of salaries will show: A second lieutenant of infantry gets $1,368 [$24,872 in 2015 dollars—poverty level wages] per year; a first lieutenant of infantry, $1,428; a captain of infantry, $1,648; a second lieutenant of cavalry, $1,467.96 per year; a first lieutenant the same as second; a captain, $1,648; majors of infantry, cavalry, and artillery, $2,160; lieutenant-colonels, $2,460; colonels, $2,748. This does not include service rations, quarters and fuel in kind, or commutation of quarters and fuel when not with troops. An officer receives a service ration for every five years he has remained in the service; it is worth $9 per month, or $108 per year. When officers are serving with troops they are provided by the Government with quarters and fuel free of charge, but when they are stationed in a city, or on staff duty, they are allowed to commute their quarters and fuel money, at a price fixed by the army regulations. If an officer is married, it is cheaper for him to be with troops, and be furnished with quarters and fuel in kind for himself and family; bit, if he is a single man, then he can board in a family in the city, and his money allowance for quarters and fuel will go a long way in paying his expenses.

TICKLING A CROW GIRL

ONE day at Fort Kearney I sent for my cook Basache, and asked her the meaning of Mock-pe-Lutah. She said it was the Indian name for Red Cloud or Bloody Hand, and that this terrible warrior had derived his name from his deeds of blood and the red blankets his warriors wore, who never moved on their enemies without appearing as a cloud, so great were their numbers. Sweeping down with his hosts on the border, he covered the hills like a red cloud in the heavens, and never returned until he had almost exterminated the tribe or settlement against which his wrath was directed.

Basache then went on to give me some most interesting information concerning the manner in which Indians obtained their names.

Ta-shunk-ah-ko-ke-pah-pe was Man-Afraid-of-His-Horses, and obtained his name from having captured a great many horses, which he was constantly afraid he would lose. On one occasion, when the Shoshonee Indians attacked his camp, Ta-shunk-ah-ko-ke-pah-pe left his family in the hands of the Snakes, to carry off his horses.

As has been said in another chapter, most Indians receive their names from some peculiarity of person or costume, or from-some misfortune. Thus, Ba-oo-Kish, or Closed Hand, a noted Crow Indian, was so named from the fact that when young his hand was so badly burned as to cause his fingers to close into the palm, and grow fast. Another was called White Forehead, because he always wore a white band across his forehead to conceal a scar that had been given him by a squaw.

The Omaha Indians name nearly every child from some incident or event that occurs at the time of its birth. Thus, a child was born on the march, and the mother having no knife to cut the naval string, broke it, and the child was ever afterward known by the singular name of No Knife, and became a noted man in his tribe.

I will here give place to a touching incident concerning a daughter of the noted chief Spotted Tail, the origin of whose name has been given in a preceding chapter. This girl, who was said to be very beautiful, fell deeply in love with an officer stationed at Fort Laramie. He did not reciprocate her passion, and told her he could never marry her; but the poor girl came day after day to the fort, and would sit on the steps of the officer's house until he came out, when she would quietly follow him about like a dog. She seemed to ask no greater pleasure than to see him, and be near him, and was always miserable when out of his sight. Spotted Tail, who knew of his daughter's love, remonstrated with her in vain; and, when he found he could not conquer her foolish passion, sent her to a band of his people several hundred miles away. She went without murmuring; but, arrived at her destination, she refused food, and pined away, until she became a mere skeleton. Spotted Tail was sent for, to come, and see her die; and being a favorite daughter, he hastened to her side. He found her almost gone but, with her remaining strength, she told him of her great love for the whites, and made him promise that he would live at peace with them. Then she seemed very happy, and, closing her eyes, said: "This is my last request, bury me at Laramie;" and then died. The old chief carried the body to Laramie, and buried it with the whites, where she wished to lie. The grave has been carefully marked, and is still an object of great interest to people who visit the fort. Spotted Tail, since the death of his daughter, never speaks in council with the whites but he mentions her request, and declares it to be his wish to live at peace with the people she loved so well.

Several romping Crow girls being present, at my quarters one day, one of them, for sport, commenced tickling another, who could not bear to have anyone touch her under the arms. The poor girl screamed frantically, and rolled over and over, but the other kept on poking her in the ribs until she fainted outright. Basache then, in great alarm, raised her up and called to me to bring quickly the scented grass; for the girl's tail was coming up in her throat and choking her to death. I brought the grass, of which Basache always kept a good supply on hand, and lighting some of it, one held the fainting girl over it while the other threw a shawl about her head. She soon revived and took her departure, when I asked Basache to explain to me what she meant by saying the girl's tail had come up in her throat. She said very gravely, "Every human being has a tail in

280

his stomach, and it is this that always makes him sick. Some have fox tails, others cow tails, others again tails of birds, and still others dog, mink, beaver, raccoon, and horse tails. The latter are very dangerous, and constantly liable to get out of order. No one can be sick while their tail is in order, but as soon as anything gets the matter with it then they are sick. If a man has cold, it is his tail; if he has fever, vomit, rash, boils, and, above all, pains in his stomach, there is something wrong with his tail."

This theory was so absurd I could not help laughing, at which Basache was very angry, and left my presence, but I called her back to inquire what kind of a tail she had in her stomach, when, to my surprise, she promptly answered, "A wolf's tail, sir." I said, "Do each of you indeed know what kind of a tail is in your stomach?" "Oh yes," she replied, "everybody knows that, and there is my sister, Ba-ra-we-a-pak-peis, who has a cow's tail, and Pen-ke-pah, whom you know very well, has a horse tail, which is constantly making her sick.. When Ba-ra-we-a-pak-peis was younger, her tail troubled her a great deal, and mother says it often came up in her mouth, and sometimes protruded from her throat, but it never does so now, since the Indian doctor gave her some bitter-herbs to swallow."

All this was very curious and ridiculous to me, but, upon inquiry among the Crows, I learned it to be a well-founded superstition, and nearly every Crow believed a tail of one kind or another dwelt in his stomach, which was the sole cause of his ills, aches, and pains.

On the 29th of June, 1868, I received orders to escort a train over the mountains, to Fort Steele, on the Platte, and as it was understood we would not return, this order occasioned no little joy. We signalized the event by starting on the 4th of July, and in due time arrived at Fort Reno. From Reno we marched to Fort Fetterman, where Major Gordon left me, and I continued to march toward Steele with Major Gregg. We arrived safely at Steele, on the 29th of July, and went into camp.

On the 6th of August I set out to return to Fort Fetterman, and had marched as far as Elk Mountain, by the 8th of the same month. Here I found the lumber-men had just lynched a white man, and I went up to see the body, but it was gone, though a tripod with a hangman's noose at the top was still standing. Under this rude scaffold was a fresh grave, and in it the unfortunate man slept his last sleep.

While marching up to Fetterman we found the hunting excellent, and killed in all forty-three antelope, three white-tailed deer, five elk, besides an immense number of prairie-hens, rabbits, and mountain grouse.

We remained at Fetterman until late in September, and while the command was out cutting hay, guarding trains, and scouting, I had some splendid hunting, and enjoyed myself better than I had at any time since joining the army.

WARS OF THE SNAKES

THERE is a people of more than common interest, living in the west, called the Shoshonees, or Snakes. They inhabit a belt of country lying on the north-west border of the territory of Wyoming. Their earliest recollection of the whites dates from 1806, when Lewis and Clarke made their famous expedition up the Missouri. In a battle with the Minnetarees, of Knife River, the Shoshonees were defeated, and several of their women and children captured. One of these, Sacajawea, the wife of a warrior, was carried far down the Missouri, and there Lewis and his companions found her. She showed them the way up the Missouri, to where the Jefferson Fork empties, which was the place where the battle had been fought. Captain Lewis, with three men, proceeded up the Jefferson, in search of the tribe, but could not find them. This was on the first day of August, 1806. On the third day of the same month, Lewis made another attempt to find the Snakes, and, although he saw fresh moccasin tracks, and knew the Indians were near at hand, and hiding among the hills, he could not induce any of the savages to show themselves. On the eleventh day of August, however, he saw an Indian on horseback, near the river, and spreading down a blanket, which is the sign of friendship among the Indians, the captain motioned the warrior to come-and sit by him, but he fled swiftly away into the hills. Taking some provisions, Lewis set out on the track of the Indian, and on the third day saw several men and women gathering berries. The men sprang upon their horses and made off, and the women hid in a ravine; but Lewis and his men captured one old squaw and a little girl. When the woman saw them near her she sat down, as is their custom, and holding out her neck, waited for death. Lewis raised her up, and cried "tabba bone," which means white man, at the same time stripping up his sleeve and showing her his arm, for his hands and face were as bronzed as an Indian's. Little by little the poor woman took courage, and looked up when Lewis put beads on her neck, and gave the little girl a pewter mirror. Then he told her to call the women who were hiding in the ravine, and she did so, but only two young squaws had the courage to come out. Lewis painted the cheeks of all three women red, with vermilion, and showed them their faces in the pewter mirror, which pleased them mightily. Presently a troop of sixty warriors were seen riding at full speed toward Lewis and his companions. The women ran out to meet them, and showed the warriors the presents they had received. A parley took place, and after some explanations, three Indians advanced, and embracing Lewis cried out, Ah-hi-e, ah-hi-e. "I am glad to see you," or, "I am pleased you have come." All the warriors embraced Lewis's men, and then they smoked the shoshonee, taking off their moccasins, which means, "If we are false, may we be barefooted forever," a terrible penalty on the thorny plains.

The whole party soon set off for the village, and when within two miles of it, they were met by the great chief, who made a friendly speech, welcoming the whites.

In the village, Captain Lewis and his party were given leathern lodges, which were nicely fitted up with the skins of wild animals, and young men came to build fires, bring water, and wait upon them. The chief came in state to smoke with the white men, first removing his moccasins, as a token of his good faith toward them. Lewis remained several days with the Shoshonees, and was hospitably entertained and pressed to stay longer, but hearing his boats had ascended to the Jefferson, he set off for the river, accompanied by the chief and his whole tribe, all wishing to see the boats. This branch of the Snakes was under a chief named, Cameahwait, and numbered about four hundred, but Captain Lewis learned that the whole nation then contained some thirteen thousand souls, and was scattered over a vast extent of territory. They claimed all the lands between the Missouri valley and the Columbia River. They spread over the upper Platte, and roamed along the Green, Bear, Sweetwater, Colorado, and Wind rivers. Their eastern neighbors were the Dakotas (Sioux), and their northern lands extended to the country of the bloody Blackfeet. West and south of them ranged the Comanches. At the time, however, of Captain Lewis's visit, the Shoshonees were at war with the Pawnees and Minnetarees, who were found as far north as the mouth of Jefferson River, on the Missouri.

Lewis found the Snakes armed with bows, arrows, and shields, but a few had fusils, which they had obtained from the Yellowstone Indians, who had got 'them from the North-west Fur Company's traders. Though they had often heard of them, and had guns, it is doubtful if ever the Shoshonees saw a white man before Lewis and Clarke's expedition.

The supposition by Schoolcraft and other Indian writers, that the Snakes are one of the primary stocks of the Rocky Mountain Indians is a mistake. They speak the same language as the Comanches, and are undoubtedly an off-shoot of that tribe. So says General Alvord, on the testimony of an American, who had lived thirty years west of the mountains; and Colonel Cady, who has been in the United States service since 1829, confirmed the statement, at Fort Laramie, in 1863.

When the division of the Snakes and Comanches took place is not so clear, but probably about 1780. Nothing is known as to the cause of separation. The Snake Indians found by Lewis, lived in the rugged and cold country bordering on the Jefferson River, and they were extremely poor and miserable, being compelled to live at times for weeks without meat, subsisting upon roots and fish. They had but few horses, but were fierce and war-like, their enemies greatly fearing them on account of their hardihood and bravery. Notwithstanding their wretched condition, they were honest, polite to strangers, and dignified in their bearing.

In 1845, we find the Snake, or Shoshonee nation, divided into the Yam-palick-ara, or Root Eaters, and Bo-na-acks, or Bannacks. They then, with the Utalis, inhabited the basin of the Great-Salt Lake, and extended as far south and west as the borders of California and New Mexico. Their numbers at this date is not known. In 1850, we find them divided into the assimilated tribes of Bannacks; Yam-palick-ara, Root Eaters; Kerlsatik-ara, Buffalo Eaters; and Penentik-ara, or Honey Eaters. Their whole number then was four thousand and five hundred souls.

General Fremont, in his expedition, came upon the Snakes first in the north latitude 42°, and longitude 109°. They had no horses, and lived principally upon roots. In the topographical maps of 1846, the land between Red Buttes, on North Platte River, and junction of Big Sandy with Green River, is laid down as war ground of the Sioux and Snake Indians. The distance between the two points thus marked was one hundred and ninety-two miles, and it was the dark and bloody ground of the west. There raged the terrible contests of the great Dakotas and the fierce Shoshonees for more than half a century. The Snake lands then began, as they claimed, at the mouth of the Sweetwater, but they seldom ventured so far east, even in time of war. Their western boundary was at the Columbia and along the Snake River, or Lewis's Fork. The breadth of these lands was one hundred and fifty miles. The eastern part consisted of sandy plains covered with sage brush, except the Sweetwater and Wind River valleys, which were rich and tolerably well timbered. The central moiety lay across the summits of mountains; and the western lands, for one hundred and forty hides, consisted of small valleys and bristling spurs of volcanic formation, through a fissure of which the Bear-River wound, and then poured into Salt Lake.

The Shoshonees, as we before said, extended under various names as far north as the sources of the Missouri, and south to New Mexico, Texas, and Arkansas. The overland route, first opened by the Mormons to the west, lay directly through the Snake lands, and, mustering all their force, the Shoshonees sought for years to drive back the pale faces. From the Sweetwater to the Great Salt Lake Basin the road is marked with graves. Here, on this lonely plain, they killed a straggler, there, by the little stream, they surprised the encampment; and yonder, in the gorge, they pounced down upon the train and murdered men, women, and children. A rude pile of stones, or a rough cross, marks where the bones of the emigrants molder with the dust.

In 1864, we find the Sualces greatly reduced in numbers (not over fifteen hundred in all), but still scattered over a vast extent of territory. Their ancient allies, the Bannacks, still lived with them, and had intermarried with the Shoshonees, but spoke a different language. Who the Bannacks are, or where they come from, is not certainly known, but, most probably, they are one of the numerous branches of the Dakota or Sioux family.

At present, the Bannacks arc divided into two bands, the most numerous of which is Ti-gee's. This chief and his warriors roam in summer from Soda-Springs, Idaho, to Fort Hall, and in winter live with the Snakes, on Wind River, in Wyoming. Pivi-a-mos, or Big Finger, who leads the other band of Bannacks, lives in summer, near Virginia City, Montana, and in winter they go to the Yellowstone River. They have fine trout fishing during the warm months, along the Snake River, and in the cold months, live on buffalo and dried salmon.

The Snakes proper are the Ho-can-dik-ara, or Lake Diggers, who live near Salt Lake City, in Utah. On the 19th of January, 1863, this band having become hostile, General Conner made a forced march with the Second Regiment of California Volunteers to Bear River, where he surprised them and almost annihilated the band. The Aga-dik-ara, or Salmon Eating Snakes, live on Snake River, and subsist on salmon.

The largest band of Snakes is Wash-a-kees, which roams in summer on Green River, and winters on Wind River, They eat deer, antelope, and fish in summer, and buffalo in winter. The Salmon River Snakes, called Took-a-rik-aras, or Sheep Eaters, live on Salmon River. As indicated by their name, they subsist on musmen, or musimen, or muffon, or wild sheep.

It closely resembles .the wild sheep of Barbara, Corsica, and Sardinia, and is supposed by Buffon "to be the sheep in a wild state."

It is of the Eastern Snakes or Wash-a-kees band I wish more particularly to speak. The chief is sixty years old, tall in stature, and of dignified manners. This noble old Indian maintains his treaty with an exactitude that would be creditable to the most enlightened ruler. Several years ago he ceased from wary and since then has done all he agreed to perform in the treaty with the whites. In 1864, some of his young men, having become dissatisfied, wished to go and fight the whites; Wash-a-kee made a speech, and tried to dissuade them Among other things, he said: "I am not only your chief, but an old man, and your father. It, therefore, becomes my duty to advise you. I know how hard it is for youth to listen to the voice of old age. The old blood creeps with the snail, but the young blood leaps with the torrent. Once I was young, my sons, and thought as you do now. Then my people were strong, and my voice was ever for war. We fought long years, and at length, when wasted by the bullet and torn by disease, the nation sought for peace. Go count the graves of the slain, and you will learn-my reasons for being anxious to save you who are still left me. Behold our women and children; if you go to battle, who will hunt and feed them? Make no more enemies, but save your valor for the Sioux, who come every year to fight ns. We said it in the council, and we wrote it on the .paper, that we would war no more. What we have signed we will keep; what we have said to the white father we would do, that we will do. No, a Shoshonee cannot lie. You must not fight the whites; and I not only advise against it, but I forbid it." Seeing the young men were determined on war, the old chief covered his head with a blanket, that he might not see them depart. For three days he mourned for them as for the dead, and then arose and denounced them as rebels against their chief.

Soon after their departure the rebel band was caught by the whites and nearly all the warriors killed. Those who escaped came back, and humbly begged to be taken into the tribe again, but Wash-a-kee refused, and bid them begone, for rebels.' For a whole year he would not see them; but, at last, softened by the lapse of time and the petitions of his people, he said:' "Wash-a-kee knows his duty, but his heart is too weak to withstand your voices. Tell the rebellious warriors to come home." He, however, deprived the chief who had led them, of his authority, and appointed a new chief over them. All this Wash-a-kee did from convictions of duty, to comply strictly with the terms of his treaty, and, as he said, "show the white father that I would do what I had promised him in the council, and written on the paper."

The present reservation of the Shoshonees commences at the mouth of Owl Creek, runs due south to the middle of the divide between the waters of Wind Fiver and the waters of the Sweetwater; thence west along the divide and crest of Wind Fiver Mountains to the longitude of the north fork of Wind Fiver; thence north to the north Fork, and up the same, thirty miles; thence east to the south bank of Owl Creek, and down Owl Creek to its mouth, to the point of beginning.

The belt of land lying within these lines is ninety miles wide and about one hundred and ten miles long. It was set aside two years ago by the Peace Commissioners, for the sole and exclusive use of the Shoshonees and Bannack Indians; but white men have already gone in and opened several fine farms.

The beautiful valleys, pure water, rich soil, excellent timber, and delightful climate of the Preservation make it a particularly desirable region for agriculture. It is, undoubtedly, the best portion of Wyoming Territory; and the Sweetwater gold mines, lying on the edge and partly in the reservation, have brought together thousands of miners, who readily buy up all the vegetables, corn, and grain that can be raised in the valleys beyond. South Pass City, Atlantic City, and Miner's Delight are fine towns, and furnish ready markets for produce. Miner's Delight is on the reservation, and husbandmen are every year coming in and opening farms. The increasing immigration will soon repeat the old story, and the white man will have the Indian's land.

Wash-a-kee, when told that the whites would soon want his land, bowed his head, and replied, with trembling voice, "I feared it, but I had hoped it would not come in my day. Look at me; I am old, and won't trouble the white father long. My people are rapidly passing away. Every year I see them falling around me. They will soon be gone. Once we owned all the mountains and valleys to the Missouri. See what a little mite we have left. We are weak; we are poor; we cannot resist the wrongs that are put upon us. Let the white father have pity. Let him spare us this great sorrow, and leave us our last home!"

And what reply did the white father make to this sad and touching appeal? In their last convention, "The People" of Wyoming "Resolved: That the proper development of the territory requires that the lands known as the Snake Indian Reservation, should be opened as speedily as possible for settlement by white men."

That was the answer sent back to the old chief and his people, and the governor of Wyoming reiterates the cry of the people, in his message, and then goes to Washington to have the Indians removed from his territory. So it has been for more than two hundred years: civilization touches barbarism, and barbarism recoils like a burnt child from fire.

The face of the white man, like an insatiable fiend, presents itself constantly before the Indian, and a voice cries, "Back, back, to the setting sun. I want your land, your game, your home, even the graves of your people; and I will have all! all!"

Some nations fight, some implore; but the result is the same—the white man becomes the possessor. So the beautiful valleys of the Snake lands will soon teem with population; towns will spring up, and the iron and coal, plaster and copper, be dug from the hills; mills will be heard on the clear streams of the Poppoagie, church bells wall ring along the silent waters of Wind River, and poor Wash-a-kee and his children, where will they be? Dead! Under the earth. Gone to the happy hunting-grounds of their fathers—with King Philip and his people, the Pawnees, the Minnetarees, the Mohicans, the Mandans, and all who have gone before.

THE PHIL KEARNEY MASSACRE

THE Powder River country, as it has been known since 1866, embraces all that unsettled tract between the head waters of Powder River on the south and the mouth of the Big Horn on the north, and between the Big Horn Mountains and the waters of the Missouri, an area that one day will be divided into several large States. This country was unknown, except as an Indian hunting-ground until 1866, when an emigrant road was opened through it to reach the Montana mines, but trappers and hunters had been familiar with it for many years, and had found it one of the best fur-producing sections in the West. Here the buffalo, bear, elk, deer, antelope, beaver, martin, mink, and white weasel, were found in abundance, and the pelts of all these wild" animals were collected by the bold trappers or Indian traders, packed on rude boats built in the forests, and floated down the Big Horn, Yellowstone, and Missouri Rivers to the great fur mart of St. Louis.

Just after the war of the rebellion, General Conner was sent into this country to chastise the Indian tribes, who had taken advantage of the state of war and the absence of troops from the border, to commence their raids on the unprotected settlements in Montana and Dakota. Conner had some Western regiments, raised on the frontier, and, though he possessed a good deal of merit and ability as a commander, and pushed his column into the center of the Indian country, he could not do 'much toward punishing or quieting the hostile Indians.

In 1866, General Pope, who commanded in the West, ordered a road opened through the Powder River country, for emigrants bound to the Montana mines and Oregon. Troops were sent into the country to protect the route, and they built three-forts, which have become historical on the border, Forts Reno, Phil Kearney [pronounced *car-nee*], and C. F. Smith, all named after distinguished officers of the Union army, who lost their lives during the war of the rebellion. Reno was built on Powder River, Phil Kearney on the Piney, and C. F. Smith on the Big Horn.

The building of these forts in the Indian country gave great offense to the tribes inhabiting it, both hostile and friendly, because the Government took possession of the country without the consent of the Indian, and in violation of the common, but pernicious system, of making treaties before going on to their lands. After two years of active war with these Indians, during which one regiment of the army lost one hundred and fifteen men and three officers killed, in various combats, the Government decided, upon the recommendation of a commission of distinguished officers and citizens, to restore this territory to the Indians for a hunting-ground, withdrawing the troops, abandoning the forts, and giving up to the caprices of a savage race a vast and fertile region, which had once been occupied in the interests of civilization, and for which many scores of valuable lives had been sacrificed. The policy of surrendering this territory to the Indians, after occupying it with a military force for years, has often been questioned, and the discussion of this matter has produced many sharp criticisms on the conduct of officials who advised and secured the abandonment of a rich, fertile, and beautiful country to a few thousand savages, who can make no use of it but to chase the lessening herds of buffalo and deer, and fit out from distant camps their yearly raids on the peaceful settlements of border States and Territories.

In the summer of 1868, the troops and settlers who were in the Powder River country, left it for the lower settlements, and since then nothing has been heard of it, except from half-breeds or friendly Indians. It is known that the Indians burned the forts almost as soon as they were abandoned, and no white men would be safe there now, unless in sufficient strength to defy the Indians.

Those people who are interested in the West will naturally wonder that the Government should withdraw its outposts, built for the protection of the border, and restore to the savage tribes what had been claimed for civilization, and it is a question that interests all of us: how long fifteen or 'twenty thousand Indians, less than the population of a farming county, shall hold for their exclusive use a valuable country as large as three or four States the size of Illinois?

So long as the Indians live by hunting alone, they will require a large country to subsist them of course, and just so long they will be vagabonds, living a precarious life, often hungry, and always poor, their hand against every man, and every man's hand (in the civilized sense) against them.

It is time the Government adopted a policy that should be beneficial to the Indians, instead of pursuing the old plan of taking their lands by treaty, in exchange for a few trinkets, and then leaving them to decay by the inevitable results of vice and poverty.

The contest between civilization and savage superstition is decided, and it is a problem for this generation to solve, whether the remnants of the savage tribes can be saved, and reduced to a state of self-supporting peace. Just how this can be done it is difficult to say, but it has been done with some tribes, and undoubtedly can be done with others. A few devoted and self-sacrificing men are now making efforts among Indians on the upper Missouri, and meeting with a success which warrants the belief that all tribes can, by proper effort, be turned gradually from their wild habits of roving, and living from 'day to day, to settle on reservations and live as herders and farmers.

Until we adopt the policy of putting the Indians upon small reservations and compelling them to stay there, we shall have constant trouble with them, and they will all the time be growing poorer in men and the means of living, for it is' well-known that large game is growing scarce every year, and before another generation comes on the ground, the buffalo, the Indian's meat and bread, will have become as scarce on the Powder, the Big Horn, and the Yellowstone, as it is now on the Platte.

The Indians understand this, and it is no wonder they are determined to fight for the Powder River country, for it furnishes the only valuable hunting-ground in the North, and they see no way but to keep the whites out of it, or starve.

Red Cloud, chief of the Sioux, one of the ablest and most intelligent Indians in the country, lately said, to an officer of the army, that he knew the white men could wipe out his tribe, but he was fighting for his home; it was a question of starving or basing killed, and of the two he had rather be killed. This is Indian philosophy, and from his stand-point it is right; but should not the civilization of the nineteenth century find a better solution to the question than starvation and the destruction of a race?

Civilization brings its benefits and its pleasures, but it brings its duties and penalties also, and the verdict of impartial history, the verdict of the higher law, in which we all believe, and to which we defer, will condemn us, unless we save and hand down to posterity at least a remnant of the race which we have' driven across the continent, and to whom our example has been evil and not good for over two hundred years.

The Indian tribes inhabiting the Powder River country are the Sioux, Crows, and small bands of Cheyennes and Arrapahoes. This country properly belongs to the Crows, or rather the western half of it, and is known in the Indian tongue as Absaraka, "The Home of the Crows." The Sioux, however, have driven the Crows from nearly all this country, by their superior numbers, and now claim it as theirs by right of conquest. The principle of *meum* and *tuum** is as little regarded among Indian nations as among white, and they rule very much as we do, the stronger taking about what it wants.

mine and thine: distinction of private property.—Ed. 2015

The Sioux are the strongest tribe in the North, and probably the strongest in the whole country. The tribe is made up of eight different bands, under different chiefs. Of these the Ogallalas, Minneconjoes, and Unkpapas are hostile, while the Brule, Yankton, Santee, Blackfeet, and Sans-arcs bands are friendly in the main, though they often send out war parties to attack the settlements and emigrants. The Yankton and Santee bands are probably as friendly to the whites as any Indians in the country. They are settled on reservations on the upper Missouri, and have commenced planting crops and raising stock in a civilized way. The Government furnishes them agents, who employ farmers and mechanics to instruct them in the various branches of industry, and two or three devoted men are living with them as missionaries, and are gaining a good deal of influence among them, even inducing them to build school-houses and churches.

This effort among the Sioux may lead to a solution of the Indian difficulty, and it is certain it is leading in the only right direction. The men who are devoting themselves to it should be sustained, and if they succeed they should be honored for the signal service rendered two races.

The hostile Sioux are led by chiefs of ability and determination. Some of them are very capable men, and fully posted on the Indian situation as affecting them and us, and it will be difficult to control them unless we can convince the thinking men of the tribe that we are sincere in our plans for their future. The Indian is naturally suspicious, but he is now desperate and revengeful, because he feels his poverty and sees no hope of better times.

The northern Cheyennes, a small baud split off from the southern tribe, are allies of the Sioux, and have joined them in all their operations against us. The northern Arrapahoes were allies of the Sioux until 1868, when they separated from them, and have since been at peace with the whites. 1866-67 were active years in the Powder River country—the Sioux, Cheyennes, and Arrapahoes were on the war-path continually, determined to drive the white men out of the country, and numberless combats ensued, involving a large loss of life on both sides.

The odds in numbers were always on the side of the Indians, but the troops generally came off victorious, owing to superior arms and discipline. The Indians could number about 2,500 warriors at this time, and there were never more than 700 troops employed against them. The engagements were always between detachments of troops, one or two companies or less, and bodies of Indians numbering from one hundred to two thousand.

The most important engagement in the Powder River country, the only one in which the Indians were successful against an organized force, was what is known as the Phil Kearney massacre, fought on the 21st of December, 1866, between a detachment of ninety-one men of the Eighteenth and Twenty-seventh Infantry and Second

Cavalry, and 2,000 Sioux, Cheyennes, and Arrapahoes. The troops were commanded by Colonel Fetterman, a gallant man, and most excellent officer, who had served with distinction during the war, and the Indians were led by Red Leaf, Iron-clad, and other noted chiefs. This fight shows a good example of Indian tactics and cunning. The garrison of Fort Phil Kearney consisted at this date of five companies of infantry and one of cavalry, commanded by Colonel Carrington. The Indians knew that trains left the fort daily for the mountains, to procure timber and wood, and that they had a small guard to escort them. So, collecting their forces, they reached the vicinity of the fort the day previous to the attack, and concealed their men belling the mountains, four or five miles distant. On the morning of the 21st December the train went out as usual, and, before it was out of sight of the fort, was attacked by fifty Indians. The attack was soon signaled to the fort by the picket on a neighboring height, and a detachment of ninety-one men, under Colonel Fetterman, were sent out to drive off the Indians and relieve the train.

See also, _My Army Life and the Fort Phil Kearney Massacre_ by Carrington's wife.

Fetterman, instead of moving directly for the train, took a line to get in rear of the Indians, and cut off their retreat; seeing this, the Indians fell back, skirmishing with the troops, and were followed over the hills, being pressed sharply by Fetterman, until about five miles from the fort, when he found his command suddenly beset by about two thousand savages, part mounted and part on foot, and all eager to fight. Fetterman's force was probably scattered at the moment the ambush was discovered, and many of his men fell at the first shock, but he drew back his party, and after retreating a mile, closely followed, he made a stand on the top of a high ridge, determined to fight it out; and here, after two hours of life-and-death struggle, the whole party of ninety-one men and three officers were killed, not even a wounded man escaping to tell the story.

All that is known of the fight, after Fetterman's party disappeared from the sight of their friends at the fort, is gleaned from the reports of the Indians, coming to us through half-breeds on the frontier, and from the position of the dead bodies when found after the fight.

The faults which led to the sacrifice of ninety-four men, well-armed and well commanded, were purely military, and should not be discussed here; but they were well understood, and were not repeated. „The Indians frequently attacked trains and detached parties of troops in 1867, but were always defeated, a small company on two occasions defeating seven and eight hundred Indians.

The losses which the Indians suffered in the Phil Kearney fight, and in other affairs with the troops, have never been known, as they always carry off the bodies of the dead or wounded as soon as they fall, holding it greater misfortune to lose the body of one of their men than to lose his life, and they will often sacrifice two or three in their efforts to carry off one who has fallen.

The Grows are the peaceful Indians of the Powder River country, and are old and firm friends of the white man. They are a fine set of people, and the best specimens of the Indian race to be found. They are superior to the Sioux in courage 'and ability, and often fight them successfully two to one. If the Crows were enlisted in our cause, armed, and sent against the Sioux, they would soon take the fight off our hands, and either subdue the Sioux or drive them out of the country.

The Government has adopted the policy of using friendly Indians to fight hostile ones, as in the case of the Pawnees, and they could not do a better thing, if hostilities are to continue, than to arm the Crows and other friendly tribes to settle the matter with the Sioux and others, who will not be quiet until they are soundly whipped.

The Powder River country is destined to be the home of a large and rich population at no distant day. It possesses all the elements of wealth, a fine soil and good climate, coal in abundance, limestone, and superior building stone, and undoubtedly great mineral wealth; iron is found in many places, and gold has been discovered by chance prospectors, in quantities to warrant the belief that the Big Horn Mountains and the Black Hills will prove to be very rich in precious metals, when they can be safely and thoroughly explored.

Abundant streams of pure water run through the country, and they will furnish more water power than all the streams of New England, when the time comes to use them.

The climate of the Powder River country is much finer than would be supposed from the latitude. From 43° to 45° it is about like the climate on the line of the Pacific Railroad, but from 45° to 46° it is much milder, being influenced by almost constant westerly winds, which bring to it the soft airs of the Pacific. The Indians call this section u Medicine Grounds because it is so pleasant and healthful. Snow falls in small quantities, and most of the winter the weather is delightful for out-of-door life.

The average temperature on the Big Horn is about that of the country bordering the Ohio. Cattle and all kinds of stock could live out all winter without shelter, and with no food but what they pick up; the grass, in this pure air, dies on the ground without losing its nutriment, and is just as good for food as that cut and cured in the usual way.

For stock raising, no country could be finer than this, for the conditions are such as to insure the minimum of expense and labor, and the fine air and water insure health to the herds. This country, including and bordering the Big Horn Mountains, is particularly fitted for sheep raising. Sheep like high land and dry air, and these, with the fine rich grasses of the mountain slopes, would produce fleeces not excelled in any part of the world. Sheep husbandry is in its infancy with us, but the time will come when the Big Horn country will be as famous for its flocks and wool as any parts of the old world, and perhaps as famous for its looms and mills too.

Game is more abundant on the Powder River than in any part of our possessions. Here the buffalo range in herds of twenty to fifty thousand together, sometimes blackening the country for miles with their huge bodies; but, though they are found in large masses, still all experience of border men shows that they are lessening in numbers, and the sections in which large herds are found are becoming narrower every year. The tribes in the North subsist almost entirely on buffalo meat, and t they probably kill a quarter of a million of buffalo every year.

As they kill cows mainly, on account of the better quality of meat, they reduce the herds much faster than is needful, with proper management. The elk, the finest of the large game, is found in large numbers, often one or two thousand in a band. Black-tail and white-tail deer, antelope; black, cinnamon, and grizzly bear; beaver, otter, and all the fur-producing animals, are very abundant. The streams are full of excellent salmon, trout, catfish, and bass; arid of the feathered game, geese, brant, ducks, and grouse are as plentiful as any sportsman could wish.

Wild fruits, such as plums, currants, gooseberries, raspberries, buffalo berries, and service berries, grow almost every-where, and are excellent. The Indians make a good deal of use of them for food, drying large quantities, and mixing them with the marrow of buffalo bones, for winter use; the dried berries are sometimes pounded up with buffalo meat and flit, making a sort of "pemican" which is packed in skins, and called towro.

The most singular of all the wild animals in the country is the mountain sheep, which-lives in the mountain ranges, the higher and wilder the better, and which are seldom seen in the low country. The mountain sheep, allusion to which is made elsewhere, is about the size of the common deer, weighing from one to two hundred pounds; the flesh is good, and very much like venison, having no flavor of mutton; the hair is coarse, like the antelope, and perfectly straight; the only resemblance to sheep is in the horns; these greatly eclipse anything seen in domestic flocks, being long, spiral, and giving the head a massive and imposing look. It is difficult to see what the animal was furnished such head-gear for, unless, as the hunters say, he uses them to break his fall when taking dangerous leaps, striking on his horns instead of his feet, whether this is so or not, he is a great leaper, and difficult to kill on account of his inaccessible haunts, and his boldness in eluding pursuit. If these animals could be caught and tamed, they would be great curiosities in our parks; but we have never heard of their being captured while young, and there are few opportunities to secure living specimens.

One of the greatest natural curiosities on the continent is the Big Horn cañon, where the Big Horn River breaks through the mountains, and when it is known, it will rival the famous cañon of the Colorado. It is about sixty miles long, as nearly as can be ascertained from those who have seen most of it, but it is not likely that anyone has seen its whole length yet.

Old [Jim] Bridger, the trapper and guide, has been through a part of it in a boat, and tells many marvelous stories of its wonders and dangers; and in 1867, Mackenzie, an adventurous frontiersman, saw a good deal of it, in attempting to run timber through for the use of the fort on the Big Horn, but he came to grief, losing his timber, which lodged on rocks, and wrecking himself and companions, with a loss of everything but their arms. The cañon is more than half a mile high in many places, and varies in width, like all breaks in the mountains, being narrow in places, and in others very wide. It is one of the most picturesque spots imaginable; its perfect seclusion gives it an air of mystery, and the slight sense of awe which creeps over one, in threading its wild paths is not lessened by the sight of an occasional grizzly.

The chief beauty of the cañon is in the multiform shapes taken by rock, and tree, and foliage; the rocks take every shape imaginable: turrets, spires, minarets, towers, and natural bridges. The timber covers the slopes sometimes from the bank of the river to where the top breaks abruptly against the sky, and beautiful streams twine themselves around the rude masses of rock, until one can often fancy he sees the old ruins of an abbey, with an English ivy creeping over it.

Whatever there is of beauty in the wildest scenes of nature, in the massive grandeur of rock, in the grace of vines and foliage, and the charm of running water, is furnished by this lonely cañon. And one of these days, when the Yellowstone and Big Horn are navigated by steamers, the traveler will seek this spot in pursuit of health and pleasure, as he now does Niagara and the Alps.

The agricultural value of the Big Horn country will be as great as Minnesota, or any of the Northern States. All the cereals will grow there without doubt. The valleys are fertile and well-watered, and much of the high land will raise the small grains.

The valley of the Powder River is the, poorest country in this section, but the valleys of Clear Fork, Piney, Goose, Wolf, Trout, Tongue, Little Horn, and Big Horn, are as fine as men need to live in, and much better land than a majority of farmers cultivate in the East.

PECULIARITIES AND HABITS

JUST west of the Powder Liver country, and north of the Snake lands is a very rich territory called Montana. The climate is delightful during the summer months, it not being too warm, and at night a person finds it necessary to sleep under one or more blankets. Much of the time the atmosphere is hazy, not unlike an Indian summer in the Eastern States. During the winter the weather is extremely cold, and people easily get frostbitten by exposure. It is never very windy, but quiet, still, cold weather, which is sometimes exceedingly pleasant.

The grazing cannot be excelled in any country, and much of the stock runs out all the winter, though there is by no means any lack of snow. In spring-time the stock is fat, and it is fair to say that no better beef can be found. Horses and cattle thrive, and look fine and sleek. There is plenty of timber on the mountain sides and in the cañons, and a thick under growth of bushes in which there is an abundance of berries. In such a country game must abound, and here are found the moose, elk, buffalo, deer, antelope, cinnamon or black bears, badgers, beavers, martins, mink, and a variety of other wild animals.

The Upper Crow Indians, who are friendly, live in the middle of the territory, in the unsettled portion, and seem to get along pretty well in their wild and savage way. Their reservation is on the Yellowstone River, in a fine game country; and a small, compact fort for the use of the agent has been built there. Here the Indians live, and hence they make their way to the buffalo grounds, and return laden with dried meat and robes.

In November, 1869, there were over three thousand five hundred Mountain Crows at the agency for the purpose of receiving the annuities given to them by the Government. The Crows had had a fight with the Cheyennes, in the country of the Sioux, in which, the Crows were victorious. They killed six adult Cheyennes and captured four young ones. These they tortured in the most barbarous manner, cutting off their hands, then their feet, and finally killing them. One Crow warrior was badly wounded, and died afterward. The daughter of "Iron Bull," a principal chief, also died at the agency, and her body was wrapped in furs and placed upon a scaffold in great pomp. Iron Bull burnt his lodge, destroyed his property, and killed his horses as a sign of mourning.

Over her and the warrior who died of his wounds, the camp was in a general state of-mourning, black paint was daubed on many hideous faces, gashes being cut with knives, and hair torn out by the handful. The Indians were mostly encamped on Bowlder Creek, near its confluence with the Yellowstone, and a great many River Crows were encamped below. After considerable difficulty about the character of the goods, the annuities were distributed.

The Crows had a very successful fall hunt, and it was estimated that there were over six thousand buffalo robes in their camp, which was also bountifully stocked with buffalo meat. The buffalo at that time were ranging within twenty-five miles of the agency, and after receiving their goods many of the Indians returned to the hunting-grounds. Tindoy's band of Bannack Indians were out hunting during the whole fall with the Crows, and brought back many robes and a good supply of meat.

The lodges of the Crows along the bank of Bowlder Creek were made of dressed .buffalo skins, and presented a picturesque appearance, half hidden as they were amid the bushes and trees. It was late in the fall, and the leaves had fallen, but the gray hues were softened, and the russet of the grass in the creek bottoms was enlivened by the presence of hundreds, perhaps thousands, of Indian ponies. Night was made hideous by the singing of the Indian songs and the howling of Indian dogs. In the daytime there was a grand display of Indian firing by the young dandies, and scalp dances over the scalps of the unfortunate Cheyennes who had been killed.

The Crows have always been friendly to the whites, with perhaps a few exceptions. They are arrant thieves, and on more than one occasion have been accused of cowardice, though that is not true of them. A more persistent nation of beggars, however, does not exist upon earth. An Indian always expects a present of some kind, but it has been remarked that few, if any, Indians make presents in return.

"Get all you can and keep all you get" is the maxim of the Aborigines. One of them never was known to give away anything that was not absolutely worthless. A squaw of the Crow tribe, or as they call themselves Absarcis, never visits a white man's house without saying in the most pitiful and drawling tones, "Awush-me; Awush-me;" meaning, "I am hungry; I am hungry;" even though she has just eaten enough food to kill a white woman outright. A more sorrowful and melancholy cadence cannot be given to any language than that given by the Crows to their own. I had the honor to become acquainted with some of the big-nosed and nobby-complexioned leaders of this nation of Indians, among whom I recollect with peculiar feelings the chiefs Iron Bull, Black Foot, Show-his-face, Old Wolf, The Coat, Black Bird, and several others whose distinguished names do not now occur to me. They have an immense idea of their own importance, "and feel so big," as the Californians say, "that a very large overcoat would only make for them a moderate-sized vest." Their highest delight is to smoke kee-nick—kee-nick from the bowl of a red pipe with a long stem. They are excessively dignified and correspondingly ignorant.

There are some excellent roads in the territory of Montana. The one leading from Virginia City to Helena, and thence to Fort Benton, is a most excellent thoroughfare. A road was made in the summer of 1869 from Bozeman across the country to the mouth of the Muscleshell, and thence back to Helena. It was thought that all freight would be brought up to the mouth of the river, by boats on the Missouri River, and freighted across the country to such points as it might be destined for, but this has been superseded by the railroad; and now, unless the cost of carriage is too high, the freighting will all be done that way, and from Corinne it will be carried up into the territory. It may cost somewhat more this way, but it is more expeditious, and .on the whole far more satisfactory.

Montana has within her borders several rivers, the largest of which are the Missouri, Clarke's Fork of the Columbia, and the Yellowstone. The former is navigable as far as Fort Benton, but this is only for an exceedingly limited portion of the year, and ordinarily boats can make but one trip from St. Louis to Fort Benton and back again during the season. In some exceptional cases, however, two trips have been made. Clark's Fork is on the west side of the Rocky Mountains, and is formed by the junction of the Bitter Root and Flat Head Rivers, the Bitter Root being itself formed by the junction of the Big Blackfoot, Missoula, and the Hellgate Rivers. The whole interior of Montana is remarkably well watered, and there are gold placers on many of the creeks, the names of which it would be useless to give, as it would only lead to confusion in obtaining a knowledge of the country. The Missouri is formed by the junction of the "Three Forks," called respectively the Jefferson, the Madison, and the Gallatin Rivers, so named by Lewis and Clarke.

These are all noble and beautiful streams, lined with fine growths of timber, and abounding in trout. In the Madison are found the "half trout," a peculiar kind of a fish, which has specks and scales, being half trout and half whitefish. The timber and underbrush along these streams is a favorite resort for Indians who are now friendly. It is somewhat singular that no hard wood, such as hickory and maple, is found west of the Rocky Mountains.

There are several ranges of mountains, as the name of the territory indicates, and long before the whites came it was known to the Snake or Shoshonee. Indians as "To-yabe-shock-up" or "the Country of the Mountains." The only considerable body of water is Flat Head Lake, in the north-western corner, and the source of the river of the same name.

As the main importance abroad given to Montana is wholly connected with the gold mines, an account of them may be interesting, though it is exceedingly difficult to convey to the reader a good idea of them. Gold is not picked up by the handful, even in the best of diggings; and long lines of sluice boxes, piles of cobble stones, and thick beds of mud in the shape of "tailings," have all to be taken into account when thinking of getting out gold in the placers. To this must be added the heavily-booted and thickly-bearded miners, who are a distinct class of people, having their own peculiar phrases, their own laws, their own amusements, and their own ways of dressing, living, and working. That they do work is certain: in no country on earth do they work so hard, and all the raining that has ever been done in the United States has not paid in coin more than ten cents per day. When people think of going to the gold mines, it would be well to bear this fact in view.

It would be useless to go into dry mining details, which at best are unsatisfactory, and therefore only the general results will be given in round numbers. It must be said that this statement has been drawn up by a warm friend of the Montana mines, and must be received with some caution. Since the discovery that gold has been found in the territory, it is supposed the following-named sums have been taken out of the placer mines in the several counties of the territory:

Total, .$92,384,200

About $603,818,300 in 2015 dollars.

In addition there are Choteau, Missoula, Muscleshell, and Gallatin Counties from which there are no returns.

In the autumn of 1869 rich gold discoveries were made in Missoula County. The new diggings are said to be very extensive, and a large mining camp sprung up there during the winter of 1869-70. A great many people left Helena and other towns on both sides of the range, and the roads leading in the direction of Missoula were dotted with eager gold-seekers bound for speedy fortunes.

As all gold discoveries run about the same course, the following characteristic letters are given relative to these mines:

LETTER TO W. H. TODD.

"Fish Creek Ferry, Missoula County,

'Montana Territory, Dec. 4, 1869.'

"About two weeks since a few Frenchmen passed here, and the report was a 'big strike' had been made somewhere near Losa's Ranch, situated some twenty miles below French town. Two or three days, more and the stampede was up in earnest, men passing at all hours of the day and night. I started at dark, and reached Losa's Ranch at 2 o'clock. Next morning we followed our guide across the Missouri River, thence five miles down, crossed a stream, and followed it up about four miles. Here we left our horses, took a little grub and our blankets, and footed it nine miles up the creek, and were in the diggings. They were discovered last summer by

French, who panned out over three hundred dollars in six days' time, from different places up and down the gulch. One nugget of eighteen dollars was found. I located claim 63 below discovery. Ten cents to the pan has been Taken out of the top gravel for two thousand feet below my ground, and, in one instance, as high as fifty-eight cents was taken out of two pans. It is thought the whole length of the main creek is good; also, the right-hand fork, which is seven or eight miles long, and empties in below discovery. Respectfully, etc.,

"Nelson J. Cochrane.

A-Missoula correspondent, writing under date of December 6, 1869, communicates the following:

"I will now come to another excitement, which, I am sure, will be of more interest to the public. I refer to the stampede now going on to the new Eldorado of Montana, and located on the west side of the Missouri River, some seventy-five miles below here, and to which place everybody has gone or is going as soon as he can. The excitement commenced last week, but little was then thought of it. Last week parties arrived in town from there, when the news spread like fire, and never, since the memorable stampede from Bannack to Alder Gulch, in 1863, have I seen the like everyone who can get a horse has gone. A creek ten or twelve miles long has been prospected, and the result shows it to be of fabulous-richness—even too rich to be told by a newspaper correspondent. Suffice it to say that it bids fair to rival Alder Gulch in its best days. I saw and talked with the discoverer to-day, and others direct from there. The gulch or creek proper was discovered by a Canadian named Louis Bassette, and the majority of the men in there are Canadians. I have seen some pf the gold, and it much resembles that from McClellan Gulch—-quite coarse and of good quality. Runners have been sent to the camps in Deer Lodge, and a general stampede from the other country is expected to commence in a few days, as men cannot hold ground unless they are there in person.

"J. N. Ringold."

In April, 1865, flour sold in Virginia City for one hundred and ten dollars a hundred pounds, or one dollar and ten cents in gold per pound. It must be confessed this was a high price, and everything else was in proportion. At that time men" lived on "beef straight," and gave the flour to the women and children.

The largest nugget yet found in the territory was one which was discovered in Nelson's Gulch, on the 3d July, 1863, which was worth two thousand and sixty-three dollars. Near this gulch the outline of the mountains present a most singular appearance. In Arizona a bold outline on the mountain side, a short distance west of Maricopa Wells, is called "Montezuma's Face," and is, indeed, a most perfect representation of the face of a man lying on his back, dead. It is looked upon with awe by the neighboring Indians.

Montana is now almost isolated from the great and stirring events which are going on in the new path of commerce which stretches across the continent. It seems to be, and really is, one of the most remote portions of our country, blocked in by the far Western States and those of the Pacific, and having for its boundary on the north the bleak and almost limitless British Possessions. It is a majestic, wild, and solitary land.

Embracing that region lying between the 45th and 49th parallels of north latitude, and the 27th and 39th meridians west from Washington, it contains an area of one hundred and forty-three thousand seven hundred and seventy-six square miles, equal to ninety-two million sixteen thousand six hundred and forty acres, extending from east to west about seven hundred and fifty miles, and from north to south about two hundred and seventy-five miles. This area is nearly equal to that of California, and three times that of New York.

Of this region the Surveyor-general, in his report for 1869, estimates, that fully thirty millions six hundred and seventy-two thousand two hundred and sixteen acres are susceptible of cultivation. This is about one-third of the territory; 'the other two-thirds comprise the main range of the Rocky Mountains, running north and south across the territory, and numerous subordinate spurs, whose peaks' often surpass in altitude those of the main range.

Among the spurs may be mentioned the Coeur d'Alene and Bitter Root Mountains, making the dividing line between Montana and Idaho on the west, between which and the main range lies the rich and productive country embraced in Deer Lodge and Missoula

308

Counties; the Belt and Judith Mountains, separating the sparsely settled Musleshell County on the north-east, and Choteau County on the north-west, from the rich mining regions of Meagher County on the south, extending to the Missouri River, which is also the north-eastern boundary of Lewis & Clark County; the Bear's Paw and

Little Rocky Mountains, still to the north; the Big Horn Mountains extending into Dakota, in the south-east, north and east of which lies the unorganized county of Big Horn or Vaughan, embracing the Yellowstone region, with Gallatin County to the north-west, and Madison and Beaver Head lying west and south-west; and the western spurs of the Wind River Mountains, on the extreme eastern border.

Coal of a good quality has been found in Montana, and as rapidly as the country settles up, and it becomes necessary to develop this source of wealth, it will no doubt be found in great abundance, and perhaps of a superior quality. Year Bozeman a fine vein of bituminous coal has been developed. Just above Benton a promising vein has been opened; above Bannack, and also' near Virginia City, and on the Dearborn, veins from four to five feet have been discovered.

The inhabitants of Montana are a generous, open-hearted people, full of life and activity, and noted for that boundless hospitality which is peculiar to the frontiers. They change their places of abode readily, build up a town rapidly, and with little or no ceremony, and abandon it as readily with no symptoms of regret. Wherever mines are there they are also. They believe in themselves; take an immense amount of stock in the Great West; do not object to whisky straight are always on hand to assist a friend in distress, and take kindly to theaters and hurdy-gurdy saloons. "Plug" hats and store clothes are their abomination. A buckskin rig is considered the height of the *ton*, with a broad-brimmed soft hat "reared back" in front,

AN INDIAN ELOPEMENT

THE British traveler, Atkinson, has already told the tale of Souk, and had he laid his story among the Ogallala Sioux, instead of the wild Kirghis, and dated it about the middle, instead of the beginning of the present century, he would have been entirely correct.

Souk, was the son of the great chief of his tribe, and a young man of remarkable ability. His father had great confidence in the sagacity of his son, and intrusted him with all important expeditions of war and diplomacy. So great, indeed, was the belief of the old chief in his son, that he would undertake no enterprise without first consulting him.

The Ogallalas and Brules had sprung from the same parent stock, and had long been friendly. They were the two most powerful tribes on the plains, and by uniting their councils and forces, gave law to all the weaker tribes. At the head of the Brules was an old and experienced chief, who often met Souk's father to consult about the welfare of their tribes, and, on all such occasions, Souk was present as the prime minister of his chief and father. The old Brule frequently noticed the young Ogallala, and seemed mightily pleased with him. On one or two occasions, he spoke to Souk encouragingly, and one day .went so far as to invite him to visit his tribe, and spend a few days at his lodge. These visits were often repeated, and it was during one of them, Souk met the daughter of his friend, who was the belle of her tribe, and, besides her great personal charms, was esteemed to be the most virtuous and accomplished young woman in the nation. It did not take long for her to make an impression on the heart of Souk, and soon both the young people found themselves over head and ears in love with each other.

The Indian girl was proud of her lover, as well she might be, for he was only twenty-eight years of age, tall, handsome, good-tempered, and manly in his deportment. Besides these considerations in his favor, he was virtually the head of his tribe, and no warrior was more renowned for deeds of valor. A born chief, the idol of his aged father, prepossessing in his appearance, already at the head of his tribe, and its chief warrior, he was just such a person as was likely to move the heart and excite the admiration of a young girl.

Atchafalaya [pronounced—Chaf-fa-ly-a] was the only daughter of the Brule chief, and the spoiled pet of her father. She was tall, lithe, and agile as an antelope. She could ride the wildest steed in her father's heads, and no maiden in the tribe could shoot her painted bow so well, so daintily braid her hair, or bead moccasins as nicely as Atchafalaya. Giving all the love of her passionate, nature to Souk, he loved her with the whole strength of his manly heart in return. Day after day, the lovers lingered side by side, sat under the shade of the great trees by the clear running brook, or hand in hand, gathered wild flowers by the shadows of the tail hills.

Sometimes Souk was at the village of his father, but he always made haste to excuse himself, and hurried back to the camps of the Brule chief; indeed, he was never content, except when by the side of the bewitching Atchafalaya. The old men knew of the growing attachment between their children, and seemed rather to encourage than oppose it. Atchafalaya was buoyantly happy, and a golden future seemed opening up before her. Souk often reflected how happy he would be when he and his darling were married; and, frequently, at night, when the stars were out, the young lovers would sit for hours and plan the future happiness of themselves, and the people over whom they would rule.

One day, Souk returned to his father's camp, and formally notified him of his Jove for Atchafalaya, and demanded her in marriage. The old chief listened attentively, and at the close of Souk's harangue) rose and struck the ground three times with his spear, declaring that he knew of no 'reason why his son should not be made happy, and have Atchafalaya to wife. The grateful Souk was so overjoyed, that forgetting his position, and the rank of his chief, he fell upon his neck, and kissing him again and again, actually shed tears. Putting him kindly aside, the father, well knowing the impatience of young lovers, hastily summoned three of his most distinguished chiefs, and said to them, "Mount your swiftest horses! go to the camps of the Brule, and when you have come to him, say, Souk, the son of his old friend, loves his only daughter, Atchafalaya, and that I demand her of him in marriage to my son. You will also say, that, according to the ancient customs of our tribes, I will pay to him whatever presents he may demand for the maiden, and that it is my desire, the friendship long existing between ourselves and our people may be cemented by the marriage of our children."

Bowing low, the chiefs retired, and were soon on their way to the Brule village, which was three days' journey distant. Rather than wait impatiently in the camp until the chiefs would return, Souk proposed to go on a short hunting excursion with some young warrior friends to whom he could unbosom himself.

Meantime, the chiefs had proceeded on their errand, and on the evening of the third day, caught sight of the Brule camp. They were hospitably received by the venerable chief, who did all in his power to make them comfortable after their fatiguing ride. On the following morning, the chief assembled his counselors, and making a great dog-feast, heard the request of the ambassadors. When they had done speaking, the Brule rose and announced his consent to the marriage, saying, he was delighted to know that his daughter was to be the wife of so brave and worthy a young man as the son of his friend. He then dismissed the chiefs, stating that he would shortly send an embassy to receive the promised presents, and complete the arrangements for the marriage of the young couple.

When the chiefs returned to their camp and announced .the result of their mission, there was great r rejoicing, and Souk, who had cut his hunt short and returned before the chiefs, was now, perhaps, the happiest man in the world. There was still, however, one thing which greatly troubled him. He knew his father was very proud, and considered the honor of an alliance with his family so great that but few presents would be required to be made. On the other hand, the old Brule was exceedingly parsimonious, and, no doubt, would take this opportunity to enrich himself by demanding a great price for his daughter's hand.

Determined not to wait the pending negotiations before seeing his sweetheart, Souk summoned a band of his young warriors, and burning with love, set out for the Brule camp. It being the month of June, Souk knew the old chief would have removed from his winter encampment to his summer hunting-grounds and pasture, on the Lower Platte. This would require some seven or eight, days more travel, and carry him through a portion of the territory of his enemies; but, love laughs at danger, and selecting eight tried companions, he set out. The evening of the second day brought him to the border of his father's dominions, and, selecting a sheltered camp by the side of a little stream they determined to rest their animals for a day before crossing the country of the hostile Cheyennes.

As soon as it was dark they saddled their horses, and, swimming the Upper Platte, set out to cross the enemy's lands. Their route lay in a south-easterly direction, and led them over a fine hilly country, almost destitute of wood, except in the' deep valleys and narrow ravines. The sun had long passed the meridian, the horses had rested, and the travelers taken their midday meal, but as yet had seen nothing to indicate that man was anywhere in this vast region.

The sun was fast going down, and they were endeavoring to reach a good camping-ground known to several of the party, when suddenly, as they were descending a mountain, they saw below them smoke curling up, and, in the distance, two objects which looked like ants on the plain. Prom their position they could not see the fires from whence the smoke arose, but the sight of it caused them hastily to dismount and lead their horses under shelter of the projecting rocks, that they might not be discovered.

Two advanced on foot to reconnoiter, creeping cautiously round the base of the rocks, and then onward among fallen masses that completely screened them. At length they reached a point from which they beheld, about half a mile below them, an encampment of over one hundred men. Three large fires were blazing, and while groups were gathered around them, others were picketing out the horses, and evidently preparing to encamp for the night. Souk's men had not long been in their observatory when they, saw two men riding furiously down the valley toward the camp, and they instantly surmised that these were the two black spots they had seen on the plain, and that Souk and his party had been discovered. They were not long left in doubt, however, for 'as soon as the horsemen reached the camp they rode to the chiefs lodge, commenced gesticulating violently, and pointing toward the cliffs where Souk and his men were. A crowd gathered around the new comers, and presently several were seen to run to their horses and commence saddling up. The scouts now hastily left their hiding-place, and hurried back to Souk, whom they informed of all that was transpiring below.

Not a moment was to be lost, and, ordering his men to mount, Souk turned up the mountain along the path he had just come. He knew he had a dangerous and wily enemy to deal with, ten times his own in numbers, and that it would require all his skill to elude them, or the greatest bravery to defeat them, should it become necessary to fight.

Fortunately he knew a pass further to the west that was rarely used, and for this he pushed with all his might. On reaching the mountain-top, and looking back, black objects could be seen moving rapidly up the valley, and they knew the enemy was in pursuit of them. All night Souk toiled along, and when the morning began to break, saw the pass he was seeking still several miles ahead. Reaching the mountain's edge at sunrise, they dismounted and began the perilous descent into the gorge. In two hours it was accomplished, and they entered the somber shadows of the great cañon. They had begun to feel safe, when suddenly the man in front reined up his horse and pointed to several pony tracks in the sand. Souk dismounted and examined them, and, on looking round, saw where the animals had been picketed, apparently, about two hours before.

Could it be possible that the enemy had reached the pass before him, and were waiting to attack him higher up in the gorge? He could hardly credit it, and yet it must be so, for who else could be in that lonely glen. Recollecting that the cañon to the right would carry him into the great pass some ten miles higher up, he still hoped to get through before the enemy reached it, and, hastily mounting, they galloped furiously forward. They had come in sight of the great pass, when, just as they were about to enter it, they saw a man sitting on a horse a few hundred yards ahead of them, and directly in the trail.

314

On observing the Ogallalas, the horseman gave the Cheyenne war-whoop, and, in a moment, a dozen other mounted men appeared in rear of the first.

Grasping his spear, Souk shouted his war-whoop, and, ordering his men to charge, dashed down upon the enemy. Plunging his spear into the nearest foe, he drew his battle-ax and clove open the head of the one in rear, and before his comrades could come up with him had unhorsed a third. A shout down the great cañon caused Souk to hurriedly look that way, when he saw about fifty warriors galloping toward him. He now knew he had reached the pass ahead of the main body, and encountered only the scouts of the Cheyennes.

Ordering his men to push on up the pass to the great valley beyond, he, with two companions, remained behind to cover their retreat. On coming to their dead and wounded warriors the Cheyennes halted and held a conference, while Souk and his friends leisurely pursued their journey. In the gorge in which he then was, Souk knew ten men were as good as a hundred, and he was in no hurry to leave the friendly shelter of the rocks. Taking up a position behind a sharp butte, he fortified the place, and quietly waited for the Cheyennes. Hour after hour passed, but they did not appear. The shadows of evening were beginning to creep into the ravines, and several of Souk's party were anxious to quit their retreat and continue their journey, confident that the Cheyennes had returned to their camp, but the wily young Sioux told them to be patient, and he would inform them when it was time to go. The evening deepened into twilight, the moon rose over the peaks and stood overhead, indicating that ,it was midnight, but still Souk would not go His men had begun to grumble, when suddenly a noise was heard in the gorge below, and presently voices and the tramp of horses could be distinguished. Souk ordered four of his men to mount and be ready to leap the rude rock breastworks when he gave them notice, and to cheer and shout as loudly as possible. He then lay down with the other four, and waited for the foe. To his delight he noticed, as the Cheyennes came up, many of them were dismounted, and leading their ponies. They came within a few feet of the barricade before they perceived it, and then Souk and his comrades commenced a rapid discharge of arrows into their midst. Three or four shots had been fired before the Cheyennes know what the matter was, or where the whizzing shafts came from. Then Souk shouted his battle-cry, and the four mounted Sioux, repeating it from behind the butte, dashed over the barricade and charged the enemy, who broke and fled in the utmost confusion down the gorge. In a moment Souk, with his remaining Sioux, was mounted and after them. The animals of the Cheyennes broke loose from .some of the dismounted warriors before they could mount, and left them on foot. Several hid among the rocks, but four, Souk overtook and killed. The pursuit was kept up for nearly five miles' when Souk turned back and hastily continued his journey to the Brule camp, where he arrived in safety on the evening of the seventh day.

He was kindly received by the father of his bride,, and given a dozen fine lodges for himself and friends. The meeting between Souk and his sweetheart was as tender as that of lovers could be, and now, that they were once together, both were perfectly happy. Near the Brule encampment were some mountain vines covered with flowers, and here Souk and Atchafalaya each day spent hour after hour in sweet communion with each other. The stream was dotted for miles with hundreds of richly-painted teepees, thousands of homes and ponies were constantly to be seen grazing in the green valley, and scores of warriors in their gay and various-colored costumes galloped to and fro among the villages. It was a pleasant sight at the home of the old Brule, and one that filled their young hearts with pride and joy, for all these herds and people were one day to be theirs.

After lingering a month in the camp, the old Brule one day announced to Souk he was about to send the chiefs to receive the presents for Atchafalaya's hand, and if the young man and his friends wished to return home it would be a favorable opportunity for them to do so. Souk took the hint and made preparations accordingly.

By the advice of the old chief, the party took another route, and, although it was two days longer, it brought them in safety to the Ogallala encampment.

At Souk's request, his father immediately assembled the council, and the negotiations for Atchafalaya's hand began. An aged Brule made the first speech, expatiating on the power of his chief, the richness of the tribe, and the beauty of Atchafalaya. This was followed by an Ogallala, who dwelt at length upon the power of his chief, his rank, and age, and upon the nobleness, bravery, and skill of Souk. Several other speeches were made on each side, in which the young man and woman were alternately praised, and the glory of their fathers extolled to the skies. The council then adjourned until the following day, the important point of the conference—the price of the lady's hand—not having been touched upon at all.

Next day the conference continued, and toward evening the Brule chiefs, after having spoken a great deal, abruptly demanded fifty horses and two hundred ponies, as the price for Atchafalaya.

The friends of Souk were a good deal surprised at the extravagant demand of the Brules, it being about three times more than they expected to give. Souk's father could not conceal hit indignation, and saying he would give but twenty-five horses and one hundred ponies, adjourned the council, directing the Brule chiefs to return home and inform their venerable head of his decision.

Souk returned to his lodge with a heavy heart, for he clearly foresaw trouble, and that his love, like all other "true loves," was not to run smoothly. Summoning his friends, he desired them to make as many presents as possible to the Brule chiefs, and before they started he added five fine horses of his own, hoping by this liberality to secure their good will. He also caused them to be secretly informed, that if they could induce the Brule chief to accept his father's offer he would, on the day of his marriage, present to each of them, a fine American horse.

Before leaving the Brule camp, Souk and Atchafalaya had vowed a true lover's vow, that come what would of the council, they would be faithful to each other, and die rather than break their plighted troth. Souk had also promised his betrothed he would return in the fall and make her his wife, with or without the consent of the tribes.

317

As the summer months wore away, and no word was received from the Brule camp, Souk became each day more restless, and, finally, calling together a few of his friends, started once more for the Brides' home.

He was received most cordially by the old chief, and as before, given most hospitable entertainment. Often, however, he thought he detected sadness on the old man's face, and on questioning Atchafalaya as to the cause of her father's trouble, the poor girl burst into tears and confessed she was about to be sacrificed for her father's good. She said that the Cheyenne chief, with whom her father had long been at war, had asked her hand, and promised, on receiving her as one of his wives, to cease from warring with the Sioux. Her father, actuated by a desire to do his people and friends good, had, after the refusal of Souk's father to furnish the required presents, given the Cheyenne a promise, and they were to be married the following year, when the grass grew green on the earth. The old chief preferred greatly to have Souk for a son-in-law, but he wished also to serve his people and old friends. The treaty was to be binding on the Cheyennes, for the Ogallalas as well as the Brides, and therefore Souk and his father would be greatly benefited by her marriage to the Cheyenne.

This astounding intelligence came near upsetting Souk's better judgment, and for awhile he was nearly demented. Taking the fond girl in his arms, he swore, rather than see her the wife of the hated Cheyenne, he would spill both his own and her blood, and they would go to the happy hunting-grounds together. Atchafalaya begged him to be calm, and she would make her escape with him and fly to his people. It was agreed that, early in the spring, before the encampment moved to its summer pastures, Souk, with a chosen band, should come over the mountains, and in the confusion, when the tribe was on the march, they, would seize a favorable opportunity to escape into the mountains, from which they could make their way to Souk's father and implore his protection.

Cautioning him to conceal, even by a look, all knowledge of her engagement to the Cheyenne, the lovers parted, and next day Souk set out for his home, apparently utterly indifferent as to the result of the negotiations for his marriage.

Slowly the winter months dragged along, and to the impatient Souk they seemed interminable, but at length the water began to come down from the mountains, and the ice grew soft on the streams. As soon, as he saw these indications of returning spring, Souk called his bravest friends together and set out from the camp. He did not tell anyone where he was going, and it was only when they began to ascend the mountains they suspected they were on their way to the Brule camp. In eight days they descended the plain into the old chiefs home.

He was greatly astonished to see Souk, for he believed it impossible, at that season of the year, for anyone to cross the mountain. However, he gave Souk and his friends a hearty welcome, and again provided them with everything they needed.

Next day the chief rode down the river to prepare the camp for moving, and Souk and Atchafalaya, being left alone in the camp; had all the opportunity they desired for laying their plans. Atchafalaya said the camp would move in four days, and that in the meantime they-must make every preparation for their flight. There was one horse in the herd, she said, that was the swiftest in the tribe, and he must be either killed or she would ride him. Her father had always objected to her mounting this animal, because he was so vicious, but, now that he was away, it would be a good time for her to ride the animal, and show to her father that she was a better horsewoman than he thought. Once upon him, she could pretend a fondness for the beast, and thus secure him to ride on the trip. Souk agreed to all she said, and the wild horse was at once sent for. He reared and plunged fearfully, but at length he was conquered, and Atchafalaya mounted his back. Souk rode by her side, and they galloped down the river, to meet the old chief, who they knew must by that time be returning homeward, as it was nearly evening. They soon met him, and when he saw his daughter on the wild horse, he was greatly surprised, but not displeased, for all Indians are proud of their horsemanship. Cautioning her to be very careful, and hold him fast, Souk, the old chief, and Atchafalaya rode back together to the village.

Next day Atchafalaya again rode the wild horse, and in the evening slyly extracted a promise from her father that she should be permitted to ride him when the village changed its camping-ground.

On the morning of the fourth day the herds were gathered, the teepees pulled down, and the village commenced its march to the summer pastures. The men had got the herds fairly on the way, and the sun was just tipping the icy peaks of the mountains, when Souk and Atchafalaya mounted their steeds and galloped swiftly forward. Atchafalaya rode the wild horse, and Souk was mounted on a splendid stallion. All of Souk's warriors had been sent the day before to Pole Creek, a day in advance, under the pretense of hunting.

Riding on until they reached the head of the herd, they were about to pass, when the herders informed the young couple that it was the chief's orders no one should go ahead of the herd and they could proceed no further. Giving the men a pleasant answer, Atchafalaya said she was only trying the mettle of her horse, and at once turned back. They had gone but a little distance, when they entered the sand-hills, and, making a wide circuit, came out far in advance of the herd. They were now on the banks of a little lake, and, giving their horses full rein, sped by its clear waters.

Long before night the young people reached Pole Creek, and found Souk's warriors. He hastily explained to them what had happened, and, charging them to remain, and if possible draw off the enemy from the trail, Souk and his sweetheart again set forward.

One of the warriors who remained behind was to personate a woman, and, if possible, make the old chief's people think he was Atchafalaya. Souk said he knew a pass through the Black Hills that would bring them to his father's country two days sooner than by any other route, and, although the way was somewhat dangerous, they must take all risks, and depend on the swiftness of their horses for escape.

All night they rode on, and at sunrise halted on the top of a high hill, to breakfast on cold roast antelope and wild artichokes.

Atchafalaya's horse bore her light weight without seeming fatigue, but Souk was heavy, and his steed began to show signs of distress.

Far in the distance they could see the blue line of the gap that still lay between them and safety, and, hurriedly refreshing themselves from a spring of pure water, they again set out, hoping to reach it before night.

It was near sundown when they began to ascend the high ridge that led into the gap, and they had just reached the crest when Atchafalaya, scanning the valley below them, descried horsemen following on their trail. They had hoped they were not yet discovered, and under cover of night might still reach the pass in safety, but the horsemen soon divided, and one-half went up the valley, while the others continued to follow the trail. Souk knew in a moment that those who went up the valley were going to head them off, and, although they had nearly double the distance to ride, their road was comparatively smooth, while Souk's lay along precipices and over crags. Calling to Atchafalaya that, they must now ride for their lives, Souk whipped up the horses, and they began to climb rapidly the rugged pathway.

All night they pushed along, and at daylight found themselves quite near the pass. Souk scanned the valley through the hazy light, but could detect no traces of the Brules people. He began to hope that they had not yet arrived, and spoke encouragingly to Atchafalaya, who, pale with fatigue, now sat upon her horse like a statue. Descending into the deep cañon, Souk directed Atchafalaya to ride rapidly for the pass, while he followed close in the rear, ready to attack any enemy that might appear. They had gone half a mile, and were just entering the jaws of the great gorge, when a cry of distress rose from the lips of the girl, and, looking to his right, Souk saw about twenty Brules rapidly closing on the pass. The noble girl whipped up her horse, and, darting forward like an arrow, shot through the pass full fifty yards ahead of the foremost Brule warrior.

Souk grasped his battle-ax, and, reaching the pass just as the first Brule came up, struck his horse on the head, dropping him on the ground and sending the rider rolling over the rocks. The second warrior, seeing the fate of his companion, swerved his steed to one side and strove to pass Souk, but he quickly drew his bow and drove an arrow through the horse behind the fore-shoulder, causing him to drop to his knees and fling his rider on the ground.

The lovers were now ahead of all their pursuers, and, urging their gallant steeds to their utmost, they soon had the satisfaction of hearing the shouts of the Brules dying in the distance behind them. In an hour they halted, refreshed themselves, and rested their horses. In the distance they could see the Brules halting by a stream, and apparently resting also. The lovers were the first to move on, and, when once in the saddle, they lost no time.

It was past noon when Souk saw some objects several miles off on the left, and soon made them out to be part of the Brules, who were making for the river, to cut him off from the ford. The race was a long, one, but the lovers won it, and crossed in safety.

On the third day they entered the great mountains, and drew near the borders of the country of Souk's father. At sunset they crossed a little creek, which Souk pointed out to Atchafalaya as the boundary of the Ogallala lands. Biding forward a dozen miles, they halted in a wild, mountainous region, and, for the first time since starting, prepared to take some rest. Souk comforted Atchafalaya with the assurance that another day would take them to his home, and that they were now well out of danger.

A sheltered spot was selected for their camp, near a stream, and, while Souk gathered some sticks to make a small fire, his bride walked down to the water's edge. He saw her turn up the stream, and in a moment more she was lost to view. The fire was soon lighted, and Souk busy preparing the evening meal, when suddenly he heard a fearful shriek at no great distance.

Seizing his battle-ax, he rushed toward the spot from whence the sound proceeded, but could see no one. Calling the name of his bride, he dashed forward through the thicket, but could see or hear nothing of her. 'He called loudly again, but received no response. The silence was agonizing, and he listened for several moments, when he heard the crackling of some branches in the distance. He rushed frantically to the spot, but his career was quickly stopped by an object on the ground. It was the torn and now bloody mantle of his beloved. The mystery was in part explained: she had retired to this secluded spot to offer up a prayer to the Great Spirit for their safe-deliverance, and, as was her custom, had taken off her mantle and spread it on the earth. On this she had knelt, when a grizzly bear, those terrible beasts of the Rocky Mountains, had rushed upon her and killed her before she could utter a second cry. His huge paws were deeply imprinted on the sand, and the trail was distinctly visible along which he had dragged his victim. Souk, taking the rent garment, plunged into the brushwood.

He crossed the thicket in several directions, but in vain; it was dark, and he could not follow the trail. He returned to the camp in a frame of mind bordering on despair. Raising his hand to heaven, he swore by the great Wa-con Ton-ka to track the beast to his den and slay him, or perish in the conflict. It seemed to him an age before the light appeared, but at length the gray streamers began to streak the east, and Souk was on the trail. Again and again he lost it, but the growing light enabled him to find it, and he pushed on. He found the lair half a mile out, where the beast had eaten a part of his beloved, and, as he looked at the blood stains on the ground, his brain seemed about to burst from his skull. Pieces of garments were left on some of the bushes, where the bear had dragged the body along. Far up into the mountains Souk followed the trail, but at length lost it among the rocks. All day he hunted for it in vain, and when night came he returned to his camp. He expected the enemy had come up during his absence, but he found the horses where he had left them, and the camp undisturbed. How he wished the Brules would come and kill him. He cursed himself, and wished to die, but could not. Then he slept, how long he knew not, but the sun was far up in the heavens and shining brightly when he awoke.

Mounting one of the horses, and leading the other, he started at full speed. He wished to leave as quickly as possible, and forever, the cursed spot that had witnessed the destruction of all his earthly happiness. It afforded him some relief to ride fast, and he dashed onward, he neither knew nor cared where. His well-trained steed took the road for him, and as the evening shadows were beginning to creep over the valley, he saw far ahead the teepees of his father's village. He lashed his horse and rode like a madman into the town. His faithful warriors had returned, but they hardly knew their beloved young chief, so changed was he. At the door of his father's lodge his brave horse fell dead, and Souk rolled over on the ground insensible.

He was carefully lifted up and laid on his own bed, where for many days he remained in a raging fever, at times delirious, and calling wildly on the name of Atchafalaya. Little by little he recovered, and at length went about the village again, but he hardly ever spoke to anyone; and for years the Brules and Ogallalas never visited each other.

THE HUNTER'S DREAM

(From the Ottawa.) THERE was once a beautiful girl, who died suddenly on the day she was to have been married to a handsome young hunter, who had also proved his bravery in war, so that he enjoyed the praises of his tribe, but his heart was not proof against this loss. From the hour his betrothed was buried, there was no more joy or peace for him. He went often to visit the spot where the women had buried her, and sat musing there for hours, when, it was thought by some of his friends, he would have done better to try and amuse himself in the chase, or by diverting his thoughts in the war-path. But war and hunting had lost their charms for him. His heart was already dead within him, and he wholly neglected both his war-club and his bow.

He had heard the old people say, that there was a path that led to the land of souls, and he determined to follow it, and accordingly set out one morning, after having completed his preparations for the journey. At first he hardly knew which way to go. He was only guided by the tradition that he must go south. For awhile, he could see no change in the face of the country. Forests, and hills, and valleys, and streams, had the same look which they wore on his native plains. There was snow on the ground when he set out, and it was sometimes seen to be piled and matted on the thick trees and bushes. At length, however, it began to diminish, and, as he walked on, finally disappeared. The forest assumed a more cheerful appearance, the leaves put forth their buds, and before he was aware of the completeness of the change, he found he had left behind him the land of snow and ice. The air became mild and balmy; the dark clouds had rolled away from the sky; a pure field of blue was above him; and, as he went forward in his journey, he saw .flowers beside his path, and heard the song of birds. By these signs he knew that he was going the right way, for they agreed with the traditions of his tribe. At length he spied a path, which led him through a grove, then up a long and elevated ridge, on the very top of which, he came to a lodge. At the door, stood an old man with white hair, whose eyes, though deeply sunk, had a fiery brilliancy. He had a long robe of skins thrown loosely around his shoulders, and a staff in his hands.

325

The young man began to tell his story; but the venerable chief arrested him before he had spoken ten words. "I have expected you," he replied, "and had just risen to bid you welcome to my abode. She, whom you seek, passed here but a short time since, and being fatigued with her journey, rested herself here. Enter my lodge and be seated, and I will then satisfy your inquiries, and give you directions for your journey from this point." Having done this, and refreshed himself by rest, they both issued forth from the lodge door. "You see yonder gulf," said the old man, "and the wide-stretching plain beyond: it is the land of souls. You stand upon its borders, and my lodge is the gate of entrance. But you cannot take your body along. Leave it here with your bow and arrows, your bundle and your dog. You will find them safe upon your return." So saying, he re-entered the lodge, and the freed traveler bounded forward as if his feet had suddenly been endowed with the power of wings. But all things retained their natural colors and shapes. The woods, and leaves, and streams, and lakes, were only more bright and comely than he had ever witnessed. Animals bounded across his path with a freedom and confidence, which seemed to tell him that There was no blood shed there. Birds of beautiful plumage were in the groves, and sported in the waters. There was but one thing which he noticed as unusual. He noticed that his passage was not stopped by trees and other objects. He appeared to walk directly through them: they were, in fact, but the images or shadows of material forms, and he became sensible that he was in the land of souls.

When he had traveled half a day's journey, through a country which was continually becoming more and more attractive, he came to the banks of a broad lake, in the center of which was a large and beautiful island. He found a canoe of white shining stone tied to the shore, and was now sure that he had come to the right path, for the aged man had told him of this. Immediately entering the canoe, and taking the shining paddles in his hands, to his joy and surprise, on turning round, he beheld the object of his search in another canoe, exactly the counterpart of his, in every respect. It seemed, in fact, to be the shadow of his own. She had exactly imitated his motions, and they were side by side, and they at once pushed out from the shore and began to cross the lake. Its waves seemed to be rising, and, at a distance, looked ready to swallow them up; but, just as they entered the whitened edge, they seemed to melt away, and they were but the images of waves. But no sooner was one wreath of foam passed, than another, more threatening still, rose up. Thus they were in perpetual fear; which was increased by the clearness of the water, through which they could see heaps of the bones of persons who had perished before.

The master of life had, however, decreed to let them pass, for the thoughts and acts of neither had been bad." But they saw many others struggling and sinking in the waves. Old men and young men, males and females, of all ages and ranks, were there; some passed, and some sank. It was only the little children, whose canoes seemed to meet no waves. At length every difficulty was gone, as in a moment, and they both leaped out on the happy island. They felt that the very air was food. It strengthened and nourished them, and they wandered together over the blissful fields, where everything was formed to please the eye and ear. There were no tempests; there was no ice, nor chilly winds; no one shivered for the want of warm clothes; no one suffered for hunger; no one mourned for the dead. They saw no graves; they heard of no wars. Animals ran freely about, but there was no blood spilled in hunting them: for the air itself nourished them. Gladly would the young warrior have remained there forever, but he was obliged to go back for his body. He did not see the Master of Life, but he heard his voice, as if it were a soft breeze. "Go back," said this voice, "to the land from whence you came. Your time has not yet come. The duties for which I made you, and which you are to perform, are not yet finished. Return to your people, and accomplish the acts of a good man. You will be the ruler of your tribe for many days. The rules you will observe will be told you by my messenger who keeps the gate. When he surrenders back your body, he will tell you what to do. Listen to him, and you shall afterward rejoin the spirit which you have followed, but whom you must now leave behind. She is accepted, and will be ever here, as young and as happy as she was when I first called her from the land of snows." When this voice ceased, the narrator awoke. It was the fancy work of a dream, and he was still in the bitter land of snows and hunger, death and tears.

JIM BAKER

BAKER was born in Illinois, and live at home until he was eighteen years of age, when he enlisted in the American Fur Company, went to the Rocky Mountains, and remained there for many years. He married an Indian wife, according to the Indian custom, from the Snake tribe, and lived with the Indians several years, adopting their habits, ideas, and superstitions. He firmly believed in the efficacy of charms, and incantations of the medicine men. He contended zealously that they could cure diseases, divine where the enemy was to be found, and foretell the result of war expeditions. Unfortunately he would occasionally take a glass or two too much whisky, and, while under its influence, would commit many indiscretions. When sober, Baker was a noble, generous, big-hearted man, as, indeed, are nearly all trappers hunters, and guides on the border. He was the friend and companion of Kit Carson, Jim Bridger, and Jack Robinson, and would divide his last crust with an associate or stranger.

"Jim Baker," as he was familiarly known all along the border, accompanied General Marcy, in 1857-58, in his expedition over the Rocky Mountains, from Fort Bridger to New Mexico, and proved himself a most valuable assistant; guide, and interpreter.

Randolph Marcy was an officer on the frontier and in the American Civil War. He was also the father-in-law of General George Brinton McClellan of Civil War fame. See Marcy's Thirty Years of Army Life On The Border.

Marcy had engaged a Digger Ute Indian as guide, and promised him many presents as soon as they should reach New Mexico. On the first day out the Indian pretended not to believe he would receive the promised presents, and in the evening announced his intention of returning to Fort Bridger. Marcy told the Indian he had the presents with him, but still seeming not to be satisfied, Baker advised the general to show him the presents. This was done, and, knowing their propensity to steal, Marcy ordered the presents to be closely guarded; yet, notwithstanding every precaution, the wily savage managed, during the night, to get hold of the most of them, and then deserted. Next morning, when Baker learned of his treachery, he was so enraged that he wished to follow the Digger Ute and scalp him, but General Marcy restrained him.

During the expedition Marcy came upon a band of Utes at the western base of the Rocky Mountains, and, as he was scarce of ponies, he tried to buy some, but, although these people subsisted on rabbits, bugs, and crickets, they could not be induced to part with their ponies at any price. The general then tried to hire one of them as a guide across the mountains, but in this he also failed, when Baker came to the rescue. He said to the chief, "Come, show us the way to New Mexico," and upon the chiefs replying that the snow was too deep for any human being to attempt the passage of the mountains, Baker slapped his breast and said, "Do you think we are old women? I at first took you for a warrior, but I see now you are a squaw," and the Indian becoming very much enraged at this taunt, Baker added: "Go home now, and cover up warm, or assist your squaw in taking care of the babies." The Ute was beside himself with rage, but still he pointed to the mountains, and said: "You think I do not tell you the truth, but look, you can see the white snow upon the peaks from here. When I crossed in the autumn the leaves were beginning to fall, and the snow was then a foot deep in the passes, but it is now above my middle, and I could not possibly wade through." Nevertheless, General Marcy undertook the passage of the mountains, and, after losing nearly all his .animals, and enduring months of suffering and privation, he forced his way to Fort Massachusetts, and accomplished what General Fremont had failed to do. This was really one of the most remarkable marches on record, and entitles its conductor to lasting fame. In saying that Baker, Tyburn, and Mariano were invaluable, and probably saved the expedition, I am only repeating what General Marcy has often himself said in both public and private.

When General Marcy first met "Jim," he .inquired if he had traveled much in the States before coming out into the mountains, to which he replied: "Right smart, Cap." Marcy asked:

"Where have you been?"

"To Chicago," was the reply.

"Have you ever been to New York?"

"No, sir."

"To New Orleans?"

"No, Cap, I hasn't been to Orleans, but I'll tell you whar I have been. I've traveled mighty nigh all over four counties in Illinois," and this, it appeared, was the extent of his wanderings before leaving home.

When sober, Baker was a mild and sensible man, but when in liquor he was violent, boisterous, and dangerous. He appeared to be very fond of his squaw and children, but on one occasion, coming into his house and finding a friend there, he pretended to get jealous, and abused his wife. His friend, seeing be had a drop too much liquor, tried to appease him and convince .him of the injustice of his suspicions, but "Jim" only became more indignant and furious, and, seizing a hunting-knife, swore be would cut off one of her ears, and it was with the greatest difficulty his friend could prevent him from doing so. This was one of the Indian methods of punishing a truant spouse, and it seemed to Jim the most appropriate for that occasion.

When Marcy's expedition reached New Mexico, Baker concluded it would be a good opportunity to cast aside his leggings, moccasins, and other mountain gear, and adopt the habiliments of civilization. He accordingly bought a full outfit of citizens clothing, and when the general met him soon afterward, so great was the change that he hardly knew him.

"Why," said Marcy, "Jim, you are so metamorphosed I hardly knew you."

"I don't know what you call it," replied Baker, "but confound these store clothes, they choke my feet like—." It was the first time in twenty years Jim had worn anything but moccasins, and his feet were not prepared for the torture of breaking in new boots. In a little while he was seen walking along in his bare feet, and carrying his boots in his hand, and when asked about it, he said, "I specks these store clothes makes me look kind o' 'spectable, but they hurt, and I feel like a durned fool." An hour afterward he came out in his mountain rig and moccasins, and said he would never again attempt to wear store clothes, or act the gentleman."

Baker had been in at the death of many a grizzly bear, and related many stories of his terrible encounters with these monsters of the mountains, but he had one great bear fight that he loved most to recount. He and his friend Bridger were one day setting traps on the head waters of Grand River, when they .came suddenly upon two young grizzly bears, about the size of well-grown dogs. Baker remarked that if they could pitch in and scalp the varmints with their knives, it would be an exploit to boast of. They accordingly laid aside their rifles and went at them, Bridger attacking one, and his companion the other. He says the bears immediately raised on their hind feet, and, squatting upon their haunches, were ready for battle. He ran around, endeavoring to get an opportunity to give a blow from behind with his long sharp knife, but the young brute was too quick for him, and turned, as he passed around, so as always to confront him face to face. He knew, if he came within reach of him, though young, he could strike terrible blows and inflict Severe wounds with his claws; moreover, he felt great apprehensions that the piteous howls of the cub would bring the old dam to its rescue, when the chances of escape from death would be small. Anxious to terminate the contest as soon as possible, he made several passes at the bear, who warded off his strokes with the skill of a pugilist. Several of the lunges cut the cub's paws, and the pain greatly enraged him. At length, exasperated, the grizzly took the offensive, and sprung at his antagonist. Baker grappled with him, and, after a most terrible conflict, in which his arms and legs were torn and lacerated nearly to the bone, the mountaineer succeeded in giving the animal a death wound.

Meanwhile Bridger was fighting a terrible battle with big bear, and had become greatly exhausted, and the odds were turning decidedly against him, when he entreated his companion to come to his relief, and, although Jim said he did not like to "meddle with another man's bar fite," he finally went in, when, to his surprise, Bridger immediately retired from the contest, and left him to fight it out alone. In vain Baker begged him to help him by shooting or stabbing the bear, but Bridger only, replied, "Go ahead, Jim; you kin kill and skulp him yourself." After a severe struggle, Jim was again victorious, and, when he demanded an explanation of his conduct, Bridger replied, "Yer tarnal fool, Jim, yer got me into yer scrape, and I got meself out. Yer wanted ter kill and skulp bars with butcher-knives, and I made up my mind I'd jest shoot mine; so as the bar fite were yours, I thort I would'nt interfere." Baker reflected a moment, and then responded, "Dod rot it, Jim, if yer ain't rite, and I'll never fite nary 'nother grizzly without I have a good shootin' iron in my paws."

Like most mountaineers, Baker was liberal to a fault, and consequently was very improvident. He had made a great deal of money in trading and trapping, but, at the annual rendezvous of traders he would spend the earnings of a whole season in a few days. He had been particularly lucky one year, and laid up the snug sum of nine thousand dollars, when he made up his mind he would abandon his mountain life, return to the States, purchase a farm, and settle down. He accordingly made his preparations to start, and was on the point of departure, when he concluded to have a little blow out with some friends, whom he never expected to see again. They got some grog, and finally wandered into a monte-bank, which had been opened in the camp. He was easily persuaded to take some more drinks and try his luck, and the result was, that the next morning Baker found himself without a cent. To a friend whom he met soon afterward, he said, "Guess I won't buy a farm this year,' and next day returned to his hunting-grounds.

After a time Baker left the Indians, and established a little store on the old Mormon trail, at the crossing of Green River. Here for some years he did a fair business in trading with Indians and trafficking with passing emigrants, but one day a Frenchman appeared and set up a rival establishment which greatly reduced Baker's profits. This terribly enraged the old frontiersman, who claimed the exclusive "rite to trade on them crossin'," and he posted a "notis" for the Frenchman "tew quit." The Frenchman, however, went on with his business, and soon all intercourse of a friendly nature ceased between the neighbors. One day Baker declared war, and sent a challenge to the Frenchman, which was promptly accepted. They both retired to their cabins, which were facing each other, and prepared for battle. Baker had no liquor, and the polite Frenchman sent over his antagonist a quart. After liquoring, up, they appeared at the doors of their cabins and fired with revolvers. Between each round they would go in and drink, and soon got so drunk and unsteady there was little danger of their hitting each other. This peculiar duel had lasted for several hours, when Baker's old friend Marcy happened by, returning from Utah to the States. He asked Baker what was up, and he replied, "Yer see, Cap, that thar yaller-bellied, toad-eatin' parly-voo over thar come here to trade agin me, and we have had a bit of a skrimmage to-day."

Marcy lectured him on the sin of monopoly, but Baker only replied, "This yer's my crossin', I reckon, Cap, and I'll raise the liar o' that sneakin' pole-cat yet. I'll skulp him, Cap, if he don't leave these diggin's, darned if I don't."

He then gave notice to Marcy to stand aside, for he was going to blaze away, but Marcy stepped up to Baker, and took his pistol away, telling him he was greatly astonished to see a man of his sense make such a fool of himself. Baker submitted quietly, but upbraided Marcy, saying he wished to disgrace him by making him take insults from a cowardly, frog-eating Frenchman.

Next morning, however, he called on Marcy, and apologized for what had taken place the day before, said he was drunk, and when he allowed himself to drink whisky he had "nary sense." He also said he would leave the country, and the "cussed toad-eater might keep the durned old crossin."

Baker is still living in Colorado, but has, left the mountains, and, being very old, is waiting to take the long journey whence no mortal has yet returned.

LAST DAYS OF BELDEN

WHEN I began writing the life of Geo. P. Belden, twelve years ago, I had little thought that a dozen years hence, I would be called upon to write a new addition to the work. But the adventurous White Chief Soldier, Hunter, Trapper and Guide, seems to have found a warm spot in the hearts of the people. Thousands and Tens of Thousands of boys have read and re-read his life with increasing interest, and to-day Belden stands as the representative of all that is manly and noble in the character of the real back-woodsman. A book of genuine adventure is a treasure, and that Belden was a real adventurer and the Daniel Boone of the West, is no longer a matter of dispute.

Since his life was first written and published, Belden has passed away—gone to join that innumerable throng who wait beyond the river. He died as he lived an adventurer to the last, and fell by the hands of the people among whom he had lived so long—The Wild Indians of the Plains.

One day soon after his life had been published, he showed me a copy of the book, and turning over its leaves said. "The reading of this book has given me a desire to renew my wild life on the plains."

"But" said I, "that is impossible; you have abandoned that life, are now a commissioned officer in the Regular Army, and have a charming young wife."

"No matter," he replied, "I long for the mountains, and for the wild, free life I used so much to enjoy."

I tried to dissuade him, but soon saw his mind was made up, and knew that before long he would quit the service, and go back to the Indians.

It was a month or more before he could muster courage to break the sad intelligence to his beautiful young wife, but finally it came and almost crushed her.

He had promised to write an appendix to his life, but instead of the promised manuscript, I one day, unexpectedly, received the following letter:

Old Fort Kearney,
Neb., March 1st, 1870.
Dear General:
Yesterday on my return from the Republican River, I received your two letters which had been forwarded to me from Wind River. I am out of the army, and once more a free man. My ponies are packed, and I am about to be off for the trapping and hunting grounds. For the present, pen writing with me is over. Good-bye, and ho for the Mountains.

Yours Truly,

"Geo. P. Belden."

Not long afterwards I heard Belden was trapping alone on the Republican, in the country of the hostile Indians. An officer of the Army who visited my camp, told me he saw a wild white man dressed in buck-skins with an eagle's feather braided in his hair, and a huge rifle on his shoulder. This man I knew in a moment from the description to be Belden, who had come into the Railroad to buy ammunition and sell his pelts. Later, I heard of a white man being on Medicine Creek, whom the Indians had repeatedly attacked and tried to drive away, but after losing two of their number, gave up the attempt, saying he was bad medicine. Soon after that I received two or three rude lines scrawled on the flyleaf of a book, and sent by the hands of a hunter. They read thus:

"I am hunting and trapping on the Medicine, and while over at the Republican and Loup, I met with a couple of splendid adventures. All safe and sound yet and my hair in the proper place.

Yours,

"Geo. P. Belden."

It was a long time before I again heard from him. I was about to engage in an Indian campaign, and while on the march received from a scout the following note:

"Hear you are coming up the Crow, and will probably go over to the Republican after the Cheyennes. I know where they are and am following their trail alone. Go across Frenchman and strike for the Forks of the Republican. Good water and grass all the way. Look in big tree at the Forks for a letter from me.

Yours truly.

"Belden."

When we got to the Forks of the Republican, I found on the limb of a tree this note:

"Cheyennes on Beaver. If you can send one company to Thickwood, I will meet them there; tell them to camp in bottom, make no smoke, and wait-for me. I don't like to suggest, but if Eagan is with you, please let him come with his company, and caution the men not to shoot me for an Indian. I am a Cheyenne now and can't speak or write a word of English.

Yours,

"Belden."

The company was sent, and about an hour after they went into camp, the pickets reported an Indian approaching. He was mounted on a pony, wore leggings, and was painted like a Cheyenne warrior. As he came up he said in good Cheyenne, "Me big. Cheyenne brave. How Cola," and then bursting into a laugh cried out in English, "How are you boys! How are you Captain!" No one would have known him as a white man, and as he sat on his pony with his back humped up as the savages ride he was the very picture of an Indian warrior.

Captain Eagan asked him where the Indians were. "On the Beaver," Belden replied, "But you see, he added, I am lame and very sick (bending over and holding his stomach with his hands) though I am one of them. But they are very sharp and keep a good look out. I have followed them every day and kept in sight, but did not care to take the risk of entering their camp until I knew something would come of it. To-night I will go over and count them if the General is ready to attack, but where and how is he?"

Captain Eagan replied, "I was on the Republican, and only waiting for reliable news to advance."

"All right!" said Belden, "then to-night I will go over to the Cheyenne camp and to-morrow bring you reliable news."

After he had eaten a hearty supper, he carefully repainted himself, and arranging his hair in the Cheyenne fashion, mounted his pony and rode away.

His story of an eventful night adventure in an Indian camp is best told in his own words; he said:

"After leaving Captain Eagan's camp, I went down on the Beaver and carefully approached the Cheyenne village. It was in a strong bend, and covered by high bluffs, on which were posted the pickets.

I crawled up as carefully as possible and called out in Cheyenne:

"Hello there!

"Hello!" came back.

"Is this the Cheyenne camp?"

"Yes," what do you want!

I am a Cheyenne, hurt by my pony and sick."

"All right?" replied the picket, pass in.

I then passed in and went down to the village; as I approached the lodges I found some squaws out attending to the ponies.

"What are you doing," I asked.

"Only taking in the ponies," they replied.

"What for."

"They say the soldiers are on the Republican and we fear an attack."

"Nonsense, I am going to leave mine here, and you leave yours too," I said, at the same time driving down my picket-pin quite near their ponies. They seemed reassured and proceeded to re picket their animals.

338

"We all then returned to the edge of the village, where I parted with them."

Just as I was entering the lodges, I met a warrior wrapped in his blanket and was passing by him, when he stopped, and said,

"Good evening."

"Good evening," I replied.

"What news have you?"

"Nothing, what have you?"

"The soldiers are at the Forks of the Republican."

"Do you believe it?"

"Yes," he answered," "and the Chief says we must look for an attack."

"Does the Chief think we can stand them off."

"No, he says there are too many of them for us."

"How many soldiers does he think there are at the Forks of the Republican."

"Five hundred."

"Well," said I, feeling the next question might expose me to discovery and instant death. "Can't we risk a battle? Where are all our warriors?"

"What!" he replied, "Fight five hundred soldiers with three hundred warriors, you are crazy to think of such a thing."

"You are right," I answered, "but I hate this continually running away, and would rather fight like a man, than retreat like a coward."

"I guess there are as good fighting men as you are in this camp," he replied contemptuously, "and the chief knows what he is about."

I now feared I had gone too far, but laughingly answered, "All right, keep your opinions and I will keep mine."

"Good evening," he said, striding away, to my infinite relief; for the situation was becoming embarrassing.

I squatted down among the grass, and drawing my blanket over my head, began to think; what should I do next? I knew the position of the camp, their numbers and intentions; what more did I desire to know? Had I not better return at once to the soldier's camp, and not risk all by further inquiry? Still, the spirit of adventure was so strong upon me I could not resist, and, rising, walked forward through the camp. I saw many Indians, but avoided talking to them; keeping my blanket over my head and walking slowly as if I was sick.

"What is the matter?" inquired a squaw, who was coming up from the creek, with a kettle of water on her head.

"Sick!" I answered, and when she stopped and put down her kettle, as if disposed to gossip, I merely grunted and passed on, knowing a brave is not compelled by savage politeness to talk to a woman, unless he wants to do so.

"Seems to me if I was sick I would go home and go to bed!" she called out, with all the spitefulness of a woman, and picking up her kettle again and placing it on her head, she walked angrily away.

After strolling through the village until I was tired, I went back to where I had entered it, and was about untying my pony, when a warrior rose up out of the grass, and inquired:

"What are you doing there?"

Like a Yankee, I knew the best way to answer an unexpected question; was to ask another, and I inquired:

"Who put these ponies here?"

"I did."

"You must want to lose them, I reckon, don't you?" I asked.

"No," he replied, "why do you say that?"

"Because I believe the soldiers are coming, and I want mine to get away on."

"You are a coward!" he answered.

"Coward or no coward!" I replied, "my pony sleeps with me this night," at the same time untying the lariat, and leading the little animal away.

The fellow merely grunted and laid down again in the grass.

Going around the outer edge of the village until I came to a dark spot, I mounted and rode out on the prairie.

I knew the real danger was still to be encountered, that of passing through the pickets, for the village was completely encircled by vigilant Indians. To slip through unobserved was impossible; so, going boldly up to the videttes, I asked one of them:

"Did you hear anything up there?" At the same time pointing up the Beaver.

"No," he replied.

"I thought I heard some shots," I said carelessly.

"We heard nothing, and I guess our ears are as sharp as yours," replied the Indian.

"That may be, but you could not hear so well up here; I was in the water."

"Well, go and tell the Chief," said the vidette.

"No," I answered, "I may have been mistaken, and he would punish me if I gave a false alarm."

"Very well," answered the vidette; "you watch here and I will take your pony and go up the stream a ways, and see if anyone is there."

"The pony is a fool;" said I; "he scares at every bush, and would throw you. You remain where you are, and I will go up the creek and bring you word.

To this the vidette readily assented, and mounting my animal I rode safely up the stream, and back to the soldier camp."

As soon as I got Belden's report, which did not reach me until noon the following day, I started for the Indian village with my whole force, but found it gone, and although we followed it for a week, they traveled so fast we could not overtake it, and it finally escaped into the mountains.

This adventure shows the desperate character of Belden as a scout, and his wonderful readiness and cunning when confronted by danger.

For a long time, Belden hunted and Trapped on the Republican, and hearing one day he was at Plum Greek, on the Union Pacific Railroad, I sent him word I wished him to accompany me to Pike's Peak. He replied with alacrity:

"Whispering George gave me your note last night, in which you ask me if I would like to accompany you on a trip across the country to the Peak. Would a cat like a dish of fresh milk? Of course I will go, old man. Why God bless you; I was just spoiling for something to turn up, and as old Straddle [General Palmer] has gone back on me, your note is a regular God-send. Count me in, and say where I shall join you."

"Belden."

I started from Old Fort Sedgwick on the Platte River with Belden, Scout Nelson and a small escort of soldiers. Fording the Platte we took the old overland trail, and followed it. Belden was in excellent spirits and full of humor; every mile of the journey had its history, and Belden chatted as we rode along. He pointed out the spot where famous ranches once stood; showed us where Indian battles had been fought, and related a thousand anecdotes of the people who once inhabited the trail, but were now all gone, and their houses in ruins. There, had stood the American Ranch, which had been burned in 1867 by Indians, even the women assisting to defend it to the last; when after eleven Indians had been slain, the ranch was captured, five men killed and scalped and the women all carried off into captivity. Beyond, was the Wisconsin Ranch, where two men had fought twenty savages, all one afternoon until night, killing five, and then escaped under cover of darkness.

At a little mound Mr. Belden showed us a head-board, larger than usual, on which was inscribed: "W. J. Morris, killed by Indians, January 10th, 1865." It was a sad legend, but such a one as is common on the plains. The occupant of this lonely grave by the wayside had a history; he was murdered at his own ranch by the Sioux, and his wife and children carried off into captivity. The Chief one day took from Mrs. Morris her little child, eighteen months old, and tried to make it play with him, but the child was afraid of the burly savage, and would not play, when the Indian became enraged, and dashing it on the ground, trampled it to death before the agonized mother's eyes.

In the evening we encamped on the site of "Old Fort Wicked." The buildings were all gone, but a sign in the grass read: "Fort Wicked, kept by W. Godfrey, Grocery Store."

Mr. Belden said; "Here lived, in 1865, a ranchman by the name of W. Hollen Godfrey, he was a native of Western New York, and came to the Plains at an early day. Keen, sharp-eyed, brawny and intelligent; he soon made his mark, and became a terror, alike to noble red-men and white horse-thieves. He had a wife and children, who shared his adventures in the far west, and the woman was no less courageous than her husband. Starting west, Godfrey halted here and built a ranch, at which he sold whisky, tobacco, canned fruits and notions to emigrants. His hut was a strong one, and answered both for a fort and residence; it had flared embrasures, and a wall six feet high, well loop-holed. The building was covered with sods to protect it from fire, and indeed, the whole place was as strong as it could be made out of the materials the country afforded.

In 1865 when the Indians broke out and destroyed nearly all the ranches along the Platte, Godfrey was advised to leave, but he declared he would stick .to his home and take the chances of repelling any attack made upon him. His place was very much exposed, and it was not long until the Indians assaulted it. One afternoon a war party of one hundred and thirty Cheyenne and Sioux warriors came down upon the ranch, and demanded that the occupants should come out and surrender. Godfrey had four men with him, and although the odds were one to thirty-six, he at once began the fight. The Indians after driving off the stock and trying in vain to draw out the men after them, made a direct assault, while some kept up a heavy fire on the ranch, others set fire to the grass, the wind blowing at the time almost a gale. Under cover of the smoke Godfrey and his companions sallied out and wet the grass so that the fire would not burn up to the ranch. At one time the Indians got into the stable which almost connected with the house, and set it on fire, but the white men drove them out, and Godfrey with buckets of water went on the roof and drowned out the flames. Sixty balls struck the corner of the stable where Godfrey was working, but he escaped unharmed. The Indians next divided their warriors and one party circled around the buildings, while the others charged up and fired at close range. It was lively work for an hour or two. Mrs. Godfrey loading the rifles and keeping them clean and cool, while the men stood at the embrasures and fired them. After five hours fighting night came on and the Indians drew off, having made up their minds that they could not capture the ranch. Godfrey said it was "the Gol-darndest wickedest fight he ever did see in all his born days," and in commemoration of the event, he named his place, "Fort Wicked," by which designation it was ever afterwards known on the plains, and Godfrey became celebrated among travelers as "Old Wicked."

An Indian had fallen during, the battle near the ranch, and Godfrey knowing his companions would make an effort to carry him off kept close watch; three charges were made to recover the wounded Indian and two more warriors fell, when Old Wicked called out to his wife, "They're coming on again Betsy, hurry up and bring me another rifle, I want to get enough hair to make yer a bed quilt." The Indians had to leave their dead in the hands of the whites, and Godfrey said, "I took more pains in skinnin' them fellows heads than I ever did in peelin' any animal in my life."

It was after the camp fires were lighted, the supper over, and the pipes filled that Mr. Belden was most interesting. He was full of anecdotes and had a vast fund of information which his varied and wonderful life had enabled him to accumulate during his long residence on the plains, and upon this he drew for hours, always talking interestingly and well.

One evening I said to Mr. Belden, "The captivities of the white people by Indians have greatly interested me, pray tell me what do the Indians do with the white women they capture?"

"Gamble for them," he replied.

"Will you explain that a little, Mr. Belden?"

"Yes. You see when they take a White woman or girl prisoner she is generally given to the Chief or the one who has the best right to her by having risked his life to take her. When her proper owner gets tired of her, which is generally very soon, he sells her, or puts her up at a raffle, and the lucky man gets her. After she has been in the tribe for some time, she is gambled off almost every day and has a hard time of it. When I was with the Indians on the Missouri, I won two girls and protecting them from outrage, sent them to their homes for which I deserve some credit I think. I could tell you many strange tales about white captives if you had the desire and patience to listen to them."

I begged him to proceed, and he then related to me the captivity and sufferings of Mrs. Morton, of Denver, Miss Roper, Mrs. Ewbanks, Mrs. Kelly, Mrs. Larimer, Mrs. Jones and many others. These stories lie before me in huge chapters which would almost make a volume, but they cannot be referred to, even in brief, in a sketch like this.

Nelson one day said Belden was a poet of no mean ability and I asked him to let me see some of his productions.

"I haven't a specimen about me," said Belden, but after we get into camp this evening if you will loan me your pencil and scratch book I will see what I can do in that line."

After the camp was made and the supper despatched, I called on Mr. Belden for a poem. "Without saying a word he rose from the fire and taking my pencil and paper went into the tent, where by the uncertain light of a tallow candle he commenced writing.

"Now," said Nelson who was an enthusiastic admirer of Mr. Belden's literary productions, you will hear poetry as is poetry; none of your slobbery, smooth, soft stuff, such as Longfellow and them other fellows down Hast write, but real story poetry of a fight or adventure full of fact and incident, and the whole thing set down just as it tuk place. He writes mighty slow, however, and not to bother him by waitin' while he is composin', I will tell you a story.

"Hello! Belden, old Alligator, draw her fine and don't hurry yourself, for I have been a braggin' on yer and I am goin' to sling a story so as to give you plenty of time," cried Nelson.

"All right! Go ahead old man," came from the inside of the tent.

Nelson then related to us the story of the life of the famous desperado, Jack Slade; how he cut off the ears of people, carried them in his pockets, and when he called for drinks offered the bar-keepers human ears in change. How he tied up poor old Jules Benard, made a target of his living body, first clipping off a finger, then an ear, then his nose, until the old man begged for death, and Slade kindly shot him through the head; but it is of Belden, and not Slade or Nelson, I am writing this sketch, so when Nelson had related his story and it was growing late, Belden came forth from the tent with a bundle of manuscript in his hand and signified his readiness to proceed. Nelson piled up the fire and when the wood burned brightly we all settled ourselves down to listen to the reading.

"Some years ago," began Mr. Belden, *ten* trappers of the plains formed a League, agreeing to stand by each other through life. They were to defend each other, come when called for, however distant and inconvenient the journey might be, and minister to one another in sickness or misfortune. They were also to meet every year until the League should be reduced to one member. Death, Indians, lightning or snow, were the only excuses sufficient to warrant the absence of a member from the annual meeting. At one of these meetings only nine trappers appeared; the tenth, Ben Harding, or "Slippery Ben," as he was called, being dead. Just as the trappers were about to disperse for their yearly hunt, a tall figure on a white horse was seen approaching and the ghost of Ben Harding appeared and took its accustomed seat in the circle at the trapper's Council. It is of this particular meeting of the League I shall treat in my poem."

When he announced the death of Slippery Ben, there were tears not only in his voice, but on his cheeks, and his tones sank away until we could with difficulty repress our own tears. When he called the roll and mentioned Nelson's name, the Scout bowed his head, and at the conclusion of the reading of the poem, I saw the tears were running down the brave fellow's cheeks. I could not but admire the admirable manner in which Belden read the verses, referring to Slippery Ben's Ghost, and it seemed as though the Dead Trapper stood before us on "his Shadowy Steed." I doubt if there are a dozen actors in the world who could read these verses well, or at least so, affectingly. I have often since tried to read the poem, but cannot do it justice and make it sound as Belden did. Since hearing this poem read, I can readily understand the strange fascination and wide popularity of Bret Harte's and Joaquin Miller's poems among this class of men. They may not be said to contain poetry, but their quaint sayings recite the everyday life of the frontiersmen and people of whom they treat, and they therefore appeal to both their hearts and understandings. They are delicious pieces of word paintings, and when properly rendered, the figures rise and troop before us as did "Ghostly Ben and his Shadowy Steed." Mr. Belden left me many of his poems, and they still lie in my desk unpublished. I have studied them for hours, but cannot read them, at least not as they should be read, or as Mr. Belden could make them sound. The accent is most difficult, and if placed in the wrong word in a single line, it throws the whole verse out of rhythme. There is one poem of Mr. Belden's on the "Lone Tree Massacre," which I think quite wonderful, but it is too long for a place in this narrative of his last days.

Next morning after the recitation of Belden's poem we began to prepare for our onward journey, when as one of the soldiers was grooming his horse, the animal suddenly kicked him, the iron-shoe burying itself deep in Iris leg, making an ugly gash and fracturing one of the small bones. The poor fellow suffered terribly, and rather than leave him behind we determined to wait over a day. Mr. Belden, among his other accomplishments, numbered that of Surgeon, and always carried with him a small chest of instruments and medicines. The man's leg was soon dressed as well as any practicing physician could have done it, and we began to cast about for amusements with which to pass the day. 'A hunt on the prairie was proposed, and we eagerly sallied forth, guns in hand; but after a weary tramp of over two hours, we took only one small rabbit and a few birds, and returned to camp fatigued and disgusted. Mr. Belden was then requested to give us an exhibition of his skill at handling the bow and rifle. A small squirrel was suspended by the tail at a distance of eighty yards, and Mr. Belden taking his bow and arrow at the first shot severed the squirrel's tail from its body. A quarter of a dollar was then put in a split-stick, and Belden knocked it out three times in five shots. Next a brass tack, highly polished, was driven into a board and set up at one hundred yards distant; Mr. Belden took his rifle and fired one shot and the tack disappeared. An examination showed that the tack had been hit exactly on the head, and had been driven through the board. Several other exhibitions of his skill as a marksman were given, but these are sufficient to show his wonderful ability. Such proficiency in the handling of deadly weapons can only be attained by the frontiersmen, whose lives often depend on a single shot.

The day passed pleasantly enough, and at night when the camp fires were lighted I was not sorry we had stopped over. Story telling was again in order, and Belden related to us the history of Black Bear and his wife, an intelligent white woman, who he had captured from a train on the North Platte in 1852. I regret that this interesting narrative must again be omitted; but I am compelled to hasten on to the conclusion of Mr. Belden's life.

In a day or two we reached Denver, where eating a mess of fresh cabbage, I fell sick, and being unable to leave my room for several days, I told Belden to take my note book and go on to Pike's Peak, make the ascent alone and write down all that he experienced and saw. I have his notes before me still, and I have always considered his account of the ascent of the Peak, by far, the most interesting ever given by any traveler. Of course it is too long to quote; but one or two extracts will show its completeness. He says:

"I verified Pike's, Richardson's and other tourist's experience with my own in order that by comparison I might get as near the truth as possible. Mr. Jules E. Coffey went with me and I hired old Gallages as guide." After describing his first days ascent Mr. Belden goes on to say, "at sun-down we encamped for the night and eating our boiled pork and bread, rolled ourselves in our blankets and slept soundly until morning." The next days' ascent was more difficult, "over two little valleys, along cañons of decomposed rock, by landslides and masses of ugly granite, to the great stone chain over-hanging the valley and hills below. We saw the rock where Richardson and his friends had taken shelter from the rain in 1860, when they made their ascent. The guide pointed out the spot where the two ladies of Richardson's party had slept and the log on which their breakfast was spread after the weary night had passed. We camped on a shelving rock hard by, and I could readily understand and appreciate the astonishing courage and resolution of these delicate women in climbing the dizzy' heights."

Next day Belden "passed through the clouds and saw them whirling about on the mountain side below." In the afternoon he says my lungs began to bleed, and I experienced great difficulty in breathing. So much was I oppressed that I had to lay down at one time and I thought I should die. I gave up all hopes of ever completing the journey, but presently feeling better, thought I would push on a little further. Mr. Coffey was taken with violent vomiting, and even old Gallages complained of being sick at his stomach. We made a cup of strong tea, and while the water was boiling, old Gallages entertained us by relating anecdotes of how people had died while making the ascent. "After that days' journey Belden goes on to say:" We had now reached the main Peak and began to ascend it. It is bleak, barren and rocky; vegetation has ceased, and pines, firs, shrubs and cedars all lay at our feet, while below them again float the clouds. The air is growing colder, and the damp forms icicles, while above, the snow begins to appear. Are follow up a little cañon toward the top of the Peak; the mist has broken away and below, the harvest fields, woods, plains and prairies in panoramas of gold and green, with lakes and streams can just be seen. We are just five miles from the town where we started up; five miles as the crow flies and fifteen by the road over which we have traveled. The men and animals in the streets of the little town look no larger than ants, even when seen through a powerful glass, and the cattle in the fields appear as mere black spots."

"We are now at the top and seem quite near the sky, and while we look at the Rocky Mountain Sheep which inhabit this lonely Peak, old Gallages the guide, slily suggests we are about as near heaven as most of us will ever get. I started a loose rock down the Peak, and as it rolls from ledge to ledge showering sparks of fire wherever it strikes, a noise like thunder comes up the Peak from a thousand feet below. Gallages showed us where Richardson and his ladies stood and sang:

"This is the way I long have sought,

And mourned because I found it not."

And as we could not sing, we gave three cheers for the brave Boston woman and her spunky companions from Denytown, New Hampshire."

"It is mid-summer but all around us lie the unmelted snow. It is cold, and a sign on a rock explains the fact by informing us that the spot on which we stand is 13,400 feet above the level of the sea. The summit of this wonderful Peak is not a cone, as most people would suppose, but a little level plain of perhaps fifty acres in extent and is covered with blocks of disintegrated granite."

"Here we sit down and look into four Territories and States, all of which we can see from the Peak; straight ahead is Kansas, to the right, Utah, to the left, Colorado, and behind us New Mexico; North is the Platte for seventy miles; West the Peaks of Colorado; East for hundreds of miles the prairie, near gems of lakes; at our feet the green timbers of the Fountain Qui Berrille, the Arkansas and Hernfano, while behind them rise the Spanish Peaks of New Mexico and stretch away for hundreds of miles."

One day I asked Mr. Belden if the Indians had any real poetry in their songs, or if they were as they sounded, a mere conglomeration of gutturals.

"The Indians, he said, have no books and their record and history is therefore wholly oral. The difficulty of handing down correct

350

traditions from father to son as a connecting link between the present and the past is very great. What may have been their literature in the past, if they had any, I do not know, but it is likely they had, and being only oral has been lost. They sang, as they now do, when Columbus landed but who would believe that the songs of those days are still sung. Probably they were replaced in a few years by new ones. Indeed, this is a fact, for even while I was with the Sioux I remember two or three "new sets of songs appeared and those sang when I first joined the tribe have been entirely superseded and forgotten."

"What are their songs all about" I inquired.

"Of war, love and the chase," he said, "these are the three principal topics, but the clouds, the sun, moon and stars, wind, rain and lightning, come in for a fair share of attention from their poets."

"Will you give us some specimens of Indian poetry" I asked.

"With pleasure," he replied, and then clearing his throat sang in good voice:

"Wagemin! Wagemin Paimosaid,

Wagemin Wagemin Paimosaid.

Bakan. Kenazee Ka. Sangizzcsee Wagemin. Wagemin Kinabowid Wagemin Wagemin Ningah. Nugamowid."

"But what is it I inquired."

"A red ear of corn," he replied, and then related the following legend: "You must know at the corn husking season there is great hilarity among the Indians, and the young people gather at social huskings. On such occasions if a young female finds a red ear of corn it is indicative that she has a brave sweetheart, and she must present it to the warrior she likes bp .. ,. ear is crooked, or tapering to a point, it is considered the image of an old man-thief who would cast his life with hers, and the whole circle is set in a roar. "Wagemin, Wagemin," they shout, and the whole troop set up the corn song.

The story of Par Kabilonocca, the God of Winter, and the song of Singebiss, is too good to lose. Par Kabilonocca froze up all the

351

country and drove the inhabitants to the south, all but one poor old Indian, Singebiss, who, in defiance of the icy God, remained by the side of the lake. Kabilonocca, offended, blew his bitterest blast, determined to drive away Singebiss but the brave man declared he would not go, and continued to subsist on fish. "He shall not withstand me," cried the enraged Ice God, and summoning all his cold, said: "I will now go and freeze him stiff." Singebiss, who knew of his coming, had a warm fire on his hearth, and when Winter knocked at his cabin door, he said, blithely, "Come in, Sir." The Ice God entered and did his best to freeze Singebiss, but he only piled on the logs, poked up the fire and never minded him. Finally, Winter, finding unless he made off, fearing that he should be melted, with tears in his eyes, cried out: "Egad! I cannot stand this— I am roasting," began his retreat, when Singebiss struck up his song of defiance.

The Frog Song, or "The Frog in the Spring," as the Indians call it, is one of their prettiest songs, and Tom Hood or Burns might have been proud to be the author of it. This song represents the winter and the coming of spring, which means much more to the Indian than the white man in his warm house.

"The Indians," said Mr. Belden, "believe the birds are intelligent creatures and that they can foretell man's destiny; they therefore regard their presence as indicative of good will and often undertake to interpret the messages they are supposed to bring.

"There," said Mr. Belden, "I think that will do for one time on the subject of Indian poetry."

I could not but thank him for his wonderful rendering of the Indian songs, and said I had not the slightest idea before that there was so much that was beautiful and wonderful ill the savage language.

"Oh! well," he replied, "white people do not understand Indians, that is all, and never will, never will, I tell you," he added emphatically.

At Denver Mr. Belden left me and returned to the Republican River to hunt, and for a long time I lost sight of him. Then I heard he was living at Plum Tree, in an Indian Lodge, and his fair young wife was with him. She was trying to assimilate herself to his wild life, but she soon tired of it, and Belden begged her to go to her uncle in Indiana, who was very wealthy, and had offered her a home. She went accordingly, and I never heard of her afterwards. She was a mere girl in 1868, when I knew her, and is probably living yet in Indiana.

A year later, Belden went to Omaha to live, and being a good compositor, was engaged on the *Republican*. He often wrote to me from Omaha, and was evidently ill at ease and discontented. I next heard of him at Sioux City, Iowa, where he was local editor of the Sioux City *Journal*. He wrote a series of admirable articles for the *Journal* on the "Western country," and sent them to me. Then he drifted to the Black Hills, and from there up the Missouri, where he returned to his wild life with the Indians. I had a flattering offer for him if he would write some Indian stories, or legends about the West, and I wrote him twice that a large Eastern firm would pay him well if he would only send for one of their periodicals, a few short articles. After a long time I heard from him at the Cheyenne Agency, on the Missouri, in Dakota, and he sent me one short story, saying he would send more, but they never came. As the story referred to above is probably the very last one poor Belden ever wrote, and it is short, I will try to give it.

THE TRAPPER'S ROCK

Just above old Julesburg on the Union Pacific Railroad is a rock at the foot of which was once enacted a horrible tragedy. The place is a deep cañon surmounted by high bluffs, and there is a loneliness and silence about the place which oppresses everyone, and makes the visitor glad to hasten away. Many years ago two young men came from the east and ascending the Missouri, engaged in the fur business near its head waters. They were bosom friends, and prospered in all their undertakings; money flowed into their pockets, and they became rich in course of time from the sale of their furs; still they stayed in the West, that had been so generous to them, and having become fond of their wild life, determined to make the Missouri their permanent home. One of the young men had lived at St. Louis, where he had a mother and sisters. It was to St. Louis the partners went annually to sell their pelts and divide the profits of their now large business. The younger sister of the brother, infatuated by the tales of adventure told her by the traders, longed to visit them in their home in the West, and begged so hard that the brother finally consented she might go. For a whole year she lived at the trappers home in the far West, and when the time came for the partners to go down the river, and sell their furs, the brother could not go. The girl was loth to leave her brother, but he urged her to return home with his friend, and see their mother, saying, he would soon follow her. Entrusting his beloved sister to his partner and friend, the two set out in a Mackinaw, well provided with every comfort for their journey. The brother, who was sick, grew worse, and the summer wore away before he was able to travel. In the meantime the partner returned, bringing with him news from home, and a division of the annual profits of the business, which was larger than ever before. The brother was pleased with the manner in which their business had been conducted, and readily yielded to the suggestion of his partner to delay his visit East for another year, devote the winter to trapping, and go down in the spring. All went well until about mid-winter, when the brother received, by the hands of a trapper, a letter from his home, which well-nigh crazed him. It was from his mother, and gave a long and circumstantial account of the ruin of his sister by his partner. It was the old story of woman's trust and man's perfidy. The girl, unable to bear her shame, had lost her reason and was a hopeless maniac. On reading this letter, the first impulse of the brother was to go and kill his partner, but dissembling, he devised a plan of revenge which no Indian could have outdone for diabolical cruelty. Keeping the receipt of the letter a profound secret, he went on with his business as usual, and every day met his partner on the same terms of friendly intimacy as formerly. When the skins were packed and all in readiness to go down the river, the brother went to Fort Benton, in Montana, and there had executed a will, leaving the name of the person who had executed it blank. He then returned to his camp, on the Jefferson Fork. Devising a cunning story, representing to his partner that on the Platte River there were to be made great profits

354

in furs, and proposed that instead of going down the Missouri, they should cross overland, descend the Platte River to its mouth and there intercept their boats on the Missouri. As an inducement, he said, if they found all as represented, they could establish a branch of their business at old Fort Laramie, where the brother had friends, and thus increase the 'profits of their trade. The partner readily assented to a proposal so manifestly to the advantage of both, and alone they set out together, taking with them only riding ponies and two to carry their blankets, and the flour and bacon they expected to use on the journey. They traveled for many days, and finally came to the Platte River, which they followed by the overland trail until they reached Jules Barand's ranch. Under some pretense or other, the brother here induced his partner to accompany him into a lonely cañon, where, quickly disarming him, he tied his partner hand and foot, and securely bound him to the rock above referred to. At first the partner thought it was some cruel joke or trick, but when the brother produced his mother's letter and read it to him, the poor man knew his time had come to die, and begged to be shot on the spot; but the brother had another fate in store for the seducer of his sister. Coolly camping y the rock, he sat down to see his victim starve to death. On the third day the ill-fated man signed the deed bequeathing all his property to the injured girl, and the brother attached a fictitious signature to the instrument, by the terms of which he was made the executor of his partners will. He then wrote a letter for his partner to sign, saving, he had fallen very ill of fever on the plains, and if he did not recover, the letter would be delivered to his friends by the hand of his beloved partner. All this the infuriated brother compelled his partner to sign, and then quietly waited for the end. Day by day he grew weaker, and the brother gloated over his misery, often reading to him the letter from his mother.

The poor man promised to marry the girl and make all the restitution in his power if the brother would spare his life; but to all his entreaties the partner turned a deaf ear and left him to die. At last he was reduced to a mere skeleton, and on the ninth day die. After burying his emaciated victim's corpse the brother resumed his journey down the Platte. At the mouth of the river he found the fleet of boats waiting, which had been there a long time, and the boatmen were wondering what had become of the owners. To the boatmen he represented his partner had died of fever, and his delay was for the purpose of nursing him. In St. Louis he repeated the same story and showed the letter to his partner's relatives. The will was also proved and the girl became the dead man's heir. As the wrong done to the girl was well known to his friends, they thought little of the matter, believing the will to be an act of restitution and justice to the injured one. After a time the brother returned to the Rocky Mountains and resumed his trade with the Indians. Two years ago he was shot by the Sioux and before dying confessed his crime. Some hunters visited the rock and dug up the skeleton. Around the neck of the poor fellow was still the chain by which he had been fastened to the rock. They reburied the bones on the spot, and the tale is still told to travelers of how the hard-hearted brother day after day eat his meals in the presence of his wretched and starving prisoner, never so much as offering him a crumb to appease his hunger, or a cup of water to slake his thirst. The sister recovered her reason and still lives in St. Louis; but after she learned of her brother's horrible punishment of her false lover, she turned over his property to his relatives and she and her mother live upon the ample fortune inherited from the dead brother and son.

Once after this, I heard from Mr. Belden. I had written him making certain inquiries about matters in which I was greatly interested, well knowing his prodigious knowledge of the west would enable him to inform me correctly. He replied from far up the Missouri river and said:

"I have been absent so long from the river and the places of civilized men, I suppose you think I am dead; but my hair is still on the top of my head. We have had some glorious sports, and I can set down one more Indian fight in my experience of the Plains, besides having had no end of hunts, bear fights and races. We went out early to the buffalo land and took a great many beasts, but they will not last long if the present destruction of these noble animals is allowed to go on as in the past few years. There are a lot of mean white men who are called buffalo skinners, and they slaughter the buffalo merely for their skins, no regard being paid to the meat, which is allowed to rot on the ground. These men are hated by the Indians, who would soon make an end of them if it were not for fear of the troops. It seems to me this indiscriminate slaughter of buffalo wrong and should be stopped. Congress ought to prohibit it by statute. Will you not write to some of your friends and urge the passage of a law to this effect: That buffalo shall only be killed hereafter for food?

Unless this is done and the buffalo skinners leave the country, there will be trouble between them and the Indians. They had a mind to drive them off this summer, but I told them they must wait until the Great Father heard about it, and then he would see their beef cattle were not wantonly destroyed.

"Now, as to the questions in your letter—1st, you were quite right in what you said in my life about the Shoshonee Indians being an off-shoot of the Comanches, and those Washington fellows don't know anything about it. How could they know better than you when they have never been west of Pittsburg, and wouldn't know a Comanche from a Sioux if they were to run against them? The Shoshonees speak the same language as the Comanches, and are like them in all respects. 'A primary stock of the Rocky Mountain Indian?' indeed. Just you write that Washington man and tell him he don't know anything about the Shoshonees or any other Indians, for that matter, and if he don't believe you and me, that the Snakes are Comanches, let him consult Col. Cady, Gen. Alvord,* United States Army, or any other old officer who knows about Indians, and he will soon find out his mistake.

*Benjamin Alvord (1813–1884) was an American soldier, mathematician, and botanist.—Ed. 2015

"As to the change of climate on the Plains since I came West, it has been material, and the rainfall has doubled and is increasing every year, especially along the line of the Union Pacific Railroad. This I attribute in a great measure is due to the settlement of the country and to tree planting. I think when the country is settled up thickly the stirring of the soil will produce humidity of the atmosphere sufficient to produce enough rain to make the crops grow and ripen well."

After this letter I lost sight of Belden and did not hear of him again, until one day I received a letter from his cousin, John W Hugus, a Post Trader, informing me Belden was dead—had been murdered by Indians on the Upper Missouri. This letter I have lost, but the facts are still fresh in my mind. Mr. Belden had been living with the Cheyennes on the Missouri in Dakota, but had gone into the interior to trade with some bands. One day he came down to the trader's establishment with his horse and pack pony, and having bought three hundred dollars' worth of beads, cloth and Indian trinkets, he packed them on his pony and set out for the interior. It is supposed some Indian saw him, and actuated by motives of cupidity, went on ahead and hid by the side of a little lake, where he knew Belden would .stop to water his animals. Belden came to the lake, dismounted and stooped to dip up a cup of water, when just as he was in the act of placing it to his lips, an Indian raised up out of the grass and fired, shooting him through the head. The great scout fell forward on his face and died almost immediately. His body was found by some hunters by the side of the lake and brought into the Agency and buried His ponies and goods were gone, the thief having made good his escape into the interior. I never heard that the murderer of Belden was discovered, and he probably never will be, or be punished if he is found out. Such events are so common on the Plains that little attention is paid to them, even at the time, and they are forgotten in a month after they have occurred, except by relatives and personal friends of the murdered man. I understand Belden's mother has had his body taken to Omaha and buried in the family burying ground at that place. Belden's father had been dead many years, but his mother, a smart, active old lady, was living a year ago at Omaha, and I believe lives there still. Belden had a brother who was a quiet farmer and resided near Omaha on his mother's farm. He had three sisters, charming women, the eldest of whom married a gentleman of wealth and position at Omaha; his second sister was married to Mr. Wallace, an Omaha banker, and resides in that city; his youngest sister, Hattie, and of whom he was very fond, is married to an army officer, and is now stationed with the Fourteenth Infantry in Utah.

Thus ends the history of Geo. P. Belden, the Daniel Boone of the West. A great many people have thought him a fictitious character, not believing any man could have so many real adventures, but I can assure them Belden was real flesh and blood, and that nothing in the following pages has been exaggerated or misrepresented. His life as he lived it is set down in the exact words of the adventurous chief, soldier, hunter, trapper and guide, and varied and remarkable as it may appear, it is true to the letter.

James S. Brisbin,

U. S. Army.

Fort Assinniboine, Montana, January 29, 1881.

THE END

BIG BYTE BOOKS is your source for great lost history!

Made in the USA
Las Vegas, NV
29 November 2024

12866536R00215